The Actor as Storyteller

AN INTRODUCTION TO ACTING

Bruce J. Miller

University of Miami

MAYFIELD PUBLISHING COMPANY
Mountain View, California
London • Toronto

Library of Congress Cataloging-in-Publication Data

Miller, Bruce J.
    The actor as storyteller : an introduction to acting / Bruce J.
Miller.
        p.   cm.
    Includes bibliographical references and index.
    ISBN 0-7674-0605-2
    1. Acting. I. Title.
PN2061.M46   1999
792'.028—dc21   99-13025
                                   CIP

Manufactured in the United States of America
10 9 8 7 6 5 4 3 2 1

Mayfield Publishing Company
1280 Villa Street
Mountain View, California 94041

Sponsoring editor, Jan Beatty; signing representative, Brenda Johnson; production editor, Linda Ward; manuscript editor, Mark Gallaher; design manager, Susan Breitbard; text and cover designer, Joan Greenfield; manufacturing manager, Randy Hurst. The text was set in 9/12 Stone Serif by TBH Typecast, Inc., and printed on 45# Highland Plus by R. R. Donnelley & Sons Company.

Parts of this book appeared in some form as articles written for *Dramatics Magazine* and *Teaching Theatre*.

 This book is printed on acid-free, recycled paper.

For my wife, Amy, who put me on the right path,
and my daughter, Emma, who provided the motivation
to make the journey.

PREFACE

What you will find in this text may not be revolutionary or earth-shattering in and of itself. I did not invent the stuff I teach. Stanislavski, the father of all acting craft, must be credited with that. But over the last ten years I have learned to articulate basic acting craft in a way that is simple, direct, and immediate. These techniques are practical and broadly applicable, and they will not need to be jettisoned when the novice actor is ready for a more sophisticated and deeper exploration of dramatic works.

My approach in teaching and in this text is simply this: The actor is responsible to serve any dramatic situation by making choices that create the best possible story of his or her character, while at the same time serving the overall story of the play, the scene, and every moment. This means that acting requires headwork first. Actors must be able to think about how they serve the plays they are in. In short, they must understand what theatre is, how it works, and how to analyze and synthesize the content of a script. Movies and television—along with the development of Method acting—have created for would-be actors the illusion that being believable and spontaneous from moment to moment is all that is required. For many aspiring actors this has translated into self-indulgent emotionalism, often at the expense of a script. It has also led actors away from the belief that acting is a craft with specific tangible, intellectual tools that can and must be developed. These tools include the use of common sense to weigh, choose, and refine one's options in order to serve the playwright's vision and that of the production being rehearsed.

Most high school actors who are serious about careers in acting enroll in college theatre programs to learn about the craft. Yet, ironically, they often come to study theatre having developed their impressions of what acting is all about by watching television and film. Many have little or no knowledge of theatre and how it works. They do not realize that an actor's responsibility is far different in theatre than it is in the other hybrid mediums where most actors end up working—if they are lucky enough to find work at all.

This text, then, is intended for serious beginning actors. The first part consists of an overview: what theatre is and how it works, the differences between theatre and its hybrid mediums, and the part an actor plays in each of those mediums. It also introduces ways that novice acting students can begin to examine the process of acting. The second part of the text focuses on acting craft itself. It introduces the concept of the actor as storyteller and then presents the specific tools an actor works with. The third part details the process an actor can use to prepare for scene work and rehearsals. It offers an organized working plan for using the tools presented in the second part. The fourth part includes discussion of mental preparation, suggestions for auditioning, a process for rehearsing a play, and an overview of the realities of show business.

A Philosophical Note

Although it is the acting student I address throughout most of this book, do understand that I've kept you, the teacher, in mind as well. In fact, I count on you to balance out what some may at first glance consider to be an unevenly distributed presentation of the process of acting. It is true that my focus leans toward the intellectual side of the acting process—to dramatic analysis and synthesis. This is intentional because I feel that the basics of dealing with a script have not been given enough attention in many other beginning acting texts and in much of the training that beginning actors go through. I do, however, appreciate the importance of inspiration, creative impulse, emotional truth, and simply being in and reacting to the moment. Where I may have underemphasized those aspects of the acting process, I fully expect that you will fill in any gaps with your own expertise and experience. It is my hope that those of you whose philosophy of acting seems to be at odds with my own, as presented in this text, will still be able to see through our differences and take advantage of what is useful to you here.

Features

You will find that this text provides

- A sequential approach to acting craft that compounds principles, concepts, and skills and culminates in a detailed representation of an actor's responsibilities to a script.

- An introduction to what theatre is, how it works, and its connection to the acting process.

- A well-reasoned argument for the study of acting through theatre training.

- An examination of the differences between stage and film acting.

- An examination of the acting process as it relates both to the script and to the audience watching.

- An examination of the rehearsal process both with regard to scene work and to the development of a role in a production.

- A detailed examination of script analysis of the overall play and of individual scenes.

- A sample of an actor's script filled with useful script notations.

- An introduction to the concept of style and its importance to an actor.

- An examination of positive ways to give and receive artistic criticism.
- A detailed examination of the audition process from selection of material to its presentation.
- An examination of ways to view theatre and the acting process intelligently from an actor's point of view.
- An examination of the skills and personality traits necessary for success in the world of theatre, including skills not necessarily taught in acting classes.
- A glossary of terms that reflect important theatrical concepts as well as acting tools that, in combination, can help actors meld their technique with the demands of a script and a theatrical performance.
- A detailed listing of other books to augment what is offered here.
- Numerous exercises that I have found to be effective in teaching acting concepts or as demonstrations of those concepts. In many cases, I have purposely avoided going into great detail about what will happen during the exercises or what will or should be learned from them. My intention has been to provide a framework for discovery and eventual mastery, not a step-by-step prescription.
- A short play at the end of the text. The play is meant to provide a common source for class discussion. However, one short play cannot possibly meet all the demands of an acting class, so in several places you will also find what I hope prove to be useful and diversified lists of plays and playwrights that can serve as sources for work in your class.
- Many references to movies and television. This is not really a contradiction. Because many of the readers of this text will be beginners, it stands to reason that they will be more familiar with the body of work in film than in theatre. Therefore, it seems reasonable to offer examples that are familiar and universal wherever necessary.

I have focused on the craft of acting—that which is learnable and can be mastered. I have made no effort to address the artist directly. Believe me, I realize that acting is also an art form, but I have no illusions about creating artists or training the artistic abilities of our most talented students. I wouldn't know how to do so. Craft, in the hands of those with such talent, can help reveal that talent in an efficient, reliable manner. For those of us who rely primarily on our craft, its mastery can go a long way toward making up for our artistic deficiencies. And in the beginning of their journey, what better gift can we give our novice actors than a bright, shiny set of tools that will help them find their way.

Acknowledgments

For me, the process of learning to teach acting has been very much like the process of learning to act itself. The biggest difference is that teachers must be able to articulate everything they see, think, and feel about the work before them, unlike actors, who can sometimes get away with simply pretending to do so. For that reason, I would like to thank every student I have had the good fortune to work with over the last eleven years or so. Each of them has helped keep me honest and taught me more about acting—and the teaching of it—than I could have ever learned from a book. My heartfelt thanks to Joel Friedman for the invaluable guidance he has provided me (and countless others) over the years. His inspiration and generosity as a teacher and the wisdom he has willingly shared about every facet of theatre cannot be measured.

Next, a special thanks to all those who supported and encouraged me in the writing of this book. Particular thanks to Jim Palmarini and Don Corathers, my editors at *Dramatics Magazine,* who told me I had something to offer and encouraged me to keep writing, and to Julie York, who helped me get my writiting clean and simple. Thanks also to Richard Glockner, my lifelong friend, who responded positively to my work (something he almost never does) and offered me many fine practical suggestions; to Stephen Trovillion, who helped keep me honest, specific, and clear; to Kate Besterman, who gave me positive and helpful feedback from the student's point of view; to Margot Moreland, who did the same from the professional viewpoint; to my colleagues at Walnut Hill and the University of Miami, who have consistently supported and believed in me; to Andrew and Jack Weiner, who held my hand through new territory; to David Mamet and his followers for provoking me and reminding me that "acting is simple, but not easy"; a special thanks, as well, to my wife, Amy, who lent me her eyes and was able to catch what I never could have alone; and to everyone else whom I have come in contact with during my years in theatre. Consciously or not, I know that I have learned from all of them.

I would also like to give special thanks to my colleagues in the field who responded positively to the manuscript as it was being written and rewritten. Their criticism, support, and suggestions were invaluable, and their many contributions are reflected in this work. They include Ashley Carr, California State University, Long Beach; Robert Dunkerly, Community College of Southern Nevada; Victoria Holloway, Arizona State University; Dale McFadden, Indiana University; Ray Paolino, University of Georgia; Leslie Rivers, California State Polytechnic University, Pomona; and Michael Wright, University of Texas, El Paso.

Finally, I would like to express my appreciation to all those at Mayfield who helped make this book possible. Jan Beatty, my sponsoring editor, believed in the project from the outset and gave me the encouragement and guidance to bring it to fruition. Linda Ward, my seemingly unflappable production editor, organized the various production stages and kept everything running smoothly and on schedule. Mark Gallaher did an outstanding job of copyediting; he managed to improve me without losing me. Others at Mayfield who contributed their assistance and expertise are Susan Breitbard, Randy Hurst, and Joshua Tepfer. To all of them, I am greatly indebted.

CONTENTS

ABOUT THE AUTHOR

I began my career in theatre as a secondary school English teacher, where I used to consider each class a unique performance—even when I taught five different sections of the same subject. During my first year of teaching, without any training whatsoever, I directed the junior high school play. Not surprisingly, it was *Arsenic and Old Lace.* I'm sure it was both terrible and wonderful, and, even if it did little else, that production whetted my appetite for theatre and, although I didn't quite know it then, hooked me. From this first experience I quickly learned that theatre was about making good choices and learning to collaborate.

After four years of teaching, I returned to graduate school to pursue a career in journalism. Yet, a year later, as a result of a picaresque series of coincidences, I found myself in an MFA program in acting. Three years after that, scars notwithstanding, I earned my degree and slowly made my way to New York. For the next ten years, I could call myself a working actor, and sometimes I actually even worked as one. I did theatre in New York and in the provinces for love, and I did commercials, soaps, television, and film work for money. Sometimes I actually made a living.

But after a decade in the business, I counted the $400 I had in the bank and called it quits. A life in theatre had become too scary for me, and I returned to education—this time as an acting teacher and director. I accepted a position as chairman of the theatre department at a private arts high school near Boston. During the years I was there, my students came to have a reputation for craft and clarity that matched most well-trained college students. Many of my graduates—who, by the way, did not all possess huge natural talent—matriculated into the finest BFA programs in the country. It was during those years that I developed the approach and vocabulary that has become the cornerstone of this book.

I received an MFA in acting from Temple University and am currently Head of Performance for the BFA Theatre Conservatory at the University of Miami. I have been a recipient of the E. E. Ford Foundation Award for Teaching Excellence and have been recognized by Who's Who Among America's Teachers. My articles on acting and theatre appear frequently in *Dramatics Magazine* and *Teaching Theatre.*

CHAPTER 1

Why the Theatre to Study Acting?

With each passing generation, fewer and fewer Americans are exposed to theatre. First of all, there may be less of it. Professional theatre is often prohibitively expensive to produce. Second, because of these costs, ticket prices—even for amateur productions—are often twice as much for theatre performances as for movies, if not more. Younger audiences, in particular, may be less able or willing to spend the money. Third, audiences find theatre more difficult than movies and television. Theatre requires more imagination and concentration than do film and TV. It has less action. It is slower moving. It challenges the intellect more than a contemporary audience may want on an evening out. In short, the viewing and listening habits that our society has developed since the advent of TV do not make for a fertile theatre climate. Yet, ironically, the number of college students who are deciding to major in theatre is on the rise.

Acting Students Today

In today's celebrity-oriented society, an acting career seems like a very glamorous way to spend a lifetime. It beckons with the allure of fame and fortune. Its appeal operates on many of us in the same way that the prince's ball did on Cinderella and her stepsisters. A single dance with the prince could change a woman's entire lifetime. On television especially, we have seen unknowns become stars practically overnight. The power of television is such that in no time at all, one actress's hairdo can become the hairdo of a nation. Consciously or not, many students decide to pursue acting in college for this reason. If this is your reason, it is not a good one. As you probably know, your chances of success are just a little better than the chances of one of Cinderella's stepsisters marrying the prince. But even for those of you who are thinking about majoring in theatre because you love acting and performing, there are several things you need to think about.

This is probably a good time to ask yourself about your own theatrical background and experience.

EXERCISE 1-1

Answer the following questions as completely and honestly as possible. You may want to discuss your findings with other students in your class.

1. Has your theatrical experience been limited to performing in high school plays or musicals?

2. What professional shows have you seen?

3. Does your familiarity with professional theatre extend beyond the national tour of that famous musical that passed through town?

4. Have you ever seen a professional production of a dramatic play? If so, what did you like about it? What moved you? What was unique about it? Were you challenged in a new way? Explain.

5. Do you like sitting through a non-musical?

6. Are you able to stay focused while watching limited action and listening to lots of words?

7. Do you like to read plays? How many have you read?

8. Can you read a play and understand the action and the story without having a teacher take you through it? Are you stimulated intellectually or emotionally? Explain.

9. Have you read any of the works of Sam Shepard, David Mamet, Caryl Churchill, Marsha Norman, or Harold Pinter? If not, are you familiar with their work? Do you know who they are?

10. Have you thought about the difference between acting for the stage and acting for the camera?

I don't intend these questions to be patronizing. The fact is that more and more talented young actors are entering theatre training programs with only the most rudimentary understanding of what theatre is and how it works. To be perfectly honest, this is appalling. In a survey conducted not long ago by *American Theatre,* a cross section of university theatre teachers were asked about their current students.

Here's a summary of their responses about today's entering freshmen in theatre programs:

- They lack an ability to understand and use language.
- They lack a knowledge of what theatre is.

- They lack a knowledge about history and culture.
- They lack role models in theatre.
- They lack the ability to analyze and synthesize.*

Some of you might be thinking, "So what? I'm a TV or movie actor, or at least I plan to be. What do I need to know all that junk about theatre for anyway? If I wanted to be a scholar, I would major in English or history or philosophy! The screen is the place I'm heading. I know how to be 'real' for the camera." I could probably fill ten chapters with solid rebuttals to that kind of thinking, but for brevity's sake, I will focus on just a few practical ones. First, whether you are planning for a career in films or in theatre, chances are you are studying acting through courses offered by your college's theatre department. Even if you study privately in New York or L.A., much of the scene work you will do in classes probably comes from play scripts. That means the focus and approach to your acting training will, at least in part, be theatre oriented.

If, on the other hand, you decide to learn the craft of acting through a school of communication and film or as a "working" actor, you'll face other problems. You may get practical experience acting in front of the camera (if you're lucky), but specific training in craft will probably be limited—a few courses at most if you're in the former category, and some random bits of advice if you're in the latter. Regardless of the category, you will probably end up spending considerable time trying to figure out for yourself an acting system that you can depend on. This may be a valid way to learn, but it is certainly not an efficient use of your time. It could also be frustrating—certainly more frustrating than having an experienced acting teacher or faculty member with a specific teaching plan bringing you along. In general, if you learn your craft through a theatre program, you will take more acting courses, get more acting instruction, and learn more tangible things about craft that can quickly help you as an actor, even as a screen actor. Even if you're out there working already, thinking about what theatre is and how it works can certainly help you develop your craft.

If you are not yet convinced that the theatre is the place to study acting, consider this: Most professional stage actors are able to make the jump to film and television. They don't necessarily have equal success (there are many reasons for this, none essential for this discussion), but they can make the jump. Far fewer actors who start out in film are able to work onstage. For some film actors, this is simply a matter of preference, but for most, the mere thought of doing stage work is as frightening as starring in the sequel to *Cutthroat Island* or *The Postman*. Many film actors realize that they do not possess the craft necessary to sustain a role onstage, so they stay as far away as possible. Other film and television actors known primarily for lightweight roles choose to train and then do stage work to enhance their professional image. The tactic has often worked.

---

*John Istel, "Under the Influence: A Survey," *American Theatre* Jan. 1996.

Cher, for example, was known almost exclusively as a singer and television variety performer until she appeared in the New York production of *Come Back to the Five and Dime, Jimmy Dean, Jimmy Dean*. This led to her being cast in the film version of the play and, subsequently, to a highly successful movie career—including an Academy Award as Best Actress for *Moonlighting*. The differences between stage acting and film acting will be discussed in Chapter 3, but for now I hope I have convinced you that learning to act for the stage is a sensible decision.

Finally, and perhaps most important, even if your career ultimately takes you into film and television, your theatre training will provide you with skills that you will bring to the set from your first day, necessary skills concerning acting choices and script interpretation. No one in the exorbitantly costly world of today's filmmaking wants or can afford to train you to think as an actor while you're standing on the set. Producers and directors expect you to come prepared. If you cost them money, they will quickly look elsewhere.

Assuming that you are going to pursue your acting training through theatre, let's examine our earlier list of deficiencies to determine what you can do to eliminate any currently in your way. Obviously, you cannot cure yourself overnight of every "lack" cited. You can, however, discover what theatre is and how it works, and you can certainly begin to get a sense of what you will need to learn over the next several years if you are going to master the craft of acting.

The Ravages of Mass Media

Many of the problems I have mentioned can be traced to the kind of culture we inhabit as a result of the media revolution. The influence of television and film on the way we perceive the world and even on the way we as a culture think is profound. The generation now entering college is a product of this reality. You have grown up on the visual and kinetic images provided by TV, movies, video games, and computers. The language and auditory skills once cultivated through reading books and listening to radio are all disappearing, as is the expectation that educated people use language with wit and sophistication. Yet the principal enterprise of theatre remains the articulation of words, first read from the printed page and then spoken for an audience. If you are going to train in theatre, you must not forget this fact, and you must not take for granted the skill required in reading and speaking effectively. In other words, starting right now you should begin reexamining your relation to words and how you use them.

Many student actors entering college think that good acting is simply a matter of being "believable": If you memorize the lines and can say them like a real person would, everything else takes care of itself. This is simply false. How you use the language to effectively tell the story is as important as being believable. This is especially true onstage, where *you,* not the film director, are responsible for making the story clear. If you currently do not have a strong affinity with words on a printed page, begin reading aloud to yourself and listen to how you use those carefully selected words. Practice adding colors and connotations to adjectives. Make the verbs you speak carry the action they imply. Use your voice to convey the dramatic journey the writer has created on the page. In short, if you do not add to what's in print, you are not doing your job as an actor.

EXERCISE 1-2

1. Read aloud a passage from a book—a descriptive passage, if possible. You may read to your class and get feedback. You could also read into a tape recorder. Analyze what you hear. Charles Dickens, for instance, is wordy. Try to connect his descriptions with specific images they conjure up for you. Attempt to make the words reflect those images when you say them aloud.

2. Find a print ad and read it aloud. Would someone hire you to do what you are doing? Why or why not?

3. Apply my earlier suggestions and the feedback you have gotten to your reading. Read the passages aloud again. Note the changes.

If reading aloud sounds daunting to you, try reading children's picture books or poems for children at first. The language is simple and specific, designed to conjure clear images. Practice communicating those images with your voice. When you can do this, then move on to more sophisticated material. You will be amazed at how quickly your abilities will grow if you commit the time and energy. By the way, if you cannot sight-read well (and many of today's entering freshmen cannot), you must develop the ability. Casting directors do not care that you read and memorize badly because you have a learning disability. They will quickly find someone else who can do the job if you can't. Your teachers will not want to hear your excuses either. Reading and memorizing come with the territory.

EXERCISE 1-3

1. Read a children's story aloud. Become the narrator, and commit to the story you are telling. Shape it. Use every word to communicate its action and feeling. Try Margaret Wise Brown, Maurice Sendak, William Joyce, Shel Silverstein, Eric Carle, or Chris Van Allsburg.

2. Practice reading a short Dr. Seuss book. Be sure to pay attention to the rhythm and rhyme. Find ways to vary the pace and tempo to achieve the maximum comic and dramatic effect. Make sure you find specific imagery for each item on the many lists in these stories. *Green Eggs and Ham* is a particularly good one for this purpose.

3. Listen to an audiotape of a professional narrator reading a children's story. What do you discover?

4. Listen to a book on tape. What do you learn from listening?

Discovering All Your Actor's Roots

It is likely, especially if you are in a BA or BFA program, that your theatre teachers will assume you have a general knowledge about theatre. You may believe that your experience with high school plays and a few drama classes has provided you with this background. It ain't necessarily so. You should enter college or begin your professional career with the ability to articulate what theatre is, how it works, its central ingredients, and its history. If you cannot do this now, then do some reading. There are many books available that can give you a start on the information you need about theatre. For a comprehensive list, see Suggested Readings beginning on page 276.

But you need to know about more than just theatre. Remember your parents and teachers telling you that everything you learn is important? If you think this is an exaggeration, think again. In the theatre, sooner or later *everything* you've ever learned becomes useful. An understanding of world history and culture is absolutely essential for a theatre person. Plays have been written about every subject under the sun and about every time period in which humans have lived. For instance, you might be called upon to act in a play written by an ancient Greek writer long before he was considered ancient. To do that kind of work justice, you must be familiar with every facet of that society—because the choices you make depend on your knowing how that civilization thought and behaved, what its value system was, what its spiritual beliefs were, and so on. Good instincts alone cannot guide you through this kind of acting situation.

I recently read a play called *Arcadia,* by the British playwright Tom Stoppard, which required a knowledge of Newtonian physics and the poetry of Lord Byron. It would be hard to find more eclectic subject matter in a single play. In the play *Top Girls* by Caryl Churchill, both real and fictional women from different periods of history sit down together for a meal in a restaurant. Each woman's story, reflecting her struggle in a world controlled by men, is slowly revealed as the table chat progresses. The actors playing these parts simply have to do their homework. Theatre people must have a broad base of knowledge from which to draw, and they must know how and be willing to do the intellectual detective work necessary to bring their characters to life. You need to start expanding your horizons. So start reading.

Going to the Source

Good theatre may be in short supply where you hail from, but the best way to learn what theatre really is and how it works is to experience it live. When theatre is good, the power and immediacy of the actor-audience relationship is truly indescribable. When theatrical suspension of disbelief is really working, it creates a magic that must be experienced firsthand to be understood—and once you've had that experience, you will likely be hooked for life. Even if you currently don't have this kind of opportunity, it is important to see as much theatre as you can. There is much to be learned, even from bad theatre, if you learn how to view it. Begin to learn to watch theatre actively. Try to figure out what it is trying to do and why it is succeeding or failing in its attempt. Try to reimagine the play in your mind, making the changes necessary for the production to work. Think in terms of the big picture as well as the details. Re-create the casting, the actors' choices, the costumes, the lighting, the settings. Thinking in this way is theatrical thinking. All theatre people must be able to do so.

If you simply cannot see live theatre, or see enough of it, there are excellent alternatives. For instance, many video stores now carry productions of plays that have been adapted for television. Although these productions have been altered slightly to play better for the intimacy of the smaller screen and the close-up, the best of these adaptations retain most of the important qualities they possessed as live theatre productions. Watching these videos will allow you to discover how theatre actors must work from moment to moment, making each new discovery clear and compelling while, at the same time, never losing the thread of the story being told.

Worthwhile theatre productions on video include *Death of a Salesman* with Dustin Hoffman and John Malkovich, *Cat on a Hot Tin Roof* with Jessica Lange and Tommy Lee Jones, *True West* with John Malkovich and Gary Sinise, *Orpheus Descending* with Vanessa Redgrave and Kevin Anderson, and *The Grapes of Wrath* with Gary Sinise and Terry Kinney. If you want the ultimate in theatre, get *Nicholas Nickelby,* featuring the Royal Shakespeare Company. This historic theatre production, though adapted brilliantly for the television screen, clearly retains the essence of what made it a milestone for the theatre. This is, to be sure, a list that barely scratches the surface of what's available. Be sure to watch some classical productions as well. The BBC (British Broadcasting Corporation), for instance, produced an entire Shakespeare collection in the seventies and eighties, many featuring some of the brightest stars from British theatre.

EXERCISE 1-4

1. Read *Romeo and Juliet.* Rent and watch the available videos of it: the recent Leonardo DiCaprio and Claire Danes version, the 1968 Franco Zeffirelli version, and the 1936 MGM version starring Leslie Howard. What do you learn by comparing these different interpretations? In class, discuss the pros and cons of each. Be sure to justify why you liked or did not like the choices that particularly struck you. Describe how each choice worked or failed to work for you.

2. Do the same with *Hamlet.* There are versions starring Laurence Olivier, Mel Gibson, and, most recently, Kenneth Branagh. What do you learn? Discuss the pros and cons of each.

3. Do the same with *Othello.* Once again, there is the Olivier version, but there is also a version starring Laurence Fishburne and one directed by and starring Orson Welles.

4. Do the same with *Of Mice and Men.* There are versions starring Gary Sinise and John Malkovich, Burgess Meredith and Lon Chaney, and Robert Blake and Randy Quaid.

5. Watch *A Streetcar Named Desire* with Marlon Brando and Vivien Leigh. Compare this version to the one with Alec Baldwin and Jessica Lange or the one with Ann-Margret and Treat Williams. Discuss the pros and cons of each.

Today, a large number of films adapted from plays are available for viewing. Often, however, the adaptations destroy the heart of what made these plays so wonderful onstage. For that reason, I can't wholeheartedly recommend most of them, unless you read the script of the play as well. When you see the differences between the written play and the film it has been turned into, some of the differences between the two mediums start to become clear. The film versions of *Steel Magnolias, Agnes of God, Crimes of the Heart, Torch Song Trilogy,* and *'night, Mother,* for example, all adapted from successful stage plays and all boasting major stars and talents, fail to translate into first-rate films. Investigating the failed transfer can be very enlightening to a student of theatre. On the other hand, the brilliant film *Amadeus* was totally reimagined by its author, Peter Shaffer, from his own play, because the author was so aware of how the two mediums differ. *Vanya on 42nd Street,* based on Chekhov's *Uncle Vanya,* is another wonderful film that completely retains the essence of theatre. Comparing the play script with the film version of these clearly demonstrates the differences between theatre and film, and suggests how the strengths of each medium can be used for maximum effect.

EXERCISE 1-5

Read some contemporary plays that have been turned into films. Then watch the films. Compare the two, and discuss the differences. Was the language of the play cut down? Why so? Were additional settings added? Why? Did the film version match your expectations? Explain.

Plays and Films to Read and View

Fool for Love, Sam Shepard
Frankie and Johnny at the Claire de Lune, Terrence McNally
   (film title: *Frankie and Johnny*)
Getting Out, Marsha Norman
Glengarry Glen Ross, David Mamet
The Heidi Chronicles, Wendy Wasserstein
Jeffrey, Paul Rudnick
Les Liaisons Dangereuses (Dangerous Liaisons),
   Christopher Hampton
Love! Valor! Compassion!, Terrence McNally
Marvin's Room, Scott McPherson

Noises Off, Michael Frayn
The Piano Lesson, August Wilson
Plenty, David Hare
Prelude to a Kiss, Craig Lucas
Reckless, Craig Lucas
The Substance of Fire, Jon Robin Baitz
SubUrbia, Eric Bogosian
The Sum of Us, David Stevens
Total Eclipse, Christopher Hampton

My last suggestion for helping you to prepare for your college theatre training is probably the most important by far: *Read plays.* Read as many as you possibly can. Read contemporary and classical plays. Read every genre and style of play. Find out who the great playwrights are and read them—American, European, ancient, and modern. Read current popular playwrights, too, both serious and comedic. You can learn from them all. Read some intelligent criticism as well—theatrical and dramatic. Find out why the great plays are considered great, and try to understand those reasons. Find out why other plays fail—commercially and/or artistically. Analyze every play you read as carefully as you can. Think about what each is trying to say and how it makes its statement. Take apart the plots, the characters, and the dialogue. Find the dramatic components of the story and analyze them for conflict. Be a mechanic and discover each play's inherent machinery. If, as a reader, you can discover how each play works, before long you'll be on your way to making each work as an actor, a director, or a designer. As a result, you might end up getting that first good-paying job. You might even do well in college. Start preparing now for that outcome, and it will be inevitable.

Suggested Authors

Aeschylus	Georges Feydeau	Arthur Kopit
Edward Albee	John Ford	Tony Kushner
Jean Anouilh	Maria Irene Fornes	David Mamet
Aristophanes	Brian Friel	Arthur Miller
Alan Ayckbourn	Athol Fugard	Molière
Samuel Beckett	Jean Genet	Marsha Norman
Aphra Behn	Oliver Goldsmith	Sean O'Casey
Bertolt Brecht	Lorraine Hansberry	Eugene O'Neill
Ed Bullins	Lillian Hellman	Clifford Odets
Anton Chekhov	Beth Henley	Joe Orton
Caryl Churchill	David Henry Hwang	Suzan-Lori Parks
William Congreve	Henrik Ibsen	Harold Pinter
Noel Coward	William Inge	Luigi Pirandello
Euripides	Eugène Ionesco	Edmond Rostand

William Saroyan	Wole Soyinka	Oscar Wilde
Peter Shaffer	John Steinbeck	Thornton Wilder
William Shakespeare	Tom Stoppard	Tennessee Williams
Ntozake Shange	August Strindberg	August Wilson
George Bernard Shaw	Luis Valdez	Lanford Wilson
Sam Shepard	Paula Vogel	
Sophocles	John Webster	

Summary

Students who want to become actors must know and understand theatre. Most acting training, and probably the best all-around acting training, is offered through a theatrical approach, so students must be able to read, analyze, and synthesize plays. They must also understand the conventions of theatre and how theatre works. They must understand what makes a play good and how drama works. They must be familiar with plays and the playwrights who write them. They must see as much theatre as possible. In short, acting, particularly acting for the stage, will require a great deal of hard work, much of it headwork. Desire and inspiration alone will not make you an actor.

CHAPTER 2

What Is Theatre?

In Chapter 1, I presented some of the reasons why the theatre is a wonderful acting training ground and offered suggestions for developing a familiarity with what theatre is and how it operates. Yet most of you are probably not aware of theatre's special demands and characteristics. Even if you have already developed, through experience, some concepts about theatre, it is a good idea that you be able to define this most ephemeral of art forms and to describe its most important qualities and characteristics.

A Definition of Theatre

Eric Bentley, the famous theatre critic and scholar, provided one of the simplest definitions of theatre that I've heard: Theatre is *A* (*the actor or performer*) *performing B* (*the script or performance*) *for C* (*the audience*). Most simply, then, any performance for an audience could be considered theatre. Peter Brook, one of the greatest theatre directors of the twentieth century, refers to theatre as "the empty space" in his essential theatre book *The Empty Space*. In that work Brook says that "someone walking across an empty space while someone else is watching him" could be considered an act of theatre.

   To make this very point, I often begin my first introduction to theatre class by sitting silently in a chair in the center of the room, usually facing my students. As the first-day arrivals begin to trickle into class, they don't realize that I am the teacher. I sit there silently until long past the time class should have begun. Eventually, the noise in the studio begins to diminish, and, one at a time, the students turn their focus toward me. The sense of expectation in the room becomes more and more palpable. Soon all eyes are on me. At that point, I pull out an apple or some other piece of fruit and begin to eat it. My class watches raptly—as though they are seeing the most amazing event of their lives. I simply eat—as I would if I were alone. Eventually, the class begins to laugh as I bite into the fruit, as I chew it, as I swallow.

Why do they react this way? They do so by virtue of the fact that the entire class has become an **audience**—a group of people joined as one to witness a singular event. They are sharing the experience of watching me perform the task of eating. A **theatrical event** is taking place. Any performance happens in continuous action. It is performed live by one or more human beings in front of an audience whose members share the experience together. Once the shared experience is over, it will never be repeated, and even if it is, it will never be exactly as it occurred at the time of the event described. This description comprises the basic characteristics of theatre.

EXERCISE 2-1

1. Create and perform a one-minute solo theatrical event in front of your class. It can be structured as a well-prepared and rehearsed assignment, or it can be something you think up on the spur of the moment and then perform.

2. Discuss your performance with the audience after they have watched it. Was your theatrical event a success? Why or why not? On what basis was it judged?

3. Discuss the performances of all class members in relation to each other. Which were considered the best? Did the best theatrical events share some common characteristics? What were they? What conclusions can you draw, if any, about the nature of theatre?

The fact that a theatrical event has taken place, however, does not necessarily mean that what was witnessed was good theatre. Some have defined good theatre as theatre that both entertains and enlightens (that is, it is both enjoyable and has something valuable to say). What is witnessed, then, not only should engage the audience but should also comment somehow on what it means to be human. In other words, good theatre is usually about something; it has some kind of point to make. **Theatre** is, after all, the one art form where human beings perform as human beings, setting out to imitate or represent our humanness—using our bodies, voices, intelligence, and spirit—to another group of human beings who witness the event. Obviously, the balance of entertainment and enlightenment that a particular piece of theatre may offer will vary according to the material itself and the production choices that have been made collectively by all those involved: the actors, directors, designers, producers, technicians, and so forth.

EXERCISE 2-2

1. Create a one-minute solo piece of theatre that has something to say. The performance should be centered around some idea or issue, or some statement that you want to convey.

2. Rehearse your piece, then perform it for the class.

3. Discuss your work with your classmates. Was the idea communicated clearly? Was your piece enlightening? Was it entertaining? What was the balance between the two? Was your piece successful? How was its success or failure tied in with its balance between entertainment and enlightenment? On what specific terms was your piece evaluated? What conclusions can you draw? About your work? About the nature of good theatre?

In the case of my fruit eating performance, clearly the audience is entertained. They watch with great interest, and they respond spontaneously. They even laugh heartily as I eat. But does my performance qualify as good theatre? The answer is subjective, as opinion on art, popular or high, always is. But even subjective judgments must be based on objective criteria in terms of the qualities of entertaining and enlightening, the E and E of theatre. Today's audiences, mostly uneducated about theatre, tend to judge E and E with the eyes they have developed through years of watching television and film, two hybrid mediums of theatre that, for the most part, focus far more on entertainment value than on the potential for enlightenment.

Suppose you were to judge my classroom performance to determine if, as theatre, it was good. On the entertainment side of the equation, you could ask the following questions about my performance:

- Was my fruit eating entertaining?

- Was it as entertaining as it could have been? As it should have been?

- Was it completely satisfying with regard to the story my performance seemed to want to tell?

- Did it offer up a good story?

- Did it make the audience suspend its disbelief? (Was the audience willing to accept the action as true while viewing it, even though they knew it was not real?)

On the enlightenment side of the equation, you could ask these questions:

- What did my performance say about the subject of eating or, more specifically, about the human condition as it relates to eating?

- Did it say something important about how an audience behaves as a group? About teaching as performance, or about performance as teaching? About the nature of theatre itself?

Again, although responses may be subjective, the collaborators who create theatrical works are responsible for anticipating their audience's answers to these questions if they are to produce entertaining and enlightening theatre. In other words, if my fruit eating was good theatre, then it needed to involve more than simply repeating rotely for an audience what I might spontaneously do in life. Although theatre must appear to be spontaneous, it rarely actually is so. Theatre, like other art forms, must select and organize pieces of reality in order to make a point or create an effect for its audience. This is part of the theatrical process that actors untrained in theatre seldom, if ever, think about.

EXERCISE 2-3

1. Create, rehearse, and perform a solo theatrical piece entitled "A Concert on Self." The piece should not be more than five minutes long. It should contain no dialogue, yet it should reveal something about yourself that you would like your class to know. Make your performance piece entertaining and enlightening.

2. Discuss the performance with your classmates, and evaluate the results.

To summarize then, *good theatre requires A doing B for C,* and, unlike its hybrid dramatic forms, *it must also attempt to be enlightening as well as entertaining for its audience.* Because of the live nature of theatre, this entertainment and enlightenment will be direct and immediate. Good theatre requires making artistic choices purposefully and with the audience in mind. This, of course, is critically important for the actor to realize, and it marks a crucial difference in how a theatrical actor must think compared to how a film or television actor must think.

The Performer

Because most theatre requires an actor to work from scripted material, it is imperative that an actor be able to interpret a script both for its story value (the first E) and for its meaning (the second E). Young actors without a theatrical background too often think that all there is to acting is speaking the words of a script in a believable manner. This approach to acting will sometimes work in film and television but will seldom make an actor a successful craftsperson or artist onstage. The many reasons for this will be discussed in Chapter 3. For now, suffice it to say that in film the actor has to get a particular moment right only once; the director is responsible for getting the story and meaning of the script across to the audience clearly and powerfully. Onstage, it is *always* the actor's responsibility to deliver the story and meaning, and that responsibility is a large one.

Let's go back to my fruit eating performance to take a better look at what I'm talking about here. Suppose my purpose was simply to entertain. Even then, as an actor, I could have done better. I created my basic script—to eat the fruit—without any thought or preparation. I knew from my past theatrical experience that eating would produce laughs. The contrast between the relatively private act of eating and the public place in which that act takes place, particularly the more or less formal environment of a first-day college class, guarantees that response. In addition, the fact that I am initially perceived as a professor, rather than as a human being, who is eating in front of strangers makes the situation even more fertile ground for comedy. However, that was as far as I went in my preparation. I could have done much better.

Which is funnier, for instance, an apple or a banana? A banana, of course. First of all, it is phallic, and it is automatically associated with comedy. Monkeys eat bananas, comedians do pratfalls because of them. Given the circumstances, then, eating a banana is the obvious way to go. If I keep in mind the phallic potential of a banana, everything from peeling it, to placing it in my mouth, to biting down, to the final swallow, makes it ripe for comedy—if I keep in mind the audience's perspective of what I am doing. Some of what I am describing to you an audience might see on its own anyway, but it is the responsibility of the actor and the production team to maximize every theatrical situation to produce maximum entertainment value.

EXERCISE 2-4

1. Rework one of your earlier exercises focusing on its entertainment value.

2. Perform the exercise for your class.

3. Discuss the results.

Now let's suppose I was after more than entertainment when I did my fruit eating theatrical event. What if I wanted to enlighten my audience as well—to make some statement about the human condition, about what it means to be a member of our species? If I had been performing a written script, it would have been my responsibility to interpret the script and find its central **idea** or **spine**, before making any theatrical choices. Once I did, I would have to find ways to make the spine clear from the things I chose to do in my performance. Since my little original theatrical event has no script, it is up to me to decide beforehand what it is I want my audience to understand or learn. And it is up to me to come up with a series of finite choices that will make the meaning of my performance clear.

For argument's sake, I have decided that my point is to demonstrate how an audience can turn ordinary behavior into performance simply by being an audience. I decide to help the audience know that what they are watching is indeed a performance. I will bow to them before I start to eat, and I will bow to them again when I have finished eating. These symbolic gestures will establish theatricality. At each step of my eating I will look at the audience, letting them know I am aware of their watching. This again will invite them to consider my actions as a performance. I will look at them whenever I think what I am doing will be funny to them. This will encourage them to respond. I will also look at them whenever they laugh at me when I am not expecting it. In this manner I will have shaped a performance emphasizing the theatricality of my ordinary behavior. I will have done so by clearly focusing on the audience-performer relationship. No doubt the performance will still be entertaining—probably even more so—and yet it will now have a point beyond its entertainment value.

On the other hand, suppose I wanted to make the point that eating is a very peculiar activity in which we all partake. I might choose to slightly exaggerate each of my eating procedures while retaining believability. Peeling could be more important than I otherwise make it: I could take great care in undressing my banana. The way I place it in my mouth could be more careful and deliberate than usual. I could chew longer than I would ordinarily. My swallowing could be more pronounced. The net effect of my exaggerated eating would probably be to make the audience more aware of the process than they might otherwise be. They might very well draw the conclusion that eating is a funny-peculiar activity. Again, the meaning I set out to convey would determine my choices as actor/performer. Were my fruit eating theatre piece to be fully produced, all members of the production team would make choices to contribute to the overall entertainment and enlightenment aspects of this fruity production, because theatre, by its nature, is collaborative.

EXERCISE 2-5

1. Rework one of your earlier exercises focusing on its enlightenment value.
2. Perform the exercise for the class.
3. Discuss the results.

The Performance

In theatre, what the performer does is always dependent on the source material, and the actor/performer is obligated to serve that material. In modern theatre the source material usually consists of a script filled with dialogue and stage directions written down by the playwright. This playwright realizes that his or her source material is only a guideline for a completed production. That leaves a lot of latitude for a production team to interpret the script and to make choices that will emphasize or underscore the meaning they decide the audience should come away with. Once the rehearsal period is over and the work is being performed for an audience, the choices made for the production must be **controllable** and **repeatable** even though moment to moment spontaneity is healthy. (There will be more on this in Chapter 3.)

EXERCISE 2-6

1. Put in writing an outline of what you did in an earlier exercise from this chapter.

2. Exchange outlines with one of your classmates.

3. Rehearse and perform your classmate's outline.

4. Discuss the performances, focusing on the differences between scripts, the first performance, and the new performance.

Most historians believe that theatre as we know it today evolved from ancient religious rituals such as sacrifices for fertility and appeals to the gods for other favors. When these ceremonies brought the desired outcomes, the religious elders were careful to repeat the ceremony in the manner that brought success. In other words, the ceremonies were ritualized to ensure that success would be repeated. Ceremonies thus became planned performances repeated each time in a specific manner, and the priests or the shamans became performers fulfilling their scripts.

Western theatre can be traced directly back to the ancient Greeks. Their religious festivals evolved into scripted performances in which actors portrayed characters who played out a series of actions in front of an audience. These scripted performances had story lines as well as dialogue and were meant to reflect to the audience some moral statement that would be familiar and important. Many of these works are still performed today and have as much beauty and validity for our society as they did for those who first watched them. The six **elements of drama** laid out in the seminal work *The Poetics,* by Aristotle, theatre's first critic, remain the basic elements that make up contemporary theatre: action, character, dialogue, idea or spine, music, and spectacle.

EXERCISE 2-7

1. Divide into groups and make a list of rituals that we engage in today (Thanksgiving dinner, birthday celebrations, decorating the Christmas tree). Create a short group theatrical piece based on one of the rituals on your list.

2. Perform the piece for your class.

3. Discuss the piece in terms of ritual. In terms of theatre. In terms of the definition of good theatre. Was the piece entertaining? Enlightening? Entertaining *and* enlightening? Why or why not?

The word **drama** can be traced back to the Greek word meaning **action**. Aristotle pointed out how plays are really about action, and a good play will move relentlessly through a series of actions or events until the final outcome of the story is revealed and somehow resolved. When we view a contemporary play, whether it centers on plot or character, it is still the story that holds our interest. If a play does not have a compelling story to tell, chances are it will not please the audience viewing it. Directors, designers, and actors are well aware of this fact, and before rehearsals begin, they make choices that they believe will best serve the production. Usually, these choices are intended to make the story of the play, along with its spine, as compelling as possible. A play with a great idea behind it will fail if that idea is not encased in a story that somehow grabs an audience.

EXERCISE 2-8

1. Using the discussion in Exercise 2-7, rework your group ritual so that it now tells a story. Keep in mind the six elements of drama put forth by Aristotle.
2. Rehearse and perform your piece.
3. Discuss the results.

The Audience

Without the audience, there is no theatre. Until an audience views a theatrical work, it is not a performance—for it is the audience, in Peter Brook's words, "that completes the steps to creation." Critical public viewing is necessary for all of the arts, popular or fine, but only in the performing arts is that response communal and immediate. Theatre (as well as dance and musical performance) is experienced by a group of people who respond collectively as one body and influence the performance in both obvious and subtle ways.

An audience gives immediate feedback to performers. This feedback often affects how what is being enacted on the stage is delivered and carried out. Actors doing a live performance can feel the audience's reactions moment by moment, and a performer cannot help but respond to those reactions. For this reason, no two performances in theatre are ever exactly alike. In my own fruit eating performance (the one that demonstrated the importance of interaction with the audience), I noted that I would play off my spectators as they responded to my actions. But even if getting the audience to respond was not my planned goal, the power of the audience cannot be ignored, nor should performers want to ignore it. The continuous interaction between performer and audience creates a magnetism and electricity that is one of the cornerstones of theatre's uniqueness—and of its **immediacy** and **ephemerality**.

EXERCISE 2-9

1. Repeat each of the group ritual performances from Exercise 2-8, but this time the members of the watching class must play the

role of audience rather than just be one. They should force reactions to the work they see, but make their reactions seem as believable as possible. They should laugh, applaud, boo, and hiss wherever appropriate. Discuss with the performers how this reaction affected their work.

2. Volunteers from the class can be selected to tell a long story or joke to the class. The class should react to the storytelling in some overt or exaggerated manner. Discuss what effect this audience reaction had on the storytelling.

3. Watch any live performance, or a live performance on tape, and study it for the performer-audience interrelationship. Discuss your observations with your class.

As I mentioned earlier, theatre is the one art form that uses humans as both the medium and the subject for its art, while at the same time commenting on what it means to be human. The events that occur onstage are selected and arranged so that they convey specific meaning to the audience. An audience responds intellectually as well as emotionally to the traffic onstage, if and when that arrangement is successfully put together by the playwright and the production team. In addition, an audience's distance from the action allows it to judge what it is seeing more objectively than it might be able to judge a similar situation in life. This paradox is called **aesthetic distance**, and it creates for an audience the opportunity to make judgments about issues intellectually while retaining some degree of emotional empathy, walking in another person's shoes, so to speak, before making judgments. This is one of the characteristics that gives theatre its tremendous power.

In spite of its empathy, an audience never completely forgets that what they are watching is fictional. Yet, when the performance is working, the audience will pretend that it is real, at least while in the act of watching. This **suspension of disbelief** is one of the consummate magical elements of the theatre. A reality far different from the one we experience in our own lives can and will be accepted onstage—as long as the reality created is consistently maintained throughout the performance. For instance, the world created when we view a production of Shakespeare is not the reality we find in our own lives. People do not speak, dress, or even behave like the characters we find in that world. Yet, for the "two hours' traffic onstage," we choose to believe that they do, in order to fully share in the theatrical experience. We suspend our disbelief, even while making judgments about the characters and the situations that reveal them to us.

When the Chorus in *Henry V* apologizes to the audience for the limitations of his theatre, he is really reminding that audience of their obligations during a well-presented theatrical event. In this speech, the Chorus asks his audience to suspend its disbelief—to believe that which might not be believed in film, on television, or, for that matter, in life. What the Chorus asks his listeners to do is to take on the special responsibility of a theatrical audience.

> Can this cockpit hold
> The vasty fields of France? Or may we cram
> Within this wooden O the very casques
> That did affright the air at Agincourt?
> O, pardon! Since a crooked figure may
> Attest in little place a million,
> And let us, ciphers to this great accompt,
> On your imaginary forces work.

Unfortunately, too many members of today's theatre audiences do not understand this responsibility because they do not understand the elements, conventions, and ingredients of this unique art form. For them, the beauty, magic, and communicative power of theatre is sometimes lost. Sadly, in an era of instant gratification, theatre has become an acquired taste. But like good wine, caviar, and Tony Bennett, theatre is more than worth the effort, and for those who make it, theatre's rewards remain timeless and universal. For those who plan to study theatre, understanding its component parts is more than an obligation—it is a privilege to be cherished.

Summary

Theatre is created when a performer performs something live and continuously for an audience. Good theatre is entertaining and enlightening. It is selective. It somehow comments on the human condition. Theatre began as religious ritual and evolved into its present dramatic form, which usually includes action, character, dialogue, idea, spectacle, and music as its basic elements. Good theatre most often centers around a good story, and what happens onstage is controllable and repeatable because actors are well trained and rehearsed. Theatre is a unique art form in that it is created and performed live for an audience. It is therefore both immediate and ephemeral. Theatre is dependent on the interaction of performers and an audience who must suspend its disbelief and watch with some degree of aesthetic distance. Unlike television or movies, theatre expects and requires some work from the audience, but the effort is well worth it for those willing to develop the understanding it requires.

CHAPTER 3

Stage Acting and Film Acting: Same Game, Different Surface

In Chapters 1 and 2, I have tried to make the point that learning to act for the stage is the best all-around method for mastering the acting craft, whether you ultimately work in film or in theatre. The craft of stage acting will serve the actor well in either medium, whereas mastering the craft of screen acting does not necessarily prepare an actor for theatrical performance. This has been demonstrated time and again by the difficulty American screen actors have when they attempt to work onstage, and by the refusal of many fine film actors even to make the attempt. Although some stage actors do have trouble shifting to meet the demands of the camera, in time most manage to do so, and many learn to do it extremely well. Far fewer successfully make the jump from film to stage.

Some Misconceptions about Stage and Screen Acting

Most British actors consider it a routine part of their craft to work in both theatre and film. Is their training and technique so different from that of actors in the United States? Some people may argue that English actors are far more external in their approach to acting—that what works brilliantly onstage looks false, technical, or too big on the screen. Yet for years, discerning U.S. audiences have been watching English actors give wonderful performances on quality PBS series such as *Masterpiece Theatre* and *Mystery*. The versatility and range demonstrated by many of our overseas cousins is a marvel, and the small screen has served to enhance the reputation of British acting here in the United States. Further, the work of gifted English film actors such as Anthony Hopkins, Juliet Stevenson, Daniel Day-Lewis, Vanessa Redgrave, Miranda Richardson, Minnie Driver, and Alan Rickman, all trained in English theatre, completely dispels the negative view of British acting.

In the United States, on the other hand, actors often consider it necessary to choose one medium over the other. Many student actors believe that the skills they acquire training for the stage will get in the way of truthful acting for the camera. Film acting is real, they think, whereas acting for the stage is not. Film acting can all be done with the eyes, whereas stage acting requires an exaggerated use of the face and body. Film acting, they declare, is intimate, internal, and natural, whereas acting for the stage is anything but—it is too presentational and totally manufactured. If you act for the stage, they maintain, you will be condemned to false acting on the screen. The fact is, however, that neither medium is more or less real than the other. The mediums are simply different—in ways that I will discuss shortly.

A closer look quickly reveals many fine actors on this side of the Atlantic who are accomplished in both mediums and who travel seamlessly from one to the other—for example, Meryl Streep, Al Pacino, Glenn Close, Robert Duvall, Kevin Spacey, and Laurence Fishburne. Clearly, acting need not be exclusive to any one medium. Rather, like the tennis player who can compete on grass or clay, the actor must be aware of the differences between the mediums and must adjust his or her game to each. Further, any young actor who thinks film and television require less technical skill than stage acting has never been in a room filled with film, sound, and lighting equipment, surrounded by an army of frantic technicians and a demanding mob called the production team. Bottom line is "tennis is tennis," if you've got the right training.

EXERCISE 3-1

1. Make a list of your own "best" actors. Don't include actors you like just for their personalities on screen. Focus on those actors you most respect *as actors*. What criteria do you use for your evaluations? Translate those criteria into qualities you think are necessary for good acting.

2. Compare your list with those of others in your class. Who are the big repeats? Why do you think this is so?

3. Which of the actors on the following list do you think could act well onstage as well as on screen? Why? (Be sure to consider how these actors use their voices and bodies to convey story and character.) Rank the actors on the list from best to worst as film actors. Rank them from best to worst as potential stage actors.

Kevin Bacon	Nicholas Cage	Whoopie Goldberg
Angela Bassett	Jim Carrey	Tom Hanks
Kathy Bates	Leonardo DiCaprio	William Hurt
Halle Berry	Sally Field	Samuel L. Jackson
Jeff Bridges	Bridget Fonda	Diane Keaton
Sandra Bullock	Morgan Freeman	Kevin Kline

Jack Lemmon	Edward James Olmos	Sissy Spacek
Jennifer Lopez	Gywneth Paltrow	Uma Thurman
Shirley McLaine	Sean Penn	John Travolta
John Malkovich	Rosie Perez	Sigourney Weaver
Walter Matthau	Michelle Pfeiffer	Robin Williams
Julianne Moore	Lou Diamond Phillips	Kate Winslet
Eddie Murphy	Julia Roberts	
Nick Nolte	Meg Ryan	

4. Research the actors on the preceding list to find out which are stage actors or have at least been trained in theatre. How do your findings correspond to your rankings?

The Actor's Medium versus the Director's Medium

If, for well-trained actors, working in both mediums is simply a matter of making adjustments to the different courts being played on, what are the characteristics and requirements of each? Perhaps the best place to begin this discussion is by acknowledging that film is a director's medium, whereas the stage is an actor's. Simply put, in film the director has almost total control over what the audience sees. Onstage, it is the actor who controls what is seen by the audience. This is one of the most significant reasons that acting training should begin with the stage. Let me explain.

In film, the director selects what an audience will see in various ways. First, the director decides what the camera will film. He or she can shoot a close-up of the person speaking or a close-up of the person listening. The director can also shoot both the speaker and the listener at the same time, either with a midshot or with a shot from a greater distance that could include some of the background set. The director decides what is most important to show aesthetically and what is most necessary to show to convey the story. Often a director will shoot a number of possibilities and decide later which to use.

Second, if the director has shot the scene from several angles, he or she—along with the editor—can choose, through cutting and editing, what to show at any given moment. In other words, during the scene, the editor can cut from one actor to another at any time, always keeping the audience focused on what is most important at the time. The editor can edit to make a moment clear and well acted even when it is not. For instance, if a weak actor cannot deliver his or her big moment clearly, believably, and with optimum dramatic impact (the obligation of all good acting), the editor can cut away to a listening actor for a much clearer and stronger reaction shot. In other words, the bad acting has been eliminated simply by technically rerouting the focus of the audience. The audience will never know that famous rock star X, making his dramatic debut, can't really act at all. Stage actors do not have this luxury. Hence, a director's medium.

Onstage, the actor is responsible for every moment, and the audience's focus can only be directed by what the actors do and say. All actors remain visible from the time they enter the scene to the time they exit. Therefore, the stage actor must be acting—and acting well—at every moment. The messages the audience receives during a live theatre performance come as a result of the specific choices the actors make and the way they use their voices and bodies. There are no cut-aways to protect the stage actor.

I define good acting for my students as *"acting that is believable and that tells the best possible story while serving the script."* After all, once the curtain goes up in live theatre, it is the actors themselves who make clear the story, propelling it forward moment by moment. And each **moment** must itself be clearly rendered: Like bricks in a building, each moment must be carefully placed before the next can be laid; otherwise, the structure will collapse. It is the actors themselves, then, who must be aware of the throughline of the scene, building it toward its climax while clarifying and amplifying each dramatic moment as it comes up. This can only be achieved *knowingly,* even though each moment must seem to the audience as though it has never occurred before. Of course, during re-hearsals, the director helps the actors flesh out the story and its individual mo-ments, but once in performance, it is the actors who make it happen night after night. Hence, an actor's medium.

EXERCISE 3-2

1. Read the following list of actions. (Note that for the sake of con-venience I've used feminine pronouns here. Male actors should substitute *he, him,* and *his.*)

- A character enters her apartment.
- She wipes her forehead.
- She fans herself with her hand.
- She goes to the far end of the room where the windows are located.
- She tries to open the first one.
- She stops trying.
- She unlocks the window.
- She tries to open it.
- She stops trying to open the window.

- She looks around the room.
- She goes to a table with drawers by the door.
- She opens a drawer.
- She looks for something in it.
- She rummages through the drawer.
- She finds a hammer.
- She closes the drawer.

- She returns to the window with the tool.
- She gently bangs the hammer against the wood frame of the window next to the lock.

- She puts down the hammer.
- She tries again to open the window.
- She stops trying to open the window.

- She picks up the hammer again.
- She bangs the window frame harder.
- She puts down the hammer.
- She tries the window again.
- She opens the window.

- She sticks her head out the window.
- She fans the cool air against her.
- She withdraws her head.
- She goes to the second window.
- She opens it.

- She goes to the door next to which is an electric switch for the ceiling fan.
- She throws the switch on.
- She stands under the fan.
- She looks around the room.

- She goes to a chair.
- She sits.
- She takes off her shoes one at a time.
- She sits back in the chair.

- She turns toward the phone on a table near the left window.
- She gets up and crosses to the phone.
- She picks up the receiver and says, "Hello."
- She listens.
- She says, "Good-bye."
- She hangs up the phone.

- She returns to her chair.
- She sits.
- She puts her head in her hands.

2. Select any single sequence of actions from the preceding list, and perform it for your class. Discuss your work. Was it believable? Why or why not? Repeat the sequence until you can do it specifically and believably.

3. Select three connected sequences from the list, and perform them in order for your class. Discuss your work. Was it believable? Why or why not? Repeat the actions until you can do them specifically and believably.

4. Why do you think there is a space between each sequence of actions in the list? Test your theory.

5. Have a class contest. Starting with the first action, a member of the class should attempt to perform as many of the actions in

sequence as he or she can. When this person fails to follow the sequence correctly, the next member of the class begins at the failed action and continues until another mistake is made, and so on. Keep a tally of the most correct completed actions executed in sequence.

6. Discuss the work you observed. Were the actions all executed in a believable manner? Why or why not? Which actions (and actors) were more believable? Why? What is the connection between this exercise and the subject of movie acting versus stage acting?

7. As a rehearsed exercise, practice doing ten, twenty, or all of the actions in sequence. Perform your work for the class. Discuss the performances you see.

EXERCISE 3-3

The following description should be read aloud by a single reader while one or more actors execute the actions being described. Again, change the pronouns to *he, him,* and *his* as appropriate. (Best results are achieved when one actor works at a time, but several actors could, if necessary, work simultaneously.) If necessary, the reader may go back and repeat parts of the description until the performer(s) can execute each action correctly.

A character enters her apartment after a long, hot commute home from work. She notices that the room is stifling. She realizes that there are no windows open. She goes to the far end of the room where the windows are located. She tries to open the first one. She cannot. She notices that it is locked. She unlocks the window and tries to open it. She cannot. She looks around the room and notices a table by the door. She goes to the table, opens a drawer in the front, and looks for something in it. She rummages through the drawer until she finds something. It is a hammer. She closes the drawer and returns to the window with the tool. She gently bangs the hammer against the wood frame of the window next to the lock. She puts down the hammer, and tries again to open the window. It is still stuck. She picks up the hammer again and bangs the window frame harder. She puts down the hammer, and tries the window again. This time it gives. The window opens. The character sticks her head out the window. The breeze blows against her face and upper body. The character fans the cool air against her. She withdraws her head. She goes to the second window. She opens it easily. She does the same to the third. She goes to the electric switch by the door and throws it on. The ceiling fan above spreads its cooling breezes. The character cools her perspiring body under it. She looks around the room. She goes to a chair and sits. She takes off her shoes one at a time. She sits back in the chair. The phone rings. She gets up and crosses to the phone on the table near the left window. She picks up the receiver and says, "Hello." She listens for some time, and finally says, "Good-bye." She hangs up the phone. She returns to her chair. She sits. She puts her head in her hands and does not look up again.

1. How did the acting for this exercise compare with the acting for Exercise 3-2? Why? Be specific in your comparisons.

2. Who did the best work? Why? What about the work made it stand out? Be specific.

3. How do the differences between this exercise and Exercise 3-2 relate to the differences between film acting and stage acting? To what you know about acting in general?

4. Discuss what you learned about acting by doing these exercises and/or observing the work of others.

EXERCISE 3-4

1. Play "Add an Action."

A volunteer steps onto the stage, or into the center of the circle made up of your class, and executes a single, complete action (something you actually do physically). This action should have a beginning, middle, and end. Once the action is completed, the actor should freeze briefly, then return to the circle. For instance, the first actor enters the space and stops, then returns to the circle. The next actor repeats the first action and adds a new action that follows logically from the first. The second actor might turn his or her head to the left and to the right, before freezing and returning to the circle. As each new actor takes a turn, the added action should develop a story that is simple, clear, logical, and dramatically interesting. The exercise is over when all actors have had a chance to contribute an action, whenever the story has been completed, or when your teacher or coach decides to stop the game.

2. Discuss the game in terms of what you learned about acting. Who were the most believable players? Why? Who were the least believable? Why? Who were the most interesting to watch? Why? Who were the least interesting to watch? Why?

3. Do you see any connection between what you learned from this exercise and the earlier discussion about film acting versus stage acting? Discuss.

Adjusting to Technical Demands

So, which medium is more realistic, more natural to act in? A medium where each moment unfolds one at a time in proper order without stopping, where one dramatic event leads to another? Or a medium where scenes are often shot out of sequence and actors have to figure out what happened previously? Where only one moment may be created at a time, where the camera must be repositioned for every angle and every moment to be covered? Where an actor may be asked to repeat that moment fifty or more times until the director likes what she or he sees and hears, until the technical obligations of the camera and sound crew are met? The answer is, neither, really. Each medium has its own technical problems that the actor must deal with, and in each, the actor must bring a different set of skills to accommodate those problems. But the fact remains that learning to act for the theatre is the most sensible route for aspiring actors to take. If you have mastered the craft of acting for the stage, you will in time be able to learn the technical aspects of acting for the camera.

Let's take a closer look at some of the technical obligations involved in each of the two mediums.

Stage Skills Do Double Duty

For young actors afraid that learning the craft of acting for the stage will destroy their ability to be natural, live theatre does have certain characteristics that might make those apprehensions appear true. What about the issues of size, of voice, of style, of language? Stage acting does require its performers to make many adjustments that seemingly make their work less real. A large theatre, for instance, requires an actor to project his or her voice so that the back row can hear every word. These words are often more important and poetical than those spoken in films, or in life for that matter. But this should be no surprise. The history of theatre is a history based in language for the ear rather than images for the eye, as in the more visual cinema. Moreover, the actor has the responsibility to make the words of the text clear and might even be required to shape those words to sound beautiful if, as in the words of Shakespeare, the material requires it. That might mean being "unnatural." Portraying the heroic passions of ancient kings and queens might also mean acting in a style larger than what we might display in real life. But will meeting these obligations destroy an actor's ability to meet the demands of a film performance? Not if the actor has the talent and training to do so. Remember the tennis player.

EXERCISE 3-5

1. Stand as far away from the class as possible. Recite a nursery rhyme. Make your class understand the nursery rhyme by how you move and how you speak, but keep your distance. Communicate the message contained in the story.

2. Stand very close to your class and repeat Step 1 of this exercise.

3. Select one person from the class, and, from a distance, repeat Step 1.

4. Stand nose to nose with a person from the class and repeat Step 1.

5. Repeat Step 4, but this time say one line at a time. For each line, change your position or your physical relationship to your listener.

6. Repeat the sequence with other actors and other nursery rhymes.

7. Discuss what you observed and learned about acting from the sequence of steps in this exercise. Discuss any differences between film acting and stage acting you might have discovered. Did your definition of "believable" change according to the exercise? Why or why not? Who did the best work? Why? Can you draw any conclusions about good acting and not-so-good acting?

The British actor Ralph Fiennes recently completed a run in the title role of *Hamlet* on Broadway. He received rave reviews from the critics. His ability to serve the text, which included at least five major monologues, while bringing a sense of excitement and energy to the role, was noted again and again. Yet most audiences are far more familiar with his work in film. His role in *Schindler's List* as the sadistic concentration camp commandant is unforgettable. Ironically, it is the understated manner of the character in the film, his cold arrogance and impenetrable silence, that makes Fiennes's portrayal so frighteningly human and real. It is a cinematic performance made compellingly clear, more through what we see than through anything else. Fiennes uses his skills as a theatre actor, carefully choosing his physical actions to convey specific meaning in each frame of film. In *The English Patient*, Fiennes played many scenes with no dialogue and bandaged so that his face can't be seen. Yet in spite of this, his physical action made clear what he was thinking and feeling. The actor's ability to work well in both theatre and film is, no doubt, at least partially based on the choices he makes about his work—choices that are clear and compelling, choices that are made in conjunction with the technical demands of the medium he is working in. But because he is a fine actor, he makes those choices seem spontaneous and real. His performances could not have been achieved simply by behaving believably while the camera was running, an approach that some film actors untrained for the stage might take.

The point is that Ralph Fiennes, like most well-trained actors, is able to adjust his work to the demands of the medium. Believability does not necessarily depend on creating the reality we experience in life. Believability onstage depends on the conventions established in any particular production. The audience for theatre suspends its disbelief in accordance with the material being watched. If the actors consistently play the conventions they've established, the audience will believe the action. It is no different in film.

The subject matter of movies and the way they are written often reflect a seemingly more literal reality, possibly because film is not restricted by stationary sets and budget considerations, nor is it language oriented. A film's means of communication is primarily visual, and through technical wizardry, film can convince us that almost anything is real. A fleet of flying saucers, a flock of homicidal tornadoes, and a dozen identical Michael Keatons can be created with or without the audience's willing suspension of disbelief. Yet in spite of all that, Patrick Stewart must still convince us with his own skill as an actor that he commands a starship. The world of *Star Trek* is a far cry from any reality Stewart has experienced in life. Making the role of Captain Picard seem believable is an acting obligation no more natural than playing Hamlet for the stage. Yet Patrick Stewart, a Royal Shakespeare Company veteran, does it brilliantly. On the other hand, film actor Sylvester Stallone has been far less convincing in the futuristic films *Demolition Man* and *Judge Dredd*. A good actor is a good actor and, in most cases, will be able to adjust a performance in accordance with the material.

EXERCISE 3-6

1. Watch the film *The Bridges of Madison County.* Compare the work of Meryl Streep and Clint Eastwood, two actors with opposite acting backgrounds and styles. Study what they do. Which performance gives more to the audience, and why? What does each communicate through what he or she does physically? Who does a better job of letting you know what he or she is thinking and feeling? Which of the two tells a better and clearer story over the course of the film?

2. Watch the film *Crimson Tide.* Study the crew of the ship, most of whom have little dialogue. By the end of the movie, do you feel you know many of those characters? Without dialogue, how was that feat accomplished?

3. Watch and compare the film versions of Shakespeare's *Henry V*— the first with Laurence Olivier, the second with Kenneth Branagh. What are your reactions? Note the differences in style. Which is more theatrical? Which is more cinematic? Branagh is one of the great contemporary English-speaking classical stage actors. Can he act for the camera?

4. Watch the film *One Flew Over the Cuckoo's Nest.* Study how Jack Nicholson and his fellow inmates continue to tell stories even when they are not speaking. Notice how Nicholson never has a moment when he isn't furthering the story. Watch how he does it.

5. Watch the film *Remains of the Day.* Study Anthony Hopkins's performance. List what he does physically that tells us what he is thinking and feeling. What do you think of his performance? Explain. Compare what he must do to get his story across with what Emma Thompson must do.

6. Read the play *Amadeus* and then watch the film version. How are they different? Why? The same writer wrote the play and the screenplay. Why and how did he change his work?

7. Watch *Death of a Salesman* with Dustin Hoffman, a video version of a stage production. Study the acting. Is Hoffman different on stage than in his films? How? Why? Draw conclusions.

The Technical Demands of Working for the Camera

Screen actors must pay attention to the technical demands of their medium as well, and by doing so, they must sometimes do things far more unnatural than projecting to the back row of a theatre or speaking lines no one in real life would ever say. For example, when Captain Picard reels from the impact of an asteroid, no asteroid exists; Patrick Stewart is pretending. When Sam Neill's eyes well up at his first sighting of a living brachiosaurus, he is watching a spot on a blue mat pointed to by some technician from George Lucas's Industrial Light and Magic Company. When the little boy in *Close Encounters* beautifully registers his awe at the dazzling light beamed from a spaceship, he is not acting at all. He is really being caught candidly by the camera as he watches Steven Spielberg dance in a bear suit. The illusion of the spaceship is achieved later by cutting. Are these examples from film work really more lifelike, more believable, more natural than those achieved when acting for the stage?

Even when not being asked to support the demands of special effects, the screen actor must continually contradict real-life behavior to meet the demands of the camera. Actors seldom look directly at each other in a two-shot, for instance. If they did, each actor would be partially blocked, and the framing for the camera would not be as interesting. Film actors must learn to "cheat" for the camera—an accepted part of film acting. Obviously, that is not natural behavior. In addition, for close-ups actors often speak to other actors who are not even there. Since a single shot must be covered from many angles, the actor without the lines is often dismissed, leaving the speaking actor to imagine the reactions of his or her partner. Or, when two or more actors appear in the same frame, they are often placed in body relationships that would never occur in life but that look good for the camera. The actors must pretend, for instance, that it is normal to stand and chat while their bodies are touching at the hips. This position, of course, doesn't show because the camera is framing a close-up of the faces.

When being blocked for the camera, performers are often asked to do things far more unreal than anything a director might ask in a stage production. In order to "hit a mark," for instance, an actor might need to time a cross in order to hit a certain spot at a specific moment or precisely as a certain piece of dialogue is being said. This often requires actors to move unnaturally fast or slow to meet the needs of the camera, sound recorder, or editor. I once had a job where, in imitation of Rocky Balboa, I had to jog up the steps of the Philadelphia Art Museum while keeping my fisted hands above my head in victory. In order to accommodate the technical needs of the shot, I had to jog in quarter speed up the steps. And it took over a dozen takes. Try maintaining your victory energy on take 12 at quarter speed while climbing a hundred steps! It eventually looked great on film, but it felt ridiculous.

Next is the problem of "continuity." Film actors, like actors onstage, often rely on "pieces of business" to keep the reality of their acting strong. **Business** consists of any small pieces of action actors do while the scene is going on. Smoking a cigarette, putting on makeup, or drinking coffee can all be considered pieces of business. Onstage, an actor times out any business during rehearsals to get the maximum effect from this physical work, sometimes using business to accentuate a moment. Stamping out a cigarette harshly to show that a character is angry is an example. Because stage acting is done in sequence, there is some flexibility to using business and room for that magical improvisational moment. But in a film scene, if an actor chooses to stamp out a cigarette, then that cigarette must be stamped out exactly in the same manner on each take from different angles. Otherwise, the editor will be faced with the impossible task of putting the scene together bit by bit where actions don't match up from one moment to the next. Being shackled by your own solid acting choice is anything but natural. If you pay attention, you'll be able to find countless examples of bad continuity on television, because a film or TV show is shot much faster (to keep costs down) than a theatrical release. Time and budget restraints can make for sloppy work, especially when actors are not technically proficient.

Then there is the issue of being too big or too small for the camera. It is true, as the cliché goes, that a film close-up might require an actor to act with nothing but the eyes. But how will the actor know what to do with the eyes if he or she is simply behaving? What must the actor as the character try to communicate in this close-up? Making the right choices is still a part of the good actor's obligation. And what about an extreme long shot? Can an actor simply rely on his or her eyes when they are not even visible in the shot? In such scenes an actor, shot with a Panavision lens, takes up only a minute part of the frame yet very well may be expected to carry focus. If that is the case, then the actor had better be able to make some strong choices with the body as well as the face. In other words, like the stage actor, a film actor had better be able to project. Otherwise, the editor will be putting in some very long workdays, and the director will end up having to be far more creative than he or she ever anticipated.

EXERCISE 3-7

1. Invent an imaginary monster. React believably.

2. Recite a poem or something else you've memorized, at the same time doing some business. Repeat the poem, stopping at each line. Pick up the next line at the exact spot you left off the business. Use your class for a continuity check.

3. Improv a scene with a partner while walking much more slowly than you would in real life. While walking much faster. While never quite looking at each other. Discuss the results.

Finally, what about those models, athletes, and other nonactors who are discovered and instantly given leads in films? Liv Tyler, for instance, whose previous claim to fame consisted of performing in an Aerosmith video (and being the daughter of the group's lead singer), has recently appeared in a spate of new films, mostly independent or foreign. In *Stealing Beauty,* for instance, she had the lead role in a film directed by Italian film legend Bernardo Bertolucci, who had nothing but praise for her. Clearly Mr. Bertolucci loved her face on screen, and for him, she possesses some kind of magic cinematic power. Because of that, he was able to build a film around her face; and through camera angles, reaction shots, and clever cutting and editing, he shaped a performance for the screen that was fascinating as well as beautiful. Yet, both *Time* magazine and the *New York Times* asked the same question: "Can she act, and does it matter?" By her own admission, Ms. Tyler has never had an acting lesson; but in the past several years, she has completed seven movies, including the 1998 summer blockbuster *Armageddon.* Right now she is hot, hot, hot. Cindy Crawford, on the other hand, has been less successful in her early film efforts. Is it the material, the director, or the talent of the actors that spells the difference? The jury is still out, but it is doubtful whether Ms. Tyler or Ms. Crawford will be offered roles in the legitimate theatre anytime soon. It is even more doubtful that they would accept the offer if one were put forth. After all, in addition to being beautiful, they're probably too smart to make that mistake.

EXERCISE 3-8

Watch again a movie with a performance you really admire. Study the performance. What things make it work so well? Now that you are looking more specifically, has your opinion about the performance changed? Why? What things do you see now that you missed before?

Summary

The mediums of film and stage are different and therefore require different skills from the actors working in each medium. This is a fact, not a value judgment. Actors trained for the stage are generally more able to work in both mediums than are actors brought up in the movies. Learning to act from moment to moment in sequence and without stopping tends to provide excellent training ground for eventual work in either field. Theatre is an actor's medium; there is no place to hide when the work is not up to par. Film, on the other hand, is a director's medium where stopping the camera and editing to achieve desired results are standard procedure. For this reason, it makes sense to train for the stage. Neither medium is more or less realistic than the other. Both require technical demands that go beyond what real people do in real life. These demands must be mastered if an actor is to work believably and compellingly in either area.

The fact remains, however, that an actor working onstage is responsible to tell the story of the play—clearly and compellingly. No one can later make that actor look better than he or she was onstage at any given performance. No one can later make that actor's individual work blend into the larger context of the story being told. On the stage, only the actor and those working with him or her onstage can accomplish these necessary goals, and they can only hope to do so if they have a thorough understanding of the craft and of how a script works—a solid argument for learning acting for the stage.

CHAPTER 4

Inside Out, Outside In: From Stanislavski to Strasberg

I strongly believe that acting can and should be taught as a **craft** consisting of a finite number of concepts and tools that can be mastered with practice and time. Once a student actor has absorbed these concepts and assimilated these tools, he or she can accomplish work onstage that not only serves the playwright's script but is also clear, believable, and exciting. The work will also be controlled and repeatable. This, I believe, is the kind of work that dedicated young actors should set as a goal for themselves.

Craft versus Art

Although I speak of acting as a craft, not as an art, there are those who can miraculously make it so. The distinction between craft and art is important: For me, craft implies a series of skills that can be mastered with practice and dedication. No amount of practice or dedication, however, will make an artist of someone who does not already possess the requisite amount of talent. Talent cannot be learned. It is a gift. I can learn carpentry skills and eventually build a bookshelf that is sturdy and aesthetically pleasing. I can master shape and shading with charcoal and eventually produce a still-life that draws praise. I can even practice chords on the guitar and eventually strum along with an Eric Clapton blues number. But it is a mistake for me to assume that if I practice enough, the cabinets I design and make will be equal to those produced by Chippendale, that my portraits will rival those by the Dutch masters, or that my guitar riffs will be confused with those of Eric Clapton or Andrés Segovia.

True artistry is something few are fortunate enough to possess. That does not mean, however, that those of us not born with a natural gift should remove ourselves from the arts. The development of craft can go a long way to compensate for the limitations imposed by any lack of innate talent. The truth is that an audience probably cannot distinguish between a highly developed craft and a natural talent. For those with lesser natural talent, craft can fill the void. For those blessed with a greater abundance of talent, craft can be the key for opening previously untapped resources, often allowing the true artist to emerge.

In either case, craft is the tangible that must be introduced, developed, and mastered. Most true artists would probably agree that the mastery of technique affords a freedom that would not be possible had that technique never been developed. Would Picasso's later work have been as successful had he not possessed the technique or craft so obvious in his early work? Would the passion and clarity apparent in the work of the great musical soloists be possible if they played totally by instinct without the technique they struggled to master in their years of training? Great English-speaking film and stage actors of the last few generations—Olivier, Brando, Hopkins, De Niro, Hepburn, Davis, Redgrave, and Streep—have all had much training. They have all greatly profited from the craft they have learned. The development of craft is obvious even in the work of our current personality stars. Isn't it apparent that Arnold has learned something about the craft of acting since his debut as Conan the Barbarian?

Technique: Stanislavski or Strasberg?

In each of the arts, proper technique is a source of disagreement and debate. The fingering technique of the violinist, the brush stroke technique of the painter, the vocal technique of the opera singer—all of these topics have provided, at one time or another, a reason for artists to vehemently disagree. Which technique is the right one? Which mentor has the one true answer? Such debates will continue long after any of us will be around to care. But of all the arts, theatre has been the setting for one of the most ongoing public battles over technique. This is ironic since until recently in the history of theatre, no objective acting technique had even existed.

The Stanislavski System

An actual system that could be taught to actors was first introduced in Russia by the great actor and director **Constantin Stanislavski** around the turn of the twentieth century. For a half century or more, Stanislavski studied the process of acting, trying always to objectify what he learned from the work he did with his fellow actors at Moscow Art Theatre. He spent his long professional life observing, theorizing, experimenting, and refining what he believed to be the usable ingredients in the process of acting. His contributions have entirely changed the way actors today approach their work. The great Russian master also unintentionally planted the seeds of debate regarding the craft of acting. In the English-speaking theatre, the debate remains as potent today as it was when Stanislavski's early work was first translated more than a half century ago.

The confusion over what Stanislavski's system really was and is cannot be blamed on the master himself. It is more a result of timing—Stanislavski's first great work on acting theory, *An Actor Prepares,* was not published in English until 1936. This was several years after the Group Theatre, arguably the most important and influential collection of American actors, directors, and playwrights ever assembled in one time and place, had begun implementing Stanislavski's theories based on the work of Richard Boleslavski and Maria Ouspenskaya. Two of Stanislavski's emigrant Russian disciples, they had been distilling Stanislavski's methods through their own classes since the early 1920s, and their work had profoundly influenced Lee Strasberg and others in the Group Theatre. Stanislavski's text appeared at the very time that the Group Theatre was searching for a unifying technique that could support the Group's theatrical goals and philosophy—a philosophy that included a desire for a truthful theatre that was realistic and relevant to the harsh times of the 1930s.

A good part of Stanislavski's early work focused on the internal (inside) aspects of the acting process. To ensure that the work was honest and believable, Stanislavski felt it important for actors themselves to experience the feelings their characters felt at any particular moment in the play. He believed that only by reaching into their own emotional memory bank could actors hope to achieve this state. Stanislavski's techniques for finding this **emotional truth** included concentration exercises and the use of **emotional memory** and the **inner monologue.** Lee Strasberg, the principal acting teacher of the Group Theatre, wholeheartedly embraced this aspect of Stanislavski's teachings, especially the elements concerning emotional memory. The **internal technique** described in *An Actor Prepares* became the cornerstone of Strasberg's famous "**Method.**"

EXERCISE 4-1

1. Recall an incident from your life that had a profound emotional effect on you. Relate the event to the class. Describe your own emotional response to the story you recalled, both now and at the time it happened. Did recalling the event conjure up strong feelings from the past? Explain. What was the reaction of the class to your story? Were they moved by the story itself, by your telling of the story, or by a combination of the two? What is the difference? Discuss their reaction.

2. Retell the story of the event. This time, while telling the story, focus your attention on what you felt at the time the event was actually occurring.

3. Retell the story again. This time, instead of focusing on the emotions you felt directly, try to recall and relate as many sensory details from the experience as you can. Don't attempt to produce emotion; just focus on the details. What did you discover? Describe your emotional response to the event you recalled. Compare it to the earlier tellings. Discuss your own reactions

with the class. Discuss the reaction of the class. What conclusions can you draw?

EXERCISE 4-2

1. Play "Add a Word."

Form a circle with your class. The first person will say and then complete the following sentence: "When my father died, he left me his _____." The first person might complete the sentence with "worn-out copy of the Bible." The next person in the circle will repeat the sentence with the completed statement from the first person and then add a new item. The second person's statement might be, "When my father died, he left me his worn-out copy of the Bible and the memory of his aftershave." The third person repeats the statement and list so far and then adds a new item. Each new item should be as specific as possible. The game continues until everyone has made a contribution.

Note that this game is not about being able to remember the list. It is not about winning and losing. It is about the actor's task of associating the words on the list with real emotional connections. Each player should focus on the specifics of the Bible and of the aftershave. What did the Bible look like and feel like? What was the smell of the cologne? How did it make you feel? When do you most remember smelling it? These are the associations that will make the items on the list have emotional meaning.

2. Discuss your observations about the game. Draw conclusions.

3. Play the game again; this time, use the following sentence: "When I get out of school, I'm going to _____." Follow the process described above.

4. Create your own start-up sentences to complete. A good start-up sentence will suggest emotional connections to build on. Replay the game and see what happens. Be sure to discuss what you observed and the conclusions you can draw from the experience of playing the game.

It is not hard to understand why Stanislavski's early work focused so heavily on the inner side of acting if we examine the theatre and society at the time he began his studies. The rise of the middle class and the development of the science of psychology combined to produce a movement toward realism in European theatre. The merchant class and the problems of ordinary people began replacing kings and queens as the subject matter for drama, and developments in set design and lighting actually made possible the illusion of reality onstage. A need arose for a new kind of acting that could reflect this new theatrical reality. Declamatory acting, with its over-the-top emotional affect, no longer worked.

Stanislavski sought a way to help actors find their way to a more real emotional center that was still dramatically exciting but believable as well.

But as Stanislavski and his Moscow Art Theatre actors continued to use the internal technique, they came to realize its limitations—it was not always reliable, and, worse, it too often produced an effect opposite to the one desired, especially after repetition. Emotional memory, he discovered, sometimes caused his actors to push for an emotion rather than helping them find a real one. Further, by focusing on the emotion of a moment, his actors sometimes became indulgent, or lost the thread of what was supposed to be happening in the unfolding story on stage. Besides, the obligation of projecting the work clearly to an audience was sometimes unnatural and interfered with the spontaneity and truthfulness of the work being produced. Eventually, Stanislavski and his company abandoned this technique as their principal approach in favor of the more external (outside) approach of physical actions.

EXERCISE 4-3

1. Be angry. Each member of your class should take a turn to demonstrate anger for the class. Discuss the results. Whose was the best portrayal? Why? Draw conclusions.

2. Do something you would do when you are angry (pound a desk, kick a chair). Commit to the action. Each member of your class should take a turn. Discuss the results. Compare the results with the anger produced in Step 1.

3. Recall a situation in which you were angry. Try to remember all the details of your outward behavior. What things did you do? Re-create those things and perform the "be angry" exercise focusing on your actions. Discuss the results.

4. Repeat the process for the following emotional conditions: sadness, jealousy, boredom, happiness, depression.

5. Compose your own list of emotions, and try the exercise with the emotions from your list. Be sure to follow the process in Steps 1 through 3.

Building a Character, Stanislavski's companion volume to *An Actor Prepares,* concerns itself primarily with physical action and the technique of *playing actions,* an approach Stanislavski came to believe was much more reliable for the actor to use. In his opinion, this **external technique** provided a clarity for work on the stage that emotional truth alone was not capable of producing. Some of this work had been described in the earlier volume, but in Stanislavski's later years he came to the conclusion that honest emotion could be produced spontaneously if actors fully committed themselves to the actions they were playing. In other words, the work was now more concerned with what an actor "does" rather than what an actor "feels." *Building a Character* did not appear in English until 1949, thirteen years after the first volume, and far too long after its theories of internal acting had made their way into the heart and mind of Lee Strasberg. Strasberg, who based his own work on the theories that Stanislavski eventually abandoned, went on to become America's most famous acting guru.

EXERCISE 4-4

1. Jump up and down for twenty seconds and stop. What do you feel? Re-create the feeling without jumping. Compare the two feelings.

2. Create the feeling of love from inside yourself. Perform the feeling of love for your class. Discuss with your class what they saw. Hug someone. What do you feel? Compare what you feel to the feeling of love that you created.

3. Engage in a silent activity for one minute in front of the class— something simple such as playing a game of solitaire or doing push-ups. Ask your class to react to what they saw.

4. Repeat Step 3. This time say aloud all the thoughts that occur to you while engaging in the activity. Ask your class to react to what they saw.

5. Again, repeat Step 3. This time try to repeat your inner thoughts from Step 4 by saying them to yourself rather than aloud as you perform your activity. Ask your class to react to what they saw. Draw conclusions.

Stanislavski eventually came to see the processes described in *An Actor Prepares* and *Building a Character* as two parts of a whole that an actor must master if the work is to have true integrity. Further, Stanislavski continued to refine and develop his own thoughts about acting until the day he died. He never believed that he had discovered the absolute right answers about the acting process, nor did he ever come to think that his ways were the only ways an actor could work. His sole purpose was to enable actors, directors, and all theatre people to produce the best work they possibly could.

EXERCISE 4-5

1. Perform one of the following actions.

   Shaving   Smoking a cigarette
   Combing your hair   Watching television
   Taking a bath   Sipping tea
   Reading a newspaper   Eating soup
   Doing a puzzle   Looking at a scrapbook
   Repairing something

2. Repeat your actions, but this time add the thoughts and feelings necessary to make your actions specific and clear to your class.

Say these aloud the first time you try it. Then repeat the action, saying them only to yourself.

3. Perform two of the actions in Step 1, one after another. Make your class believe that it makes sense to do the two actions in this sequence. Discuss the results.

4. Select three actions from the list in Step 1, and perform them one after another. Make your class believe that the three actions are logically connected. Discuss the results.

The Strasberg Method

As an acting teacher, **Lee Strasberg** was not as flexible as Stanislavski in his approach to acting, even though his "Method" was based on his reading of Stanislavski's early work. Strasberg demanded that each of his actors develop, master, and employ only his specific techniques. During the Group Theatre days, Strasberg's demands caused rifts among the Group's members that probably helped lead to its eventual dissolution. These rifts certainly helped generate the various schools of acting that developed in the United States as former Group members started their own acting studios. Among these famous acting teachers are Robert Lewis, Harold Clurman, Sanford Meisner, Paul Mann, and Elia Kazan.

But Strasberg's most famous adversary during the Group Theatre's existence and later was **Stella Adler,** his preeminent rival acting teacher in New York. As an established actor from a famous acting family, Adler resented having Strasberg's technique pushed down her throat during acting classes at the Group. She was never comfortable with its premises, and no matter how hard she tried, she could not master the technique. She felt it was silly to use emotional memory since living in the circumstances of the play had always worked well enough for her in the past. She felt it was the actor's job to pretend, and she saw no need, at least for her, to introduce elements from outside the play.

During a trip abroad in 1937, Adler met in Paris with Stanislavski for several weeks of lessons. On her return, she reported on what she had learned to the Group and to Lee Strasberg in particular. She told Strasberg that he was misinterpreting the Stanislavski system's early work and that a newer set of principles was already being used by the master. Strasberg responded that he was not using the Stanislavski system, but rather the Strasberg "Method," and the name as well as the technique stuck.

In 1982, on the morning after Lee Strasberg died, Stella Adler ordered the members of her class to stand up. She told them that a "man of the theatre" had died the night before. After a full minute, she harshly told her class to sit down. When they had, she told them it would take a hundred years to undo the harm Strasberg had done to the art of acting. No doubt, this was an overstatement—a statement made by a vituperative rival—and many of the most respected actors of the era following World War II would argue that Strasberg was the greatest teacher of acting since Stanislavski. An army of fine actors—including Marlon Brando, Al Pacino, Paul Newman, Robert De Niro, Dustin Hoffman, Marilyn

Monroe, and Ellen Burstyn—seems to have developed brilliantly under Strasberg's tutelege, and many have chosen to carry on his classes.

Choosing Wisely

So, here is the point: Inside out or outside in, it doesn't really matter in and of itself. What matters is the work and your ability to do it the best you possibly can. If your natural gifts are enormous and your instincts never fail, then don't impose on yourself training techniques that don't help you. And if, like Stella Adler, you are being forced to master a technique that requires you to simply throw away all the things that work for you, think twice before you do so. If parts of something you learn from one technique help you but others do not, use only what works. If your product is outstanding, no one will criticize you because of how you got there. Craft is not religion; it is meant to serve you, not the other way around. Perhaps that is what so upsets those who criticize Lee Strasberg. They argue that he came to believe he alone possessed the answers to all acting questions. In truth, no one does.

Keep in mind, however, that if you are a student just beginning your training, it is your responsibility to avoid any premature judgments about the craft you are learning. Perhaps the following incident from one of my sophomore scene study classes best illustrates that caution: Two of my students had been working on a scene from the play *All the Way Home* by Tad Mosel in which their characters waited for confirmation of the death of one of their husbands. Questions about playing actions (outside) and playing emotions (inside) continually arose, and the students struggled in particular with the scene's emotional content. After several reworkings, the actors finally brought in a scene that was simple, clear, and believable because of the strong use of **physical actions** and clearly played objectives. The story within the scene had finally become apparent. However, the scene still lacked the emotional punch needed to make it work completely.

I surprised my class by announcing that we would begin doing some emotional work to enhance the scene. They were shocked and began arguing that this kind of work should not be necessary if the actors were playing fully. They even began to indirectly insult the two actors working on the scene by suggesting that "good actors" can automatically bring out the proper emotions if they are fully playing the given circumstances of the scene. In my mind, the actors were playing as fully as they could at the moment but needed more than what I had so far been offering. My class, however, felt betrayed: I was violating what they perceived to be my "unassailable" technique, a technique that had helped them quickly improve and that they had confidence in. In spite of the fact that I had always told my class that I am eclectic, that I will do whatever works to get the best possible results, my students had already become so dogmatic that they were unwilling to try something new. A monster had been created, though not consciously, by my hands. I eventually got my message across to my students, but it was difficult, and feelings were hurt along the way.

The point here is an important one, one that needs to be remembered: *Your mind must remain open.* Acting is not geometry. Art is not science. There are no absolutes. If the great Stanislavski could remain open and receptive to new ideas until his death, certainly you, still at the gateway to your art, can afford to do so. Perhaps finding your own technique will come as a result of mastering those of others. The search never completed is probably the most effective search of all.

Summary

The study and mastery of acting craft, like the study of technique in any art form, is intended to help aspiring artists use their innate talent to maximum effect with maximum economy. The tools of any craft, unlike intrinsic talent, can and must be learned, for their mastery ensures that an individual's talent will be consistently and reliably applied. The craft of acting, first explored and developed by Stanislavski, can be approached through inner (creating emotions) or outer (playing actions) techniques, or any combination of the two. Though some teachers are doctrinaire and demand that their students commit fully to a rigid approach, developing actors should never forget that the purpose of studying craft is to make them the most effective actors they can be. That means that all actors must be responsible for mastering and applying the aspects of craft that work best for them. Implied in this, of course, is that all student actors will give every concept they encounter an honest reception and trial before making any decision about its effectiveness. Though the approach offered in this book is clearly oriented to the playing of actions rather than of emotions directly, there is no doubt that an eventual exploration of deeper emotional truth can be an invaluable tool for any actor. It is my belief, however, that head-first acting is necessary if the actor is to best serve the script.

CHAPTER 5

The Actor in Service of the Script

What is good acting? Most people have an opinion on the subject. Almost everyone can name a favorite actor, and most people enjoy debating over who are the "best" actors. In fact, though, most viewers' opinions about acting are based more on the personalities of the actors than on the work itself, and even a discerning viewer might define good acting simply as acting that is "believable." The actors we most often recognize as the best, however, do much more than act "believably."

What is it that makes Dustin Hoffman, Daniel Day-Lewis, or Meryl Streep stand out from so many others who also act "believably"? It can't be simply personality, since these three actors seem so different from role to role. Even Jack Nicholson, a charismatic personality actor like the great stars of an earlier era, is sometimes much better than he is at other times. Why is it that Harrison Ford, so effective in *The Fugitive* or *Air Force One*, was noted more for his bad haircut than for his performance in *Presumed Innocent*? Why was he panned in *Sabrina*? This chapter may provide an answer.

EXERCISE 5-1

1. Select some of your favorite actors. Think about the roles you have seen them in. How were they different in each role? Were they more effective in some roles than in others? Why?

2. Make a list of actors you consider outstanding. Write down the film or television roles in which you found them most memorable. Try to isolate the reasons these actors made your list. Why do these roles particularly stand out in your mind?

During the past several years, I have auditioned and interviewed hundreds of student actors. In almost all cases, when I discuss their audition monologues with them, the students talk in terms of "character" and "feelings." For most beginning actors, it seems, the process of acting is centered on and controlled by these two ideas. The influence of the Strasberg "Method" and of the actors associated with it has no doubt nurtured and mythologized an actor's focus on feelings and character. It is certainly not surprising, then, that so many young actors think about their acting in those terms.

Consequently, it is ironic that in spite of these attempts to produce emotion and to develop character, most of the pieces I see at auditions fail. Even the work from students who are obviously very talented is generally unexciting—that is, during the course of the monologue, nothing new happens, nothing changes, there are no surprises, no twists, no payoffs. Very often, because of certain misconceptions, students choose to do the very things that make them seem "actorish."

Good Actors Tell the Story

"This piece is a sad piece," the student actor says. "The character's mother has just died, and the character loved his mom very much. The character is very sensitive, and since the character I'm playing is so sad, I have to be very sad."

"Have you ever been this sad?" I ask the actor.

"Sorta," the actor responds. Or, "Sure, that's why I connected so strongly with this piece."

"And did you ever speak to someone while feeling so sad?"

"Yes. Of course."

"And when you spoke, was what you had to say meaningless because you were in so much pain?"

"No, of course not. I wouldn't have spoken unless I had something important to say," the young actor responds indignantly.

"Then why were you busy emoting, rather than trying to *communicate* your thoughts and feelings? If you focus on what you're trying to do, those emotions will still be there!" To that I might get an argument, but after working a short while, the actor discovers that his or her work is vastly improved when the *doing* rather than the emoting is the focus.

"You see?" I ask. "Isn't what you are doing and needing more important than what you are feeling? And, by the way, wasn't it more comfortable having something to do besides be sad?"

Almost without exception, the answer to that question is yes.

By focusing on the doing, the actor can project the emotion more believably and more effectively, and the work overall has more spontaneity, variety, and context. What all this demonstrates is that actors must always concern themselves with the story going on. More than that, they must continually help unfold and tell the story.

Watch Harrison Ford in *The Fugitive* or *Air Force One* telling stories about his character at every moment. He finds ways to do this in spite of the fact that he has little dialogue to work with. Then watch him in *Presumed Innocent.* Ford appears unchanged, hangdog fashion, from the first frame we see him in to the very end of the film. His performance, in my opinion, is dull because his choices leave him no room for telling the story of his character. In spite of the fact that before the character is accused he has every reason to be happy, Ford finds no moments to show this. As a result, his character always seems disgruntled, leaving him no place to go when things begin to turn bad.

Every choice that actors make on stage or in film *must be selected to help convey the story.* In other words, actors are in many ways like playwrights and authors. Everything that the characters say and do must add to the telling of the story. When this is accomplished, the acting and the production always benefit. Since most audiences go to the theatre or to the movies to see a good story, it is essential that the actors focus on making that story as clear and exciting as possible.

EXERCISE 5-2

1. Tell a story to your class, one that really happened to you. Was your telling successful? Why or why not? What are the elements that make an oral story work?

2. Listen to several other people tell their true stories. Which of the stories were compelling? Which were boring? Why?

3. Listen to several people tell jokes to your class. Which were successful? Why?

4. List the ingredients that you think make a story work.

5. Play a game such as hopscotch, one in which some kind of concentration and physical skill is necessary. Be sad, or angry, or happy, or another emotion of your choice while playing. Observe what happens to you during the game. Analyze your results, and draw conclusions.

6. Play the same game focusing only on playing as best you can. Compare the results.

Finding the Conflict and Playing Objectives

So how does an actor go about telling the story in a compelling fashion? As you probably already know, stories are composed of characters, plots, and settings. They also have points of view and usually convey some idea beyond the story itself. Plays work the same way, although point of view and theme are less obvious given a play's structure. All plots, however, are built on **conflict.** If actors can identify the conflict in any given scene of a play or create some kind of conflict in any given moment onstage, they are well on their way to interesting and clear acting—acting that tells the story.

There are four basic types of conflict:

1. A person struggling against himself or herself

2. A person struggling against another person

3. A person struggling against nature

4. A person struggling against society

In each of these situations, characters pit themselves against a force that is trying to keep them from some objective, something that they need or want, something that is extremely important to them.

EXERCISE 5-3

1. Think about several books and movies that have made a strong impression on you. What was it about these books and films that left this lasting impression? What were the main elements of conflict in each? How did the conflicts in these works contribute to your enjoyment of them? How were the other elements that made up the book or movie affected by the conflict?

2. Select a specific conflict from a movie or book. Be sure your selection is well known. Perform its central conflict somehow (without dialogue) for your class. Discuss the results. Was your class able to identify the work? What enabled them to do so? What might have better enabled them to identify the work? Was the performance interesting to watch? Why or why not?

3. Working with a partner, think of four different conflicts, one from each of the basic four types. Find a way to dramatize each without using dialogue. Perform each for an audience. Discuss the results. Which conflict was clearest to your audience? Draw conclusions.

This term **"objective"**—or **"intention,"** as it is sometimes called—was co-opted by Stanislavski (that great Russian acting theorist) and today provides actors with their basic acting tool. In acting terms it is loosely defined as *"what the characters need,"* and it is the actors' responsibility to spend their entire stage life pursuing that objective. Unlike in life, Stanislavski pointed out, where people spend most of their existence unaware of what they want, *actors must know at all times what their characters need and must continuously make choices that will lead their characters to these goals.*

In other words, a character's life onstage is much less complicated than that of people in real life. For most of us, life can be confusing and unclear, and we are indecisive. Actors, however, must prioritize and choose constantly. To most beginning actors, this essential concept seems too confining, if not ridiculous. But an audience fills in the gaps, and a good script protects actors by providing them with the necessary complexity.

EXERCISE 5-4

1. Walk across the floor while the rest of the class watches. Describe how it felt.

2. Place a long strip of masking tape across the floor, and walk across it while the class is watching. Discuss how this was different from the walk in Step 1.

3. Pretend the masking tape is a tightrope, and walk across the floor while the class is watching. Discuss this experience in relation to the previous steps.

4. Walk a tightrope that is high above the ground while the class is watching. There is no net. Discuss the experience.

EXERCISE 5-5

1. Play "Freeze Tag." Where was your focus? Did you feel emotions? Connect your experience to the acting process.

2. Play "Steal the Bacon." Discuss the game in terms of playing objectives. Connect your experience to the acting process.

3. Play "Red Light, Green Light." Discuss the game in terms of playing objectives. Connect your experience to the acting process.

Building Dramatic Conflict

In well-written plays, things happen dramatically. As characters pursue their objectives, **obstacles** appear that keep them from their goals. Conflict results, requiring characters to search for new ways to get what they need. When one tactic fails to achieve its goal, characters try another and another until they achieve success or until they give up their objectives altogether and find new ones. This continuous struggle toward some goal keeps characters multidimensional and interesting. It also makes them understandable and therefore extremely important to the telling of the story.

Unlike in the short story or novel, the dramatist has only dialogue and limited stage directions to work with. Therefore, a script itself is only a skeleton for the action that unfolds during a play. Although an audience sees characters moving through their lives onstage, what these characters think and the manner in which they go about their physical lives may not be explicitly stated, or even implied, in the script. It is the responsibility of actors and directors to bring to life the details of the unfolding story. *The more conflict that the actors can invent, the more interesting the work.*

For instance, suppose the author states in the stage directions to a play that a character picks up a pen and begins to scratch out words on a manuscript. That seems simple enough. But consider for a moment the literally thousands of ways a person could pick up that pen and begin to write. Which is the correct way? Which is the most dramatic way? Which is the best way? There is, of course, no right or wrong answer to this question. But it is up to the actor to tell the best "pen" story possible given the overall story of the play.

In the last act of Chekhov's *The Seagull,* Treplev picks up his pen and begins to scratch out sections of his manuscript. He is in despair over his failure as a writer and over his inability to have his love for others returned. The actor playing Treplev must find physical choices that will communicate Treplev's mental state and situation to the audience. The actor who simply picks up the pen and begins to delete words tells us very little about the situation. However, if he picks up the pen and poises it above his manuscript as he reads, he reveals a bit more. If he writes furiously in the margins, or haltingly while crossing out many times, he reveals more still. If he crumples a page and throws it disgustedly on the floor, he tells a lot. If he picks up the entire manuscript and throws it across the room, he is very revealing. In fact, these actions, if put together in sequence, tell a climactic little story that does not appear in the script but is certainly dramatic as well as valid given what we know of Treplev's nature and situation.

In the example of Treplev, the character's internal conflict is demonstrated in a dramatic (if less than original) way. Had the actor chosen to simply scratch out words, his acting would have contributed little or nothing to the audience's understanding of the character and situation. With the choices that I have suggested here, however, the audience will more fully understand Treplev's character and predicament and be better ready to accept the suicide that he commits a few pages further on.

EXERCISE 5-6

1. Select an historical character and choose a famous moment of conflict in his or her life. Without the use of dialogue, try to tell the story of that moment. Perform your work for an audience. Don't play the cliché by trying to do an impression; instead, handle the conflict the way you think the historical character might.

2. Get feedback and discuss the strengths and weaknesses of your performed work. What was usable criticism, and why? What worked, and why? What did not work, and why?

3. Rework the performance after considering your audience's comments.

Physical Actions: Beginnings, Middles, and Ends

Actors often find themselves in onstage situations that may have no apparent conflict. Even then, good actors take responsibility for telling some kind of story, a story that will ideally contribute to the audience's overall understanding of the characters and the plot development. Remember that every story has **a begin-ning, a middle, and an end.** If actors can execute all three of those steps, their work will be clear and interesting.

EXERCISE 5-7

1. Improvise the following scene with an acting partner: You are in love with each other. You may or may not be aware of each other's feelings, but neither of you has yet expressed them. Each of you in turn will say, "I love you." That's it. Try it, and read on only after you have worked on this for a while. (*Hint:* Don't for-get about what you need in the scene.)

2. Perform the scene for an audience.

3. Get feedback from the audience and discuss.

You might have thought that since you and your partner love each other, there is no conflict in this scene. If you based what you did solely on the dialogue pro-vided, your scene was probably very dull. But scenes and plays are not about di-alogue. Rather, the dialogue, like the physical choices in the Treplev scene mentioned earlier, is just another tool that the actor must use to tell the story.

For Exercise 5-7, good actors would have asked themselves, "Why haven't these two characters said they love each other?" There must be a reason, and it is up to the actors to find it. Could it be that these words are just too hard for these two characters to say? If so, why? Or, are the characters afraid of the repercus-sions of actually saying these words?

EXERCISE 5-8

1. With your partner, make a list of all the possible reasons two characters might find it hard to say "I love you."

2. Select the reason that seems to hold the most conflict.

3. Improvise and perform an "I love you" scene based around that conflict.

4. Get feedback from your class.

5. Compare the two scenes and draw conclusions.

Establishing a reason that keeps the characters from speaking their feelings will provide the key to the conflict in the situation. It will require either or both of the characters to tackle the obstacles that keep them from their goal. *Finding ways to overcome obstacles and inventing ways to physically demonstrate them on stage is the actors' responsibility.* Doing so can go a long way toward enriching this deceptively simple two-line scene.

EXERCISE 5-9

1. Enter a stage on which an object has been placed. Tell a story without words that involves the object on stage. Make sure your story has a conflict.

2. Discuss the exercise. Was the story clear? Did it make sense? Was it interesting?

3. Try the exercise with the following items: a penny, a quarter, a dollar, a $20 bill, a wallet, a baby doll, a gun.

Don't read on until you have tried the exercises.

Telling Good Stories

In the case of the penny, the first actor to perform the exercise in my classes will usually choose to ignore the penny even if he sees it. The actor will enter and exit the playing area without stopping. After completing the exit, the actor will usually look toward me, anticipating some kind of praise.

"You seem very satisfied with your work," I begin.

"I thought I did a good job," the actor responds. "That's what I would have done if I passed a penny."

"But it wasn't very interesting."

"Neither is a penny. It wasn't a very interesting situation you gave me."

"You chose to make it uninteresting. You created and settled for an obvious situation. This is *your* exercise! Who said the character had to be you? Your responsibility as an actor is to be compelling by telling interesting, exciting stories. In this exercise, you are the playwright. You could have invented anything you wanted—could have *been* anything you wanted, but you didn't. A smart actor will always create the best he or she can from any given situation."

Suppose the actor had entered the stage in a hurry, but the penny caught her eye. She stopped, reached down, picked up the penny, and checked the date. Suppose it was valuable? She could have chosen physical actions that demonstrated this. As a result, her exercise would have been far more interesting because, as an actor, she had chosen interesting things to do. The exercise as I just described it had a conflict (in this case, internal)—the character's need to be somewhere in a hurry against her desire as a collector to check the date on the coin. It also had a beginning, a middle, and an end—the seeing of the coin (beginning), the picking up and discovery of the coin's value (middle), and the decision to keep it (end)—each step essential to the telling of any story. Each of those parts could and should be further broken down by the actor so that she can make physical choices that clearly demonstrate each element of the unfolding action and that provide her with specific and interesting things to do. The more valuable the discovery, by the way, the more dramatic the reaction of the character and the more interesting to act and to watch.

EXERCISE 5-10

1. Go fishing. Without dialogue, improvise a scene where you are fishing. There is no one else in the scene. (*Hint:* Use what you have learned so far.) You can do this exercise alone or with several others at the same time, but imagine that you are alone.

2. Discuss the improvisations. Which ones worked best and why?

Read on only when you have completed the exercise.

If you have been paying attention up to now, you probably figured out a location for your fishing and invented rods and reels for yourself. You might have been standing or sitting in a boat, or sitting onshore or on a dock. Almost everyone comes up with some kind of fishing process. But the big question is, Did you invent a fishing *story* for yourself to tell? Most students given this exercise do not invent a story—or if they do, the story doesn't go anywhere near far enough. As I sit and watch a roomful of mimes going through the motions of fishing, what I see, for the most part, is boring—usually because of the lack of a watchable story. When I stop the exercise, my first comments will reflect that fact.

"But fishing *is* boring," someone says.

"Not always."

"But my experience was. I wanted it to be boring to demonstrate that fact."

"Good!" I say. "You succeeded!" The student gives me a look of satisfaction, but only for a moment.

Reflecting a boring reality might be believable, but is this the best kind of choice for an actor to make? Given the vast number of things an actor could select from, why choose to be dull? Isn't the "business" of acting hard enough without making it more so? Producers, directors, and casting agents can hire anyone they wish, so why train yourself to be boring onstage? It is far better to find things to do that are interesting—that are still believable. Remember, good plays are seldom written about the ordinary or the mundane. Things happen in a play. Plays tell stories; so should you.

What could happen while fishing? What conflicts could arise? Think in terms of the four types of conflict mentioned on page 47, and list all the things you can come up with that apply to each category. Then compare your list to the following suggestions: In the category of a person struggling against nature, there are conflicts with weather, tides, waves, currents, wind, insects, heat, cold, the sun, and the dark. The conflicts of a person struggling against himself or herself might include being seasick, having to deal with live bait, fighting off boredom, and coping with the problems of a beginner. (The third and fourth kinds of conflict—a person struggling against another person and against society—are best left for a time when you are working with another actor. It is better not to create believability problems by dealing with people who are not there.)

There are literally scores of things that could provide the raw material for an interesting situation. Use them. Your acting will be easier and more fun to do—and to watch.

Using Each Other: Where the Story Lies

Plays most often deal in conflicts between characters. It is no accident that most plays are composed of scenes primarily involving two actors at a time. The structure of scenes is such that a single conflict is usually worked through by these two characters. Including more than two primary characters makes a scene more difficult to write and to execute. It is like giving a juggler more balls to handle.

In any climactic scene, the conflict is usually very obvious. Since it is the climax, the stakes had better be high. But good storytelling requires that every moment be as dramatic as possible while still supporting the overall dramatic flow. When actors in a scene know what the conflict is, they can then figure out what they need from the other actor and try to get it. *What a character needs in a scene should always involve the other actor sharing the stage.* Otherwise, the playwright wouldn't have put these characters together. Young actors very often ignore this obvious point and exclude the other actors onstage. It is unlikely that this is what the playwright had in mind, and it is not a choice that leads to exciting storytelling.

EXERCISE 5-11

1. Select an objective from the following list or from a list you have composed with your class. Find a partner, try to get your partner to fulfill your objective, and see what happens.

   Possible objectives: to make your partner smile, laugh, frown, get angry, cry, sit, stand, move, jump, close his or her eyes, lie down, beg, kneel in front of you, feel bad, feel scared, feel excited.

2. Discuss the results of these improvisations. Which were the easiest to accomplish? The most difficult? Why? Did you notice anything about specific objectives versus vague ones?

Any number of conflict improvisations can be done with an acting partner. The one in Exercise 5-11 is a basic one. The trick is to develop the ability to pursue a single objective with no detours or tangents. There must be nothing extraneous. Good actors can do this; yet, at the same time, they are listening and responding at every moment to the input they are getting. Good actors know when a particular tactic is not working, because they are listening to those sharing the stage with them. As a result, they know when to give up an old tactic and begin another. Good actors also realize that getting what they need from someone else requires give-and-take. You may not be able to get your partner to do what you want without giving him or her something in return. That can only be mastered by staying in the moment.

Masters Doing the Basics

If you would like to see some great actors doing what I have just described, watch the videos of *New York, New York* or *The Shining*. In the opening scene in *New York, New York*, Robert De Niro tries to get Liza Minnelli to go out with him. She resists, but he refuses to take no for an answer. Minnelli is adamant, but De Niro eventually breaks her down. The story of his getting his objective at the expense of hers is thrilling and clear each step of the way, and the scene has the seeming spontaneity of real life. What higher praise could a scene between two actors receive?

In a scene in Stanley Kubrick's *The Shining*, Jack Nicholson attempts to get the baseball bat that Shelley Duvall is wielding to protect her son and herself from the deranged Nicholson. In some of Nicholson's most inspired, simple, and direct acting, he uses every tactic in the book to get that bat from her. The buildup of storytelling suspense is breathtaking. This scene is unforgettable because the conflict is life and death and the scene builds beautifully to its climax. Once again—actors telling stories brilliantly.

Despite that inspired scene, *The Shining* is not fully successful (especially if you've read the book). One of the main reasons might be attributed to Jack Nicholson's overall performance—not that he isn't "believable" (remember that definition of good acting?), because he is. However, Nicholson failed to tell his story in the most compelling way. From the first scene in which he appears, he seems troubled and on the edge of a breakdown. In fact, he seems a bit crazy. Wouldn't the story of *The Shining* have been stronger had Nicholson not tipped his acting hand so early in the film? By appearing a little crazed from the very beginning, Nicholson shortened the road he traveled from nice guy to monster. There is far less suspense because the story of his losing struggle against the house is a foregone conclusion: Of course the house will make this guy crazy; he practically is already.

In *As Good as It Gets*, Nicholson is far more successful—so much so that he received an Academy Award. Melvin's struggle to overcome his obsessive-compulsive behavior in order to gain the love of the character played by Helen Hunt provides a textbook example of using conflict to tell a great story. Scene by scene, Nicholson defeats his demons in order to get what he desperately wants. We are absorbed by the character's journey toward normalcy, and by Nicholson's clearly etched portrayal of that journey.

Actors must be believed, certainly. But they also must know how to tell their stories compellingly, and stories are crafted carefully, a brick at a time. In a magazine article in the early nineties, Harrison Ford was interviewed by David Halberstam. Known for his reticence with the media, Ford was surprisingly candid because he was permitted to talk about the "craft of acting." And acting is a craft, in his view. He did not talk about inspiration and emotion. He talked about building a performance by making choices. Ford summarized his job by saying that it is the actor's job to "move the story along." What he does is to "take the script, study the story, and see what he can do to make his character advance the story." Doesn't that sound familiar?

Summary

Good acting requires an actor not only to be believable but also to tell the best possible story. Actors must discover and play the conflict of a situation or, if there is none, find one to play. From the conflict, actors can determine an objective for their characters to pursue, one that is a direct outgrowth of the conflict itself. By pursuing this objective, the actors will face and attempt to overcome obstacles that will keep the story dramatically interesting for themselves and for the audience. Actors must also make and execute physical choices that both make the story clear and let the audience know what their characters are thinking and feeling. A story is told through portrayal of actions, not emotions, and actions must have beginnings, middles, and ends if they are to make each moment and the unfolding story clear. Finally, most dramatic situations involve characters interacting and, usually, needing something from each other. Most dramatic conflict is, at least in part, built on this kind of conflict. Actors must be willing to listen and interact with the other actors onstage in order to tell the most compelling and believable stories.

CHAPTER 6

Given Circumstances and Playing the Action

Imagine yourself having one of those actor's nightmare, but not the usual fare, where you find yourself naked onstage or alone with no idea what you're supposed to be saying. No, in this one you have the entire script memorized. The problem is, there are only four lines of dialogue in the script! The two characters, of which you are one, say "hello" to each other and then "good-bye." And that's it. That's the whole play—at least as written. A pretty short play, you're no doubt thinking, but worse, it's also a play with no plot, characterization, or point. And yet, there you are, standing under the lights, with an audience who have paid fifty bucks a ticket waiting for you to entertain and enlighten them. So what do you do?

In Chapter 5 I discussed the need for finding conflict and using objectives to make sense of a script and to guarantee that your work will be clear and compelling. However, as I also pointed out, conflict and objectives only serve the actor who has a clear idea of what goes on in the playwright's script. In your nightmare, no such information is available; the four lines of dialogue offer no specific information about the circumstances of the play. So what do you do?

If your answer is, "Make them up," then your nightmare is coming to an end.

Given Circumstances

In any improvisational situation, the players quickly decide on a few **given circumstances** and use them as the starting point for creating a dramatic situation. You've probably seen comic improvisational groups, either live or on television, operate in just this manner. They usually ask the audience for suggestions and, after selecting the most appealing ones, begin to play, using those selected given circumstances as their guidelines. The audience's suggestions about the characters to be played, their relation to each other, the situation, the location, and the time give the players enough material to create a dramatic event.

The instantly created given circumstances for an improvisation are not unlike the given circumstances gleaned from a script when preparing a play for production. Any set of given circumstances requires the actor to discover the *who, what, when,* and *where* of the play overall and of its individual scenes. Until all of the given circumstances are determined, an actor would be hard pressed to make acting choices that serve the play and the characters in it. Further, unless all actors are in agreement about those given circumstances, the choices they make can turn out to be inconsistent, unclear, and ultimately confusing, even unbelievable.

EXERCISE 6-1

1. Do an improvisational scene with a partner. Do not discuss any of the circumstances before beginning. Describe the experience.

2. Do an improvisational scene with a partner, this time discussing the given circumstances before beginning. Compare the two experiences.

3. With a partner, select and read a scene from a play you have not read before. Don't discuss the circumstances of the play until after you have read the scene. Describe the experience.

4. Discuss the scene you chose for Step 3, making decisions about the who, what, when, and where of the scene. When both of you are in agreement as to the details of the scene, read it together again. Was this reading different? Was this one better? Why?

Once decisions have been made about or interpreted from a script, the given circumstances become the catalyst for creating a compelling dramatic story. Suppose, for instance, that in the nightmare that began this chapter, you decide that you are a character, not unlike Fox Mulder from *The X Files*. The other speaking character is a humanoid alien. (This character information is the *who*.) And, suppose, after a long and frustrating string of unsuccessful searches, you have finally encountered this alien face-to-face. The alien, in turn, has been waiting a very long time for the proper moment to connect with you. (This background story information is the *what*.) And suppose this encounter takes place in the present in the middle of the night in the middle of winter. (This time information is the *when*.) And, finally, suppose this encounter happens in the Mojave Desert, where temperatures drop considerably at night, during a noisy dust storm that impedes visibility. (This location information is the *where*.)

Obviously, this set of given circumstances provides the limited dialogue of the play with many possibilities that did not exist before. In fact, those hellos and good-byes now stand like bookends between which dwells an encyclopedia of dramatic potential. Now that you know you are an Agent Mulder, for instance, you realize this is no ordinary "hello" situation. Rather, it is the meeting of a lifetime. In acting terms the stakes are high, the situation climactic. Your years of obsession about alien infiltration and UFO conspiracies are about to be rewarded. For actors willing to find it, "The truth *is* out there"—all of it contained in the given circumstances. Yet, so far, you have used only the who and the what.

You can find further amplifications by thinking about the when and the where of the situation. The time—the middle of the night—suggests many things that you can turn into useful acting choices. On the simplest level, it's difficult to see at night. The fact that few people will be out and about might affect your sense of security. If you feel unsafe, what things might you do? Things seem less real, more frightening at night. How might that inform your behavior?

A desert at night in winter is cold. This certainly can affect the choices you make physically and can provide obstacles that you can play against. What would you do to avoid freezing, for instance? And the dust storm potentially adds several more obstacles that, in turn, can provide wonderful dramatic possibilities. Is the swirling dust playing tricks on your eyes? Is the noise generated by the storm interfering with your ability to hear accurately? Maybe it's not a spaceship you hear at all, but just the wind and dust howling. How can the questions raised by these circumstances manifest themselves through your actions? What things can you choose to do physically that will help define the situation for the audience and give you actions to play?

The "Magic If"

Before you tackle the issues raised in the previous section, you must consider one more very important thing. Remember, even though it is you, the actor, executing the choices you decide on, it is not quite you in the situation described. It is the character you are playing. Therefore, you must ask yourself a critically important question before you proceed: *"What would you do if you were this character in this set of circumstances?"* We call this question the **"magic if,"** and your answer to it could result in a completely different set of actions from the ones you might choose as yourself. The term *actions* refers to both physical actions (the things you physically do) and **psychological actions** (the choices you make in order to pursue and obtain what you need). Note that what you might do as yourself may be far different from what Fox Mulder might do. His personality is probably very different from yours in the same way that Mulder's is very different from that of Dana Scully, his skeptical partner at the FBI, or that of their even more wary boss, Skinner. Of course, all the FBI agents from the show *The X Files* are radically different from their evil adversary, "Cancer Man." Every character in a drama or in life has his or her own set of characteristics and behavior patterns that are both unique, yet somewhat predictable—once they have been properly analyzed.

EXERCISE 6-2

1. Select an ordinary activity, something you do regularly. Engage in the activity fully and specifically in the manner you would ordinarily do it in real life. Activities might include reading the paper, listening to music, tying a shoe, or drinking a beverage.

2. Select someone you know well—a friend, a family member, even someone famous (provided you do not do a caricature). Engage in the activity you did in Step 1, but do it as that other person would do it. How were the activities different? Be specific.

3. Select a favorite character from a novel. Engage in the activity from Step 1 as the character by using the "magic if." Perform the activity. Discuss the results. Justify your choices.

4. Participate in an imaginary group shower with several members of your class. Make it a communal shower, one in which there are several showerheads but only one shared area. Create the given circumstances, and play the situation as believably as possible. Play the scene as yourself. Keep in mind the "magic if."

5. Consider and then play the following variations of the imaginary group shower:

Grammar-school-age kids of both sexes
Old people of both sexes
Teenagers of both sexes
Both sexes of age thirties and forties
Married couples of the same age

I discussed discovering a character's needs or objectives by determining the story's conflicts in Chapter 5. Obviously, Mulder both wants and needs to make contact with an alien being. He has spent his professional life looking for such an opportunity. But all the things we learn about a dramatic character from our reading and viewing must eventually be translated into tangible actions, because physical actions are by far the clearest way to communicate thoughts and feelings. Asking the "magic if," once your character analysis is under way, could end your acting nightmares forever.

It was Constantin Stanislavski who invented the "magic if," and that essential question works like a master key, unlocking every acting door. Focusing on what you would do *as the character*, after you consider what your character needs, is the cornerstone of clear, compelling acting. It not only makes acting controllable and repeatable, but it also guarantees that the internal life of the character you are playing reads to an audience. It is the audience, after all, for whom you are working. Playing emotions directly, as many beginning actors attempt to do, does not necessarily tell the story of the character or of the play, and emotions are certainly not reliable tools to depend on.

Learning the Score

If the actor's primary job is to tell the story of the play, then he or she is responsible for telling it moment by moment, beat by beat, and scene by scene. Actors are the principal medium through which a good story is told onstage or in film, and everyone, from the playwright to the director to the audience, relies on the actors to move the plot forward as well as to reveal the inner workings of their characters. If the play is to work, this must be accomplished with imagination, clarity, and simplicity.

In addition, if the story of the play is to unfold with dramatic precision, the actors must portray these physical actions through a logical, step-by-step sequence. So let's go back to the four-line nightmare play at the beginning of this chapter and apply some of the concepts discussed in the last two sections. Since the conflict, objectives, and given circumstances (the who, what, when, and where) are now clarified, and we have asked ourselves about the "magic if," we are ready to continue. Here is a **score** of physical actions that, when put together step by step, might tell the story of Mulder's encounter with the alien—simply, clearly, and compellingly. Note that this score is for Mulder only. The alien character's score is the other actor's responsibility. You might try executing the following score of actions in order to determine if this is an effective way of working.

Physical Action Score—Mulder

Beginning

Pace with arms crossed and hands on opposite arms.
Pace while rubbing opposite arms.
Stop pacing.
Look at watch.
Bring watch arm closer to eyes.
Read time.
Put arm down.
Rub arms.
Pace.
Stop pacing.
Stand still.
Tilt head in direction of sound.
Slowly move toward sound.
With hand, flick air in front of eyes.
Stop moving, squint eyes.
Put hands with fingers spread in front of eyes.
Move toward sound again, bending forward as if against a strong wind.
Stop.
Stare with hands still protecting eyes.
Slowly drop hands from eyes.

Middle

Slowly straighten body until upright.

Rub eyes.

Rub mouth.

Blink several times.

Rub mouth.

Lift right hand slowly as if in greeting.

Say "hello."

Slowly smile.

Tilt head as if listening.

Periodically nod slightly but affirmatively several times
    while head remains tilted.

Slowly and strongly nod one time.

Raise hand as if in farewell.

Say "good-bye."

Sigh.

Ending

Continue looking.

Squint.

Tilt body forward.

Move forward a few paces.

Protect eyes with hands.

Slowly move head upward until head is almost straight up.

Lift hand as if in good-bye.

Slowly bring head to normal position.

Drop hands.

Slowly drop to ground by bending knees.

Bring hands toward face while bending head toward lap.

If you read this physical action score without attempting to execute it, you probably still picked up the story. If you actually marked through the physical actions listed, you probably got a pretty good sense not only of what the character was doing but also of what he was thinking and feeling. So would an audience. Rubbing your eyes and wiping your mouth suggest thoughts and emotions, respectively. Nodding your head suggests a telepathic conversation. Dropping to your knees is a powerful climactic gesture, while collapsing your head into your lap clearly relays to an audience the tumultuousness of your experience.

Notice the layout of the Mulder score. The actions are divided into a beginning section, a middle section, and an ending section. This division suggests the storytelling properties of the score. The beginning section sets up the major plot elements and the conflict. The score establishes that waiting is more than a passive action. The waiting also involves actively searching for the alien as well as overcoming the obstacles created by the given circumstances. These obstacles include the difficulty of seeing at night, the challenges presented by the dust storm, and the coldness of the nighttime desert. The beginning section ends at a major transitional moment—when Mulder actually sees the alien. This is conveyed by the action of the slowly dropped hands. The searching and waiting are over.

The middle section covers the heart of the plot up to and including the climax. It is about sharing, communicating, and overcoming one's disbelief. The head nodding clearly demonstrates that telepathic communication is occurring and that Mulder is agreeing to the things the alien has to say. The final big affirmative nod suggests that the communication is complete. Sharing information is usually considered to be a weak acting objective, one that creates little conflict; but it is effective in this situation because of the extraordinary circumstances of this encounter. Again, because of the given circumstances, the good-bye gesture following the contact becomes an extremely powerful and climactic physical action.

The ending section represents the falling action following the actual encounter. It is about Mulder's realization that his dreams have been fulfilled. The conflict is resolved now, but the character still has to process the extraordinary event. Before he can do that, however, he needs to hold on to what just happened as long as possible. The physical actions of watching the alien ship lift off into the night sky and disappear, along with making the final good-bye gesture, accomplish that part of the story. When the vessel is gone, Mulder's dropping to his knees makes clear the dramatic power the encounter has had on him.

If, while you played out the physical action score, you committed yourself to the situation by keeping in mind the given circumstances and your acting objectives, you probably discovered that your playing generated seemingly real emotional responses. Since you knew what the situation was, your body, mind, and emotions played along. With a few repetitions of the physical action score, you'll probably discover that the emotions you generate seem no less real than those of an actual experience.

As you continue to work, you may also discover that other physical actions should be added to the score to convey more specifically what you are thinking and feeling or to enhance the story. Good. Add them. Your job is to tell the best possible story while serving the script. You might also discover that some of the physical actions on my list do not serve you well because they are not clear for you, or that you can think of other actions that would work better than mine. That, too, is fine. Change them. Working on a play or scene is not like a math test. You don't need to find all the answers immediately. Preparing your work is a process of discovery, of trial and error. Enjoy, and be challenged by the process.

EXERCISE 6-3

Write and execute a physical action score that clearly tells the story of the alien in this encounter with Agent Mulder. Be sure to consider the "magic if" as well as the given circumstances from the alien's point of view. Also, determine the alien's specific objective in this scene, and keep it in mind as you develop your score. Rehearse and perform your score for your class.

A detailed physical action score can be a very effective device for creating clear and compelling work on the stage. It is important that you master the skill because it will help you develop your craft. Ultimately, not every actor works in this fashion. Some actors develop a physical action score through trial and error during the rehearsal process. This physical action score comes as a result of working with other actors in the scene and following the advice of the director. The markings you make in your script while rehearsing reflect this process. Some actors create a physical action score on their own and then adapt it according to what is going on in the scene—once the director's suggestions, the set, and other characters' choices become more clear. Whatever process you use, remember that the mastery of physical actions is an essential acting tool.

How can you develop your ability to use physical actions? The best way is by practicing with them. If you are currently working on a play in rehearsal, or if you are working on a scene from a play in your acting class, you could use that play to provide the source material for creating your own nonverbal scene. From *The Glass Menagerie,* for example, what might be Laura's preparation for going to the business school she desperately wants to avoid? What might it be like for Tom to read a newspaper or magazine detailing the exciting adventures of others? What might Jim, the gentleman caller, do while dressing to succeed? What might Amanda Wingfield do during her private moments away from her children? Remember, the purpose of creating your physical action score is to tell an interesting and enlightening story about your character that also serves the play.

EXERCISE 6-4

1. Imagine a scene not specifically in the play you're working on. Based on that scene, create a physical action score for the character you are playing. It could be a scene alluded to in the script or one not mentioned in the play at all. It could also be a nonverbal section of the play—one that might have more meaning than the script seems to suggest. Make sure, however, that the scene you create somehow adds to what the audience knows about the story or character.

2. Write out a specific physical action score for your scene based on the Mulder example. Be sure the physical action score has a beginning, a middle, and an end.

3. Rehearse and perform the physical action score.

Action and Emotion

Another useful exercise to develop your abilities with physical choices is to turn an emotion into a tangible, controllable, and repeatable series of actions. For example, you might select the emotion of frustration. A series of actions involving trying to thread a needle—a series that builds toward a climax of frustration because you are unable to complete your objective—could make an entertaining comic or dramatic story. You get the idea.

EXERCISE 6-5

1. Select an emotional state or condition, and create a story that could make clear that emotion. Remember, emotions should not be played directly. Your job as the actor is to tell the story. Be sure to consider the given circumstances very specifically.

   Possible emotional states: anger, jealousy, hate, love, lust, boredom, disdain, fear, nervousness, shyness, embarrassment, tranquility, ecstasy, agony, insecurity, panic, affection, exhaustion, tiredness, amazement, fascination, carefulness, obsessiveness, spitefulness, happiness, shock.

2. Once you have developed the story, create a physical action score with a beginning, a middle, and an end that will tell the story clearly. The score should structure the sequence of actions in such a way that the audience understands the emotion through the story that suggests it.

3. Perform your physical action score.

Here is a variation of Exercise 6-5.

EXERCISE 6-6

Put yourself in a specific situational setting, and then assign yourself an emotion. Try to create a story that makes clear the emotion by creating a series of physical actions that will make that emotion tangible for you and for the audience. Be sure there is a conflict to work through. The more specific you are about the given circumstances, the more clear and specific your physical choices will be.

Possible situational settings: staring out a window, exercising on the floor, waiting by a telephone, staring at a letter, repairing something, packing or unpacking a bag, searching for something, looking into the distance, looking at some photos, reading a magazine, channel surfing, putting on nail polish, getting dressed, getting undressed, waking up, hearing something, perusing something, looking in a mirror.

It is essential that actors know the given circumstances of any acting situation. It is also essential that they understand the conflict and their characters' needs in the play, in the scene, and in every moment. They must consider the "magic if" in order to stay on course. But remember: Except for dialogue, it is only through actors' specific physical choices (physical actions) that these circumstances, thoughts, and needs are communicated to an audience. If actors find ways to physicalize the story that is unfolding, and do so without clouding it up with all that unnecessary forced emotion, their work will be clear and interesting, and the story will get told. Exercises 6-1 through 6-6 offer opportunities to work on the basics you need in every acting situation. So, what are you waiting for? Let's have some action!

EXERCISE 6-7

1. With a partner, rehearse a scene that begins with "hello" and ends with "good-bye." Fill in the rest of the scene using only physical actions, no additional dialogue. Be sure that the story is a good one. All given circumstances should be made clear through what you and your partner do.

2. Watch a video of Rowan Atkinson as Mr. Bean or of another comic who brilliantly creates a story without dialogue. Study how these silent masters accomplish their work. Discuss what you see.

3. Create a silent story of your own. Make the laughs come out of the situation. Don't try to be funny. Play the scene.

4. Select a favorite character from a play or novel. Write out a physical action score for that character—one that will reveal who the character is. Perform the score.

5. Select a well-known work of art by a famous artist. Write a physical action score in which you examine this work of art at a museum. Rehearse your score. Use no dialogue in the exercise. Your goal is to make clear both the artist and the work of art by creating a series of actions that will reveal them to an audience. (*Hint:* Think of Seurat [pointillism] or Van Gogh [thick swatches of paint].) Be sure to make choices about the given circumstances and the "magic if" before you begin your score. Your job is to tell a clear and compelling story through what you do physically.

Summary

Acting out the story of the play requires that actors not only discover and play their conflicts and objectives fully but also that they be aware of the given circumstances—the who, what, when, and where of the play, the scene, and the moment. Only then will the choices they make best serve the story. Further, it is not enough that these choices be believable; an actor must be certain that each choice clearly reflects the character he or she is playing. Physical actions, the things a character literally does, can reveal what a character is thinking and feeling. These physical actions reveal as much to an audience as does the dialogue a character speaks. Actors must learn to select and use physical actions as a means of making clear their every moment.

CHAPTER 7

Acting with Conflict

In Chapter 5 I defined good acting as "acting that is believable and that tells the best possible story." What I mean by this definition is that good actors must not only seem believable to the audience; they must also make choices that are as interesting as possible—choices that create and move a story forward. More simply put, actors have the same responsibility as a playwright—they must keep the action* moving in a clear and compelling manner. Whether a story is plot-centered or character-centered, it is the answer to the question "What will happen next?" that most keeps an audience's interest. And keeping an audience's interest should be as important to an actor as it is to the playwright.

Here's an example of what I mean. Suppose your agent sends you on an audition for a toothpaste commercial. You get to the casting agency or studio and ask the receptionist or production assistant for the **sides** (the script you will actually audition with). You are told by the receptionist that there are no sides. The audition will simply consist of you brushing your teeth for the camera. Simple enough, right? The receptionist then directs you to the waiting room where you are to remain until you are called. Nervously, you find a seat in the crowded lobby. Once you settle in, you furtively scan the faces of your competition. You make a horrifying discovery. Everyone waiting to audition is beautiful, many even more beautiful than you. The hundreds of teeth that surround you are all gloriously white and straight. It is obvious that many thousands of dollars have been spent on the teeth sharing this room with yours. So then, how are you going to land this commercial? You desperately need the money it will bring in, but clearly you are not "the fairest of them all." If only the audition had lines, at

---

*It should be noted that the term "action" can be used in several ways in theatre. It can refer to the ongoing development of a plot, it can refer to the physical action executed by an actor, or it can refer to the objective or goal an actor as character is pursuing. In the reference above, it refers to the developing plot.

least you could show the casting agents you could act. But there are no lines. What to do? Give up? Go home? Take that waiter job you've been avoiding?

The situation described here is not an unusual one for any actor trying to make a living in New York or L.A. Commercials can pay the rent for a while. It would be easy to rationalize and say you didn't get the job because of your looks, and sometimes that is indeed the case. But since you have relatively little control over your looks, it is your acting alone on which you must rely. The truth is that my definition of good acting could serve you well, even in a commercial audition (and one without dialogue, no less). It could even get you that national commercial, in spite of your not being the "fairest in the land," and in the following section I'll tell you how.

EXERCISE 7-1

Consider the audition situation above as an acting exercise. Decide what you would do in that thirty-second slot, and then practice your audition. When you have completed your rehearsal, read on.

The commercial audition I describe is one I actually went to, and there were scores of others I went to that were very much like that one. I didn't get that toothpaste job, in case you're wondering, but I later saw the actor who did— when I had the opportunity to watch the finished ad countless times on TV. The actor who bagged that job did turn out to be very handsome, but—and this is a very important "but"—he was also believable and told the best possible story. At this point you may be thinking that the commercial, as I described it, had no story. That is true. But the actor who got the role had invented one, and he told that story within the confines of the time allowed him on screen. He had put his learned craft to good use. I had simply brushed my teeth as believably as I could. My last brush stroke was essentially no different from my first. I had been hoping that somehow my looks would be what they were searching for. Relying on such hope is no replacement for using acting craft, I promise you.

Using Conflict

The actor cast in the commercial, however, chose to begin as though he had just gotten out of bed. Struggling into the bathroom still half-asleep, he put the toothpaste on the brush and lifted the brush to his mouth. Magically, as the taste of the paste hit his taste buds, his head lifted and lightened. His brush stroke increased in speed, in tempo. His scowl turned to a smile. He was alive again, invigorated. He began to hum. Life had become bearable—more than bearable as his brushing continued. Life was turning grand, even glorious. This toothpaste was changing his life.

The premise of the scenario the toothpaste actor acted out has been used countless times in TV ads. I'm sure you could make a page-long list of similar commercials. Off the top of my head there's the Toyota jump and any number of breath mint and chewing gum commercials. But in basic actor language, each of those commercials creates a story—a story that is presented quickly and efficiently. The actor playing the character is never the same at the end as he or she was at the beginning. The character has taken a **journey**, one in which some obstacle has been overcome, some conflict has been resolved. An actor who makes this journey is invariably more interesting than one who does not. And so, the actor as storyteller.

EXERCISE 7-2

Create your own original thirty-second commercial without dialogue. There should be only one character, you. Be sure that your commercial:

- Tells a story.
- Is based on some central conflict.
- Is one in which an obstacle is overcome.
- Has a character (you) who is different at the end than he or she was at the beginning. In other words, a journey has been taken during the commercial's thirty-second length.

Finding the Story

The journey an actor goes on, however, must be more than simply a journey; it must be an interesting one. After all, a car trip through the repetitive rolling hills and prairie of the Midwest quickly becomes boring unless something happens—unless some kind of interesting conflict presents itself. Conflict is the engine of storytelling. Until there is a conflict or an obstacle, a story line or plot is just like an interstate drive through Kansas. Nothing happens. But once conflict is added, those endless plains completely change in character. Suppose the car begins to make strange noises? Suppose the car is getting low on gas? Suppose the sky turns dark? Suppose you have to go to the bathroom? Each of these suppositions provides a conflict or an obstacle to overcome, and no playwright would ever dream of trying to write a successful piece about a drive through Kansas without one. It should be no different for an actor.

Conflict is a playwright's best friend, and should be the actor's as well. Too often, unfortunately, particularly in the United States, young performers think that emotion is where their acting energy should go, and that the storytelling aspect of a script is the province of the playwright only. They often believe that when they are in a play, a film, or even a commercial, the story will simply take care of itself. In our country, mistaken ideas about the work of Constantin Stanislavski, and the influence of Lee Strasberg and the "Method" school of acting, are in part responsible for this misconception.

Generally speaking, young American actors approach dramatic material with the question "What is my character feeling?" rather than with "What is my character doing?" But even when an actor asks the latter question, he or she is still putting the cart before the horse. The first question an actor should be asking is that same one the playwright asked while writing: "What is going on here?" In other words, what is the *action* of this play, this scene, this beat, this moment? Actors must ask themselves, "What is the story that we are trying to communicate to the audience, and what is our role in making this happen?"

EXERCISE 7-3

Put together a one-minute exercise during which you are doing one of the following:

- Fishing
- Taking a shower
- Eating
- Reading
- Exercising
- Watching television

After planning and rehearsing, perform the exercise for your class. Ask your audience to give you feedback.

Was there a journey in your exercise? Was there conflict? Did it tell a story?

Remember, even when an actor is working without a script, as the example of the toothpaste commercial points out, the fundamentals of storytelling must always be observed. And fundamental number one is *the need to identify the conflict that already exists or to invent it when necessary.*

It is an actor's responsibility to serve the script (even if it is a script you are creating yourself improvisationally), as well as his or her character, by making choices that support the story being told. Since this is the case, the definition of good acting that began this chapter should be amended to read "acting that is believable and tells the best possible story *while serving the script.*" After all, when an actor can communicate what is going on in the story as written (or improvised), the audience will usually be able to tell what the character is feeling.

The actor who got the toothpaste job managed to turn brushing his teeth into a story because he found the essential conflict. At first the commercial appeared to represent a habitual situation requiring no active mental or emotional investment. The morning brush can certainly be a mindless activity, and almost never is it an upbeat one. Had the auditioning actor merely chosen to wear a smile (because commercials require happy people), the situation would still have lacked the ingredients that make it a story. There still would have been no throughline to play with, no conflict to resolve, no obstacle to overcome. The character would simply have been "happy."

In the work of the actor who got the job, however, it was the toothpaste that made the character happy. What better selling point could the ad agency wish for? A toothpaste that can make the brusher happy! The actor had made choices that would certainly have occurred to the copywriter, had there been one. The actor had created an action based on the important points behind the story. In other words, the actor as storyteller had created a throughline of action based on the message the ad agency would want to get across—that using this brand of toothpaste will make a positive difference to its user. But that discovery came as a result of resolving a conflict that well served the commercial's ultimate message.

Types of Conflict

The conflict that was the engine for the toothpaste story was primarily an internal one. The character had to overcome his own tiredness and his foul morning mood in order to get on with the day. At the beginning of the ad, this seemed to be an overwhelming task. But the use of the toothpaste resolved this conflict and our hero was able to re-achieve the demeanor that makes his life so wonderful— a happy mood! Of course, the scenario I just described is simplistic, if not downright silly, but, nonetheless, it contains the same ingredients that actors face in any acting situation, and the actor in the commercial used his acting tools well. His little story, like all stories, had a beginning, a middle, and an end—a conflict was discovered, confronted, and resolved.

Besides internal conflict, remember the three other basic conflicts that provide the springboard for storytelling. One is the conflict that pits a character against nature—snowstorms, fires, natural disasters, and the like. Another is the conflict that arises when a character goes against the rules of society—taking a stand against a political or religious institution or a set of unjust laws, for example. The third is when a character finds himself or herself in opposition to another character who provides an obstacle that stands in the way of achieving some goal.

This last kind of conflict along with internal conflict are the two most useful for actors. These are conflicts that characters can actually deal with moment to moment onstage or on screen. They provide dramatic situations that characters must face and resolve directly and clearly at the time they appear in the story. When a character is in opposition with nature, that, too, can be useful to an actor, but the situation often involves an internal conflict as well. In the play and film *K-2*, for instance, a stranded mountain climber is in conflict with the steep height of the mountain slope, the lack of oxygen where he is stranded, and the nasty weather conditions he must endure, but the character must also face and overcome his own fear, a conflict that is internal.

Political, religious, and philosophic conflicts, on the other hand, are usually part of a story's theme or a play's spine and often cannot be confronted directly by an actor. They are usually resolved as by-products of an internal conflict or a direct conflict with another character. Although Scotsman William Wallace in the film *Braveheart* is in political opposition to the tyrannical rule of the English monarchy, we are held at first by his internal conflict over whether to take up arms; later, his man-to-man confrontations hold us dramatically, even though we may be aware of the movie's political content. When Otto Schindler in *Schindler's List* decides to save as many of his Jewish workers as he can, again the audience is first interested in his internal struggle. Later, it is his cat-and-mouse strategies to fool the concentration camp commandant that hold us, not the fact that Schindler is going against the political and philosophic forces of Nazism. The actors playing these roles successfully demonstrate to the audience their internal and external conflicts from beginning to resolution. They make choices at each dramatic moment that clearly reveal these conflicts, and thereby become compelling storytellers for their audiences.

EXERCISE 7-4

1. Make a list of several movies you have seen recently. Try to identify the type of conflict or conflicts found in each. How did the story line in each of those films relate to the conflicts you have identified?

2. Create a one-minute, silent story for each of the four kinds of conflicts. After you have done so, try to figure out which was the hardest to do. Which was the easiest? Why?

3. Create a one-minute silent story with a partner involving as many conflicts as you can. Keep the work believable. Perform the story for your class. Discuss the work.

Conflict to Objective

Stanislavski, on whose theories most contemporary acting craft is still based, understood the power of conflict. Even in his early work, the great Russian master noted the important connection between what an actor chooses to do and its relation to the script being brought to life on stage. He believed, in a nutshell, that what a character does in a play is the result of choices made by the actor, but these choices must be guided by the overall idea behind the play and the action the playwright sets down to support that idea. Because the playwright has carefully interwoven action and idea, the strength of their interconnection will be operating at every moment and in every element of the work.

In Chapter 4 I discussed the development of Stanislavski's theories of acting. Although Stanislavski acknowledged the importance of action and story in his early work, his focus at the beginning of his research was on emotional truth. In his later years, however, you will recall that Stanislavski came to believe that playing actions and performing specific tasks onstage, and not emotional truth, were the cornerstones of the acting craft. In fact, most of his later work centered on the storytelling aspects of acting, and, specifically, on conflict. His discovery of what is now one of the basic tools of acting—playing objectives—came directly from his understanding of dramatic conflict and his own appreciation of its use by good playwrights.

Most young actors today are familiar with playing objectives (also known as intentions, needs, and so forth) but very often find it difficult to work with them. Many have no idea how to go about choosing an objective, or they choose ones that are ineffective and quickly forgotten as they are working. An actor's inability to use objectives often results from failing to use the script as a guide. Too often actors select their objectives without fully understanding what is going on in the play, in the scene, or even in a particular moment. Playwrights write scripts consisting of a throughline of action where conflict is faced and resolved, and actors must be able to recognize that action. Only when they do, will they be able to select objectives that serve them well.

EXERCISE 7-5

Create a one-minute silent story using only a chair. Make sure the story has a conflict that will provide the basis for a plot with a beginning, a middle, and an end. Be certain that your choices will be clear to an audience so that they can clearly understand what they are seeing. Rehearse the scene and present it.

Remember, a character's need or objective usually comes as a result of the conflict he or she faces or the obstacles that stand in the way. The actor must determine what the character needs to do in order to triumph against that opposing force or obstacle. But, before doing that, the actor must first recognize and understand what the conflict is. And that insight comes only from understanding the action of the script as written.

For instance, more often than not, an actor works onstage with another actor. In scene work for class this is almost invariably the case. Since the playwright knowingly writes with conflict in mind, the two-character format practically screams out, "The conflict is person-against-person, Dummy! Why do you think the two of you are standing here on stage!?"

In other words, if you can figure out what the conflict is between you and your acting partner in a scene, you will be able to figure out what you must do to gain what you need. That is your objective. The script, of course, predetermines whether you ultimately end in **victory** or **defeat**. But the struggle to overcome your adversary (the dramatic conflict), not the winning itself, is what is interesting to the audience. It makes clear the conflict that is already contained in the script as written. Further, if you, as the actor playing the character, keep in mind that winning what you need is a full-time job onstage, you will be less likely to forget your objective while playing out the scene. All your choices will be clear and strong and interesting—because they are serving the script, not going against it.

EXERCISE 7-6

1. Find a partner and have a western gunfight. There should be no talking. Tell the story fully, clearly, and believably from beginning to end.

2. Find a partner and have another kind of duel. Somehow, create the period in which the duel occurs. Tell the story fully, clearly, and believably from beginning to end.

3. Find a partner and engage in some other kind of contest. Tell the story fully, clearly, and believably from beginning to end.

Discuss the performed exercises with your class. Draw conclusions.

Conflict and Character

A good script, remember, unlike life, is not a series of random events. The playwright has organized the action so that it is dramatically interesting. Part of your storytelling responsibility is to recognize what the playwright has done. The character you play onstage is not telling only his or her own story. On the contrary, your character is contributing to the telling of a greater story, one that unifies the actions of all the play's characters into a single larger action.

Not long ago I was blocking a scene for a production I was directing. One of my cast members, a gifted young sophomore doing her first big role, politely refused to carry out an action I thought was obvious for her to do.

"My character would never do that," she told me.

"Why do you say that?" I asked patiently, in spite of the fact that several other more seasoned actors in the cast looked very annoyed at the delay.

"Because I have worked very hard on my character's biography, and because of something that happened in her childhood, she would never react that way."

"Where did you get that piece of information?" I asked.

"I made it up!" she said proudly.

After a brief discussion, my actor came to realize that many of her biographical choices, though interesting and imaginative, could not be supported by the actions her character was called upon to do in the script. By making up choices inconsistent with the script, she discovered she was actually making her acting task much more difficult. She would also have been weakening the action of the play (by diminishing its built-in conflict) as well as distorting its meaning.

By accurately distilling the conflict from a script, actors can well serve the play they are performing and ensure that their work is clear and interesting. By finding the objectives that best support that conflict, actors can also illuminate the characters they are playing. What a character needs, what he or she is willing to risk to get it, and the manner in which those needs are pursued reveal far more about a character to an audience than any amount of biographical research, makeup, or physical peculiarities could ever hope to do. In the chapter to follow we will examine how.

EXERCISE 7-7

Examine several monologues, either from plays you know or from monologue collections. Do the following with each monologue:
- Determine who the speaking character is.
- Determine who the character being spoken to is.
- Determine the conflict.
- Determine what the speaker is trying to get from the listener.
- Determine how the listening character is reacting to the speaking character as specifically as possible.
- Determine the story of the monologue, and chart the journey the speaking character makes during the speech. (How is the character different at the end than he or she was at the beginning?)

Summary

The definition of good acting now stands as "acting that is believable and tells the best possible story while serving the script." If there is no script, then the actors themselves become totally responsible for the creation of a good one. Any story starts with conflict, the engine of drama. A playwright writes with this fact in mind. He or she knows that conflict is created by having opposing forces move toward, and eventually confront, one another. This journey becomes a story's plot. By learning to recognize the conflict in a story, actors can figure out their objectives (what they need) and find simple, clear choices that will not only make their individual work compelling but also contribute to the overall telling of the story.

CHAPTER 8

Finding and Playing Objectives

Remember what it was like to play a game of tag as a kid? A boy who was "It" would chase you as though his life depended on it. His footfalls on the sidewalk thundered in your stomach like a drum. You ran as though this chase were the most intense moment of your life. The monster was fast approaching. Facing a gladiator in the arena could have been no more dangerous. Your heart pounded. Your temples surged. The sweat on your brow flowed freely. The reserve of strength and speed you suddenly drew from was an adrenaline surprise. If "It" caught you, the feel of his heavy hand was crushing. The time you spent anticipating that touch—infinite. If you eluded that hand, the victory of escape proved tremendous. Your moan or laugh came from deep inside you, generated from a very real place.

One might think that to produce an emotional reaction that strong and that real would take enormous concentration and preparation, not to mention talent. But the fact is that when we were kids we didn't think about such stuff at all. When we played sports like football and games like hide-and-seek, we focused on the action in the game or, more specifically, on the winning. We never thought about what we should be feeling. Any emotional by-product was just that—a by-product. No jock I knew ever focused on his feelings—those only came as a result of catching the pass or hitting the ball, or failing to do so; and when the action was completed, the emotions surged—very real and all by themselves, spontaneously.

Actions Make Emotions

This is one of the basic principles behind actors' use of objectives. As games and sports so clearly demonstrate, humans have the capacity to generate seemingly real emotions even when they are engaged in pretend activities. The thrill of victory and the pain of defeat can be tremendous. The completed pass or landing on Free Parking when the kitty is filled with money can be as exhilarating as the joy we experience when we win an election, get a promotion, or receive the Christmas present we never thought we'd get. When we put all our energies into getting what we need, there is almost always a commensurate emotional response when we achieve our goal, or when we fail to do so. And no one doubts the sincerity of these responses.

EXERCISE 8-1

1. Make up some kind of contest to engage in by yourself and commit to it. Play the game or contest.

2. Now, in order to up the stakes, give yourself a set amount of time to complete the activity. Play the game or contest again.

   Examples: Try to hold your breath for one minute, then try to hold your breath for two minutes; attempt to do fifty sit-ups, then a specific number of sit-ups in one minute; try to toss twenty cards into a hat, then give yourself only one time through the deck or only one minute to toss the cards in; try to sink three baskets in a row, then three baskets in a row in one minute; catch three pieces of tossed candy in your mouth, then do the same thing in thirty seconds.

3. Arm-wrestle a friend.

4. Knee joust someone. (This is a mock duel using your hand as a sword to try to tag your opponent's knee without being touched there yourself.)

5. Thumb-wrestle.

6. Play tag.

   Play one or more of the contests again, but this time play as though something were at stake. Act as though you believe the stakes are real, that there is something big to win.

   What feelings did the games produce in you? Which games worked best? Why? When were they less successful? Why? How do you account for your overall reactions? Were you fully concentrating at all times? Why or why not?

It is ironic that so many actors, especially beginning actors, put all their energy into generating emotion directly. How many actors talk about their scenes and monologues in terms of what their characters are feeling? And how often does the resulting work seem unclear, superficial, or dull? More to the point, how often does the generated emotion seem unbelievable? The answer, unfortunately, is all too often. It may be true that highly skilled actors, or actors with enormous natural gifts, can generate convincing emotional responses to acting situations by actively using emotional recall or substitution. But the fact remains that most of them, either intuitively or purposefully, also use objectives whether or not they refer to them as such.

1. Arm-wrestle a friend. Remember the sequence of actions that occurred. Arm-wrestle again trying to re-create what happened the first time. How is this second experience different?

2. Arm-wrestle with a partner in front of an audience. Do this several times. Let some of the matches be spontaneous; let others be enactments. See if your audience can tell the difference. Solicit their responses. What conclusions can you draw?

Selection, Control, and Repeatability

Many people, including many students of acting, think that acting is a process in which the performer pretends to be someone else so commitedly, so completely, that the actor and the character simply merge. Some magical thing happens that allows the actor to become completely lost in the character he or she is playing. Some intuitive process takes over, one in which every thought, feeling, and action the actor exhibits is the absolutely right one. In reality, some actors have had such an experience, but for most actors, this is simply not the case. The simple truth is that good acting is not synonymous with real life behavior. When it is done well, acting might be mistaken for real, spontaneous behavior, but there are most often tremendous differences between the two.

In the first place, good acting requires **selectivity and control**. That means, as with most good art, that the actor does not make random, intuitive choices. Unlike in life, where most of us don't think about what we do and say until after it's done or said (and often can't explain the reasons for our behavior), *actors must make choices about what their characters think, feel, and do, even when the characters they are playing are completely unaware of these things.* Further, unlike in life, an actor playing a character has the responsibility to be able to repeat what he or she has created for the stage or screen time after time. This requires a control of thought and action that no one in real life would be expected to possess. The ultimate trick, however, is that in performance the actor is so prepared that he or she consciously focuses only in the moment. Everything an actor needs to do for the scene has already been absorbed during the rehearsal process.

Playing the Dramatic Situation

Chapter 7 centered on finding and using the conflict built into a playscript. Using conflict marks another significant difference between behavior in life and the illusion of real behavior an actor must create. It is the actor's responsibility to make choices for his or her character that serve the play being acted. Further, if the play is a good one, these choices will make the play interesting and exciting and will allow the actor to create a clear and effective characterization as well. In addition, by focusing on the objectives that grow out of the conflict the playwright has created, the actor makes choices of behavior that are much less complex than the behavior we often observe in life. Unlike the moment-to-moment struggles people face in real life, the actor can make choices based on the outcomes the script provides. Because they are distilled from the conflict already provided, these choices serve to heighten the dramatic effect and clarify the reasons behind a character's behavior. In life we have no obligation to be clear and exciting. The actor, of course, owes at least that much to the audience.

What all this means, then, is that actors must think about the dramatic situation they are going to be in onstage. They must understand how the story progresses in the overall play and in each individual scene specifically. They must be able to identify the conflict that exists in any acting situation that is scripted, or they must invent conflict in any acting situation that is not. Without conflict of some kind, a story is simply not a story.

It is not unusual for beginning actors to read through a scene by playing the lines rather than the situation. In other words, they let the lines dictate the way they read the dialogue rather than making the dialogue reflect what is specifically going on in the story at that particular point. More often than not the scene being read will sound boring, if not completely unbelievable. Starting with the lines without an understanding of what happens story-wise in a scene is generally acting suicide.

On the other hand, when scene partners accept the fact that the two characters in a scene were put there by the playwright to work through some conflict with each other, those actors will have taken the first steps toward creating a scene that is clear and exciting. Defining the conflict between you and your acting partner automatically creates a story situation on which the dialogue can be developed.

In *The Glass Menagerie* by Tennessee Williams, for instance, Laura goes to her collection of animals and talks about them to Jim, her gentleman caller. On face value, not much is going on here. If, however, the dialogue is read in the context of Laura's need to escape the discomfort she is feeling in the presence of her long-time fantasy beau, then its purpose becomes far more dramatic. In another example, *The Bald Soprano* by Eugène Ionesco, characters engage in **absurdist** conversations that seem to circle endlessly. The characters are unable to draw logical conclusions from the simplest sets of information. Ionesco, in fact, got the idea for his play from the foreign language exercises that he was reading for a class. The repetitive exchanges of the play make sense only when seen as the language exercises they are.

EXERCISE 8-3

1. Read through a short section of *The Glass Menagerie* with a scene partner. Once familiar with it, try to act the scene while reading.

2. Read through a short section of *The Bald Soprano* with a scene partner. Once familiar with it, try to act the scene while reading.

If you tried reading from *The Bald Soprano,* you probably found the scene and your work dull, superficial, and, perhaps, directionless. You were, in all likelihood, playing the lines rather than the situation. Unfortunately, your instincts were correct—the dialogue of the play literally does go nowhere. However, if you had, as the characters, chosen to try with all your might to make sense of the information being put forth, your struggle would have been interesting to the audience, even though the logic remained nonexistent. Characters struggling with each other to make logical sense out of illogical facts becomes an interesting conflict. How could these characters not know each other, yet share the same address, the same room, the same child, and the same bed? When each actor tries to prove to the other that only he or she is right, the conflict becomes exciting as well as hilarious. The scene also develops a throughline that gives the actors something specific to do and the audience something to watch.

EXERCISE 8-4

1. Attempt to read *The Bald Soprano* scene again. This time play the situation rather than the lines. Try hard to find answers to the confusing set of facts that are before you. Focus on the conflict that the lines create between you and your acting partner. Be sure to listen and react to any new information that affects you.

   Note the differences from the first reading. What were you trying to do this time?

2. Find and read a two-person scene with a partner. Try to discover the conflict in the unfolding story. What do the characters need from each other? Using the lines and your imagination, determine what the characters do to get what they need.

Discovering Objectives and Stakes

Once actors accept the premise that it is necessary to define or create conflict in all acting situations, they are ready for the next step. The conflict must be translated into objectives the actors can play. Most of the time the conflict exists between the two characters sharing the stage. Sometimes, however, characters join forces to face an outside obstacle together. Either way, the conflict must be faced and dealt with. Actors who have trouble recognizing an objective to play should ask themselves the questions "What do I need here, and what can I do to get it?"

Most of the time these questions will lead actors to objectives and tactics that will make the scene work. Whatever the need turns out to be, it should be greatly needed. Otherwise, the conflict in the scene will not be dramatic. In other words, the **stakes** should be as big as possible.

EXERCISE 8-5

1. Create an argument with a partner using only the alternating lines "yes" and "no." Your objective is to win the argument.

2. Repeat the above, but this time give yourself a compelling reason to win. In other words, make the stakes high. Note the differences this time.

3. Repeat the exercise one last time. This time the stakes are life and death. What conclusions can you draw?

The Basic Objectives

There are times when an actor is simply unable to find a strong objective to play. When that happens, it may be useful to start with some generalized objectives that can be more specifically defined later. There are six basic objectives that actors can play.

1. To give information

2. To get information

3. To make someone do something

4. To keep someone from doing something

5. To make someone feel good

6. To make someone feel bad

Every possible acting objective will probably fall within one of these six broad categories. Which do you think offers the least in terms of dramatic conflict? If you guessed "to give information," you have started to absorb the basic premise regarding finding and playing conflict on stage. Simply to give information generally requires very little of the actor/character and provides little in the way of dramatic conflict. Giving information is achieved as soon as the information is given. Task completed, mission accomplished, objective won. But as a starting point for finding or developing an objective, even "to give information" can be useful.

Take a messenger speech from a Greek play for instance. By definition this role is that of an information giver. However, the actor playing the messenger role has an opportunity to do much more. In fact, messenger roles in Greek plays are usually wonderful showcases. Take the messenger from *Oedipus the King,* for instance, who reports of Jocasta's death and of Oedipus's self-inflicted blinding. The actor playing the messenger role might turn his objective from "giving information" to "making the listener see the event as he saw it." This would up the stakes considerably and make those sharing the stage with him a vital part of his objective. Getting others to see the event as he did would require a great deal of coloring and shaping in order to display all the emotional upheaval the messenger felt as he witnessed the horror. The actor who commits to that objective fully will be on the way to creating a memorable sequence onstage.

EXERCISE 8-6

Improvise a scene with a partner in which you must give him or her some information. Be sure to create some kind of conflict before you begin that is related to the information you will be offering.

Did the scene work? What did you learn? How was the conflict related to the information? Was there an obstacle? What was it? Did your partner have an objective to play? What was it? How was it related to your objective? To the obstacle? To the overall conflict in the scene?

The other five basic objectives give the actor more to do because they require a response from the other actor or actors sharing the stage. If you keep in mind that objectives come out of the conflict written into a scene, and the conflict almost invariably involves two characters in that scene, then it's a short jump to realizing that the best objectives depend for their fulfillment on the other character. In other words—*verb, receiver, response.*

"To get information" requires getting the receiver to respond—if you want the information badly enough. You might even say you need "to make the other character give you information." Notice I have just upped the stakes again. "To make someone do something" or "to keep someone from doing something," even in the stating, suggests a strong conflict and a strong need. If the objective is pursued with commitment, the other actor will have to respond. "To make someone feel good or bad" directly connects an action to the receiving actor and certainly will produce a response of some kind. Further, the actor sharing the scene with you will have his or her own objective to play, the pursuit of which will interfere with your own, either directly or indirectly. This will either provide an obstacle to the completion of your objective or be in direct conflict with yours. In either case, each objective must support the conflict in the scene.

EXERCISE 8-7

Improvise a scene with a partner for each of the five broad objectives you have not yet used. Make sure that you clearly lay out the situation before beginning and that you are clear about what the conflict is.

Did you notice that as the scene unfolded your tactics to get what you needed became more specific? Did this happen as a result of learning more about the situation as well as your partner? What conclusions can you draw?

The more you work with **analysis,** trying to find the conflict and then determining objectives, the more skilled you will become. But whether an actor initially finds the objective that solves the problem of the scene or not, playing an objective, even one that ultimately does not work, is far better than not playing one at all. As the example of reading *The Bald Soprano* demonstrates, failure to play an action (the objective you pursue) will force you to play generalized emotions —guaranteed to make your work superficial and stagy, guaranteed to make the story go nowhere.

Making Objectives Specific

Here is a short list of sample verbs that could serve as strong objectives to play. They are all transitive verbs in that they require a receiver in order to complete them. They can provide, in grammatical terms, just what actors need in an objective—a verb, a receiver, and, potentially, a response.

to convince, to encourage, to destroy, to punish, to reassure, to fool, to belittle, to insult, to help, to seduce, to hurt, to ridicule, to tease, to torture, to inspire, to prepare, to share

Notice what happens, however, when an actor starts his statement of objective by saying "to *make* him/her [do something]," rather than simply using the infinitive verb forms on the list. Doing so opens up an enormous number of choices in objectives. It also makes the objective seem more important than the actor might first have thought to make it. Adding the phrase "to make" causes the objective to be more imperative. That is good, since high stakes and big choices make for exciting drama. Further, phrasing the objective in this form forces the actor to connect the objective with the other character or characters sharing the stage. For instance, notice how the following examples all seem to provide the raw material for exciting action onstage. Each connects a receiver to the specific objective.

to *make* someone: laugh, cry, feel guilty, feel empowered, accept your advice, change, forgive you, reward you, obey you, make love to you, beg you, love you, hate you, admire you, pity you, help you

You might want to try to come up with your own set of exciting objectives that will no doubt prove useful in the future. I have observed, by the way, that the more clearly and specifically you develop your objective, the more clear, specific, and exciting your work will be onstage—provided you stick to playing your objective. Invariably, actors who cannot state their objectives tersely and clearly will not put up scenes that are clear and dramatically interesting. These actors have not yet come to understand what their scene is about.

EXERCISE 8-8

1. Without prior discussion, select an objective and play that objective in an improvised scene with a partner. Be sure to deal with your partner in a believable manner while pursuing what you need.

2. Select both a physical activity you can do during an improvisation and a strong objective to play. Engage in the activity while your partner plays his or her objective. For example, you might be working out while your partner is trying to get you to help with a chore. Don't give up the activity until your partner makes you give it up. Reverse roles.

Building the Story through Objectives

An acting teacher I had many years ago insisted that we always state our objective in the following form: "to make someone _____ in order to _____." For instance, "to make John laugh in order to get him to like me"; you could continue this further by saying "to get him to like me in order to make him want to leave me his fortune." This little process points up the fact that a character's **throughline** in a play (his or her journey, objective by objective, from the beginning to the end of the plot) consists of a series of objectives, large and small, that are completed and/or abandoned during the course of a play while the character pursues his or her overall goal. Stanislavski referred to that one overall objective a character tries to achieve as the **superobjective.** In order to complete this superobjective, a character must achieve many smaller objectives that result from the conflicts and obstacles he or she faces as the plot unfolds. The section of script during which a single objective is played is called a **beat.** Each beat is followed by a **transition,** an acting moment that precedes the new objective that the character will pursue. A transitional moment is reached when a character's objective is won, lost, or abandoned due to some change in the circumstances of the story.

For instance, the actor playing Oedipus, in *Oedipus the King,* might determine that his superobjective is to find and remove the cause of the plague destroying his kingdom, that is "to rid Thebes of the plague that is destroying it." The throughline of action provided by the script requires Oedipus to alter his **tactics** (smaller objectives used to achieve larger ones) time and again as new information is revealed to him. Each new piece of information Oedipus learns during the course of the play is earth shattering. Each new piece of information causes him to reevaluate the situation and take new steps. But the superobjective, to rid Thebes of the cause of the plague, remains constant. The actor playing Oedipus must adjust to each new piece of information during a transition to the new given circumstances. First, Oedipus tries to find out whether and why the gods are angry. When it is revealed that the gods *are* angry because of the unavenged murder of King Laius, Oedipus then tries to find out who the murderer is. Oedipus becomes a detective tracking down witnesses that slowly begin to provide the answers to the mystery. Each new piece of evidence is shocking and hard to accept. Each new episode provides Oedipus with a new conflict to face or a new obstacle to overcome—until the climax is reached, until he discovers that it is he, himself, who killed King Laius, his own father, and then married his own mother. At the climax, this tragic figure discovers that it is he who must be punished, who is the cause of the gods' anger.

Playing objectives strongly does more than make the action clear, believable, and exciting. More than makeup or physicalization, it is action, or the manner in which a character pursues his objective, that reveals character. If the tragedy of Oedipus is to work, the audience must feel pity for him at the end of the play. We must see him as sympathetic if we are to be moved by his change of status from King to exiled pariah.

EXERCISE 8-9

1. The previous description of Oedipus suggests that he should appear "sympathetic." Now, that would require playing an emotion rather than an objective. How can you convert "sympathetic" into a playable action? When you have an answer, demonstrate the physical action that would reveal the concept "sympathetic" to an audience. Get feedback from the class.

2. Compile a list of descriptive qualities. Try to convert those qualities into playable actions and objectives.

3. Play an improvisational scene with conflict and objectives. Incorporate through actions some of the descriptive terms you listed for Step 2.

4. Select a favorite character from a play, novel, or film. Describe the character in a paragraph. Convert that description into playable actions and objectives. Perform a short, silent scene that reveals your character to an audience.

Character through Actions: Tactics and Risk

I recently saw a production of *Oedipus* on video. It was a filmed version of a legendary stage production from the fifties. I thought it was laughable. What may have worked onstage played as hammy for the camera. But what troubled me most was the portrayal of Oedipus. This king struck me as totally contemptible. He was a power-crazed egomaniac who found it hard to listen to anyone other than himself for more than a moment. When the climactic secrets were revealed to him, instead of pity, my reaction was simply "serves you right, sucka!" If this is the reaction I have to the tragic hero, then something is seriously wrong.

The source of the failure can clearly be traced back to acting choices. The actor playing Oedipus chose to play his tactics in such a way that the audience could never find sympathy for him. The Oedipus of this production ranted at Creon, attacked Tiresias mercilessly, never showed kindness or love to Jocasta even when she was trying with all her might to help him. The lesson here is clear: *the tactics an actor selects to achieve his or her objective create character.* Had the actor found beats where he could pursue his needs with some sensitivity to others or to the situation or to the dangers that surrounded him, his humanity might have had a chance to show through. The audience might have seen beyond his kingly trappings to the feeling human being within. We might have grown to like him, or respect him, or even admire him in spite of his flaws. Unfortunately, this actor did not find those moments. He did not *do* things in a manner that might create a feeling of sympathy.

By the same token, this Oedipus was willing to risk everyone and everything at every moment of the play in order to solve the mystery, in order to achieve his objective. He simply did not care what others believed or what they thought of him. His complete disregard for the feelings of others was his pre-eminent characteristic. One might argue that the actor playing Oedipus is trapped by the dialogue. How can he seem sympathetic when the lines he must deliver are so obviously without feeling for others? The answer lies in the manner in which the lines are delivered as well as with what the actor does physically to convey what he is thinking and feeling. If, for instance, his high-handed treatment of his subjects weighed on him more, we would see, through his apparent conflict, that he cared about others. The point is that *what one is willing to do, what one actually does, and what one is willing to risk to get what one needs will demonstrate character compellingly.* Most experienced actors realize that what a character does, how the character chooses to do it, and the **risks** the character is willing to dare make up at least three-quarters of characterization.

Simplicity and Playing the Positive

Let me conclude with a few notes on objectives and simplicity. First of all, I hope I have made clear my belief that acting is not the same as behavior in real life. It only looks like real life if done well. Acting is more focused, more selective, and more controlled. Pursuing an objective allows an actor to focus on a simple goal specifically and clearly. Since human beings are basically able to focus on only one thing at a time; for the actor, that focus should be on achieving his objective. Many untrained actors worry that focusing only on objectives will make their characters seem too simplistic. What they don't realize is that both the script and the audience will fill in the dots to make their characterizations seem as complex as real human beings actually are.

Second, simplicity means that an actor should never complicate the pursuit of objectives by making **negative choices.** A negative acting choice is any choice that does not help you get what you need. Play only the **positive.** If you want to make the girl love you, don't give up until she loves you. Don't play your anger, don't play your disappointment, don't sulk. Don't play emotionally negative states. Play your objective. Respond to her rejection during a transitional moment, act the defeat, and then begin to try and win her again. On the other hand, if you want to make your ex-girlfriend hate you so she will finally leave you in peace—don't smile at her, don't be charming—that too is a negative choice. It prevents you from obtaining your objective. Keep trying different tactics until the script requires you to stop. Never play your defeats while pursuing your objective. Your feelings of defeat won't win your objective for you. Remember, it ain't over 'til it's over. You haven't lost until the script requires it. And then, when it does, make it one hell of an acting moment.

Finally, keep in mind your overall superobjective as actors—*be believable and tell the best possible story that serves the play.* By keeping your own superobjectives in mind, your work is sure to grow in clarity, believability, and excitement.

EXERCISE 8-10

Turn one or more of the following actions into stories by finding the conflict and playing an objective:

Reading a book	Waiting for someone or something
Looking out a window	Looking for something
Putting on makeup	Straightening up a room
Dressing	Preparing a meal
Wrapping a present	Eating something
Sweeping the floor	Building something

EXERCISE 8-11

As part of a group improvisation, decide on a situation and a conflict, then determine your individual objective and a single dominant personality characteristic that can be converted into playable actions. Ask yourself what you are willing to risk to get what you need. Play out the scene.

Suggested Settings

An airport	A singles club
A train station	A New York audition for actors
A bomb shelter	A New York audition for dancers
A police station	A New York audition for singers
A dance	A Titanic cruise

EXERCISE 8-12

1. Read several scenes from scripted plays. Determine the conflict of the scene. Determine each character's objective. Find and list as many tactics that each character uses as you can. Find the transitional moments (the places where one tactic or objective is given up and replaced with another). Note where those places occur. Are the tactics positive? Explain.

2. Improvise a scene based on your analysis. Don't worry about getting the words right. Focus on the conflict, objectives, tactics, and transitions. Play only the positive. Discuss the improvised resulting scene.

Summary

The story of a play or a scene is told through the actions of its characters, not through their emotions. By recognizing conflict and making decisions about the appropriate objectives to play, actors are ready to build the story. Through a process of selection and control, actors employ a series of tactics to get what they want from the other actors sharing the stage. These tactics create conflict and put the characters at risk because of their high stakes. The combination of carefully selected actions builds a dramatic throughline. This throughline clearly maps out the story while revealing who the characters are. Actors who play specific objectives that can be fulfilled by the other actors sharing the stage guarantee the creation of a strong conflict and an interesting story both to tell and to watch. This story will be clear and interesting because the actions are.

CHAPTER 9

Listening and Staying in the Moment

In the previous chapters of this section, I've discussed many of the basic tools that actors use to build consistently first-rate work. Among these are conflict, physical actions, and the "magic if," as well as the playing of objectives and given circumstances. When actors use these tools, their work is more likely to meet the definition of good acting—acting that is believable and tells the best possible story while serving the script. But even when actors are making good choices regarding these tools, there is still an additional acting obligation that they must always meet, an obligation as important as anything already mentioned. If your work is going to be completely believable, you must be able to employ your acting tools and still listen carefully and react to your fellow actors at every moment of your stage life.

The Importance of Listening

It is one of the great ironies of acting training that students doing an improv so often demonstrate an uncanny ability to listen and react; yet when these same actors read a scripted scene, the results are far different. In an improv, it is not unusual to see young actors brilliantly playing off of each other, skillfully demonstrating the ability to pick up on each other's thoughts and actions quickly and accurately. They are able to do this because they are **listening** with their other senses as well as their ears, looking constantly for clues that will help them stay focused on the scene and on each other. An improvisational scene can be built in no other way. Since there is no script, actors have no choice but to stay completely connected with each other. If they are particularly good at improv, then their in-the-moment contributions bounce off each other as if they had already read the script or seen the movie. Situations are created and developed faster than in a nighttime soap opera.

Yet, it is not unusual that when these same students are asked to do a reading from a written scene they seem barely aware that another actor is present. Their focus goes no further than the words of the script. There is no interaction between the actors beyond listening for the cue to say the next set of lines; and when the cue is delivered, no matter how fraught with information, dramatic possibility, or surprise, the next line is returned as though its predecessor had barely existed. No dramatic moments are realized or acted out, no **new information** or **discoveries** are reacted to, and the scene is invariably unclear, flat, and without any dramatic movement.

This inability to listen and react is often what keeps a polished high school production looking like high school. Perhaps, if you think about it, even some of your own performances have been affected by this very lack of listening. Too often, when a high school performer turns on the charisma in a production, what we get is just that—a performance. The actor is focused on delivering, to the letter, everything he or she has worked out during the rehearsal period—so much so, that the actor can throw that show biz switch, and, like a pro, reproduce the goods at every performance. This ability is laudable, but it seldom results in good acting.

The question that needs to be asked is, Was the work believable? The truth is this—if an actor's performance takes place in a vacuum, believability is practically a lost cause. As an actor you can never ignore what happened onstage the moment before the one you are in. It irrevocably affects the present. Further, it is essential that you acknowledge and deal **moment to moment** with the actors who are sharing the stage with you. Otherwise, you will be making choices and completing actions that may have nothing to do with the story unfolding on the stage. This unfolding story must seem spontaneous, as though it has never happened before. It must create the illusion that it is being composed moment by moment through the interplay of all the actors—through their actions and reactions as much as by the words being spoken.

In life, when we interact with others, we adjust everything we do and say in accordance with the input we are receiving. We listen to the words we hear, of course, but we also listen in many other ways as well. First, there is the manner in which information is delivered by the speaker. There is also information in the body language of the speaker—gestures, eye contact, movements. We rely as much on our processing of this information as on the words themselves. In fact, it is often this subtextual information that keeps us from making fools of ourselves time and again.

EXERCISE 9-1

1. Have a conversation with a partner during which each of you speaks for one minute without interruption. At the end of the two minutes, each of you should report to the class all the information you received from your partner. When each of you has finished your report, find out from your partner how accurately each of you remembered what was said.

2. Do the same exercise one pair at a time in front of the class. Was the listening less accurate this time? Why? Discuss the results.

3. Repeat the exercise again, but this time report what you heard as if you are your partner giving the information rather than simply reporting what you heard as yourself. What changes occurred? Why? Discuss.

The same level of listening must be maintained by actors in the world of the play. An actor cannot simply perform a role. You must be connected with the other actors in the same way you would be in life. You must listen with your eyes as well as your ears—in fact, with all your available senses—and act accordingly. After all, an audience sees and hears the same things the actors do onstage, so it is essential that the actors react to the things that an audience will certainly find significant.

Here is an example of what I mean. Not long ago I was doing an exercise with a group of adult actors who work professionally. Two of them were asked to play robbers attempting to gain access to a house where a ten-year-old child, played by another actor, was at home alone. One of the robbers tried to entice the child into opening the door by claiming she had been sent by the child's father to deliver the boy's lunchtime favorite—a Big Mac. A good con, right? Except that the woman told the boy she had just come from Burger King (they don't sell Big Macs) with the sandwich, which the actor playing the boy accepted without any problem whatsoever. But the actor playing the boy had already established himself as a very smart young man. What then is wrong with this scenario? Later in the scene, the same actor did not challenge an inaccurate description the robber gave to the police about her partner. Why would the boy not be bothered by this? The answer is simple—he would be. It was the actor who accepted the inaccurate description and the faux pas about Burger King, not the character. Why? Because he wasn't listening. The character certainly would have been. His safety and perhaps his life depended on it.

One of the unfortunate truths of acting is that too often the audience is smarter than those working on the stage. The fact is that, when we are acting, we suddenly tend to get stupid. The things that are obvious to us in life become amazingly obscure to us when we are onstage. Ultimately, however, good actors manage to train themselves to master the ability to see and hear the things that would be obvious were they sitting in the audience. My class, by the way, immediately recognized both blunders in the acting exercise, yet none of the actors doing the exercise did. Listening is essential for believability onstage.

EXERCISE 9-2

1. Improvise a short scene with a partner and perform it. It can be on any subject. When the improv is over, tell your partner all the things he or she said to you, and report on all the things he or she did during the scene. Solicit feedback from the class. Find out

whether they felt you were listening to each other. Was there good interaction?

2. With the same partner read a one-minute selection from a scene from a play. Tell your partner all the things he or she said to you, all the things he or she did during the scene. Solicit feedback from the class. Find out whether they felt you were listening and interacting well.

3. Compare the listening and reacting in the improvisational scenes to the scenes that were read. Draw conclusions.

Improving Your Listening Ability

So, if you are like so many other actors, professional as well as student, what can you do to improve your ability to listen while acting? One thing you can do is to literally take the time in your scene rehearsals to make sure you really are listening. Here's an easy way to do just that. It's a very simple technique called "What Did You Say?" Every time your partner completes a speech, just ask, "What did you say?" This forces your partner to rethink what he or she just said, and it gives you an opportunity to hear and think again about the information your partner is communicating. (In life, by the way, you have no obligation to respond to what is being said, but onstage, a failure to react keeps you from telling the best possible story and communicating that story to the audience.) The repeated lines need not be exactly as written in the script, but they must contain all the information in the original lines. Make sure that during the repetition you catch not only the verbal information but the subtextual information as well. Doing this will help both you and your partner better recognize all the things that are worth reacting to the next time you go through the scene.

A variation on this technique is the "What Is That Supposed to Mean?" game. Here, you and your partner may interrupt each other at any time during the rehearsal to ask the question, "What is that supposed to mean?" This forces you and your scene partner to explain objectively as well as subjectively what you are actually saying and trying to achieve with the line. It also helps each of you to hear what the other intends to communicate. Consequently, you will both be better able to build the scene in accordance with the underlying story. And the story being told, rather than the dialogue alone, is where the real dramatic throughline lies.

You can also play the "What Did I Just Say?" game. Here, you or your partner can ask, "What did I just say?" at any time following the completion of a speech. Your partner must then repeat what you have just told him or her. This will definitely let you know whether listening has been going on. You can also ask your partner what your speech meant, in order to see whether your acting choices are getting through. If they're not, you and your partner will have to figure out whether the failure is a result of poor acting on your part or poor listening on your partner's.

Remember, when people speak to us in life, we can usually repeat, sometimes even verbatim, what has just been said. We can almost always interpret what we have just been told as well—for subtext, for nuance, for connotation. We can do this because we are sensitive to tone, rhythm, body language, and a host of other indicators that all come under the category of listening. We do this automatically. It is part of our built-in system of communication. When actors can't do this, it is usually a result of not paying attention to the speaker. When that is the case, believability is a lost cause.

EXERCISE 9-3

1. A volunteer from your class should speak extemporaneously to the class for two minutes or so. The subject can be provided, or the speaker can select the topic.

2. When the talk is over, the class should compose a list of things they learned from the speaker during the speech. This information should be derived not only from what was said but from all other sources of information provided by the speaker as well.

3. Draw conclusions and discuss.

4. Repeat the exercise with each new speaker.

So if you're not listening to your acting partner, what are you doing? In most cases of nonlistening, unfortunately, you're busy preparing to say your next line. But unless you clearly hear the inspiration for that line, the line you speak will never have more meaning than what simply lies in the words. If that is all the audience gets from your acting, they might as well be reading the play to themselves—because that individual reader's imagination will probably be acting with more colors than the nonlistening actor on the stage.

Here is another exercise for improving your listening skills.

EXERCISE 9-4

1. Divide into partners or small groups.

2. Select an initiator for each group.

3. First, the initiator says, "I like you" to one of the players in the group. That person then repeats the phrase back to the initiator. The initiator goes on to say, "I like you" to the next person, who will repeat it back as well—and so on through the group. The important thing is that the initiator should say the phrase differently each time. If each member of the group is listening, then each repetition of the phrase will be different as well—reflecting the way the initiator sent out the message.

There are thousands of ways to say "I like you," and each one conveys a particular meaning. If the initiator's "I like you" is passionate, the person spoken to should take note of that and respond in a way that reflects the passion being communicated. If the "I like you" is sexual, the response should reflect that fact. Every return should somehow play off of the transmitted message and actively reflect what has been taken in by the listener. Otherwise, the response will not sound believable. As the game proceeds, take turns initiating the charged statement.

Before you start your repetition game, you might make a list of emotionally charged phrases that you could say to each other instead of "I like you." If any response does not reflect the initiating statement, the initiator should simply repeat it until he or she gets an appropriate response. Remember, the statements will only be charged if they carry new and interesting information—information provided by the manner in which the initiator delivers the line. The delivery should demand that the responding actor receive the information in a particular way and then process the message before making his or her response.*

---

* **Sanford Meisner,** one of several great acting teachers who sprang from the Group Theatre (which I discuss in Chapter 4), recognized that listening and being in the moment were two of the most important attributes of good acting. As a result, he focused a good part of his teaching career on developing and working with a series of sequential **repetition games** intended to improve the actor's listening skills. If you are interested in trying his sequence of repetition games, you might check out one or more of the several books listed in the Suggested Readings that focus on his techniques. They will provide you with ample material to continue the development of your own listening skills.

Listening and Playing Objectives

Of course, playing objectives at all times while onstage will also improve your listening skills—if those objectives are connected to the actors sharing the stage with you. Your effective pursuit of objectives depends on whether your tactics are succeeding with the other actors/characters. If you are listening with your eyes and ears to what they are doing and how they are responding to your tactics, you will automatically adjust according to your effect on them and their effect on you. In other words, playing your objective effectively depends on keeping in touch with everyone who shares the stage with you.

Here is a classroom exercise I use to demonstrate the power that listening well onstage can have. It also demonstrates how playing strong, simple objectives onstage can lead to strong, clear, compelling acting. The exercise also points out the interconnectedness of the two. Ironically, the exercise is done with no talking at all. The listening takes place with the eyes because all the communication is written. The exercise is called "Instant Playwriting," and it goes like this.

EXERCISE 9-5

1. Find a partner. Then each of you should select a strong objective that you can obtain from your partner. State your objective in the form of a verb phrase starting with "to make him/her ____."

   The phrase "to make" guarantees that the objective you select will be a strong one. Including your partner's name guarantees that you must engage him or her in order to obtain the objective.

2. Write your objectives down to ensure that you have been specific. A written objective might say "to make my partner feel better," or "to make my partner help me," or even "to make my partner kiss me." If you have picked a weak objective, you will soon learn from experience the importance of going into a scene armed with a stronger one.

3. One of you begins by writing a first line of dialogue on a piece of paper. Your partner should not be able to see what you are writing. Your written dialogue should be a first step toward obtaining your stated objective. When you've completed your piece of dialogue, hand it over to your partner.

4. After reading the dialogue, your partner must respond to it in writing, trying to pursue his or her own objective.

   There is now an obstacle for your partner, who cannot pursue his or her objective without acknowledging what you have put on the table through your dialogue. In other words, your partner's dialogue must somehow incorporate the information contained in your line and at the same time try to redirect the conversation in order to find a way to fulfill his or her objective. Suddenly, it becomes clear that strategy will be necessary if either of your objectives are to be obtained.

5. When your partner has written a response, he or she then passes the paper back to you, and so on until the scene is completed. (The scene is completed when some logical resolution has been reached. You'll recognize the moment that happens. It's part of good storytelling.)

   Each new piece of dialogue should be short. The purpose of the game will be destroyed if you write long monologues in order to redirect the flow of dialogue. One sentence at a time is probably the best way to go.

6. Discuss with the class what you discovered by playing the exercise.

7. Read your scene with your partner aloud for the class. How much spontaneity were you able to retain? Did you retain the way you acted out victories, defeats, and discoveries the first time? Why or why not?

Very early into the exercise you probably noticed that you were responding emotionally to each new line of dialogue presented to you, mostly because it surprised you. You probably also noticed that you were going through a clear-cut process during and after your reading of each new line. In the first stage, you read the line—the equivalent of hearing a line spoken in an acting situation. Then you reacted to the line. Finally you initiated a response by writing a new line of dialogue. This happened sequentially and fully with each new line introduced. Clearly each new reading had a beginning, a middle, and an end. Magically, in a very short span of time, you began to realize that you were strongly connected to the material—as strongly as you are when performing a well-rehearsed script.

While writing and reading the new dialogue, you probably found yourself registering and reacting to each new piece of information, each new discovery, each little victory and defeat. Since there was no dialogue beyond what the two of you wrote in the moment, you were not distracted by anticipating your next line. And because you were truly in each moment, you reacted with a level of spontaneity usually reserved for real life. There were clear-cut beats, transitions, and a steady throughline of conflict leading toward, and culminating in, one or more climaxes. The exercise should make eminently clear the importance of listening onstage.

However, the connection between the impromptu script you create and a script written by a good playwright will probably be less apparent. Yet, in good dramatic writing, the playwright has written only what is absolutely necessary to tell the story. If something doesn't serve a specific purpose, the good playwright will omit it. In most cases a playwright is intentionally creating and developing conflict at all times because he or she is interested in making a compelling story for the stage. Consciously or not, the playwright is pitting one character against another, and for the actor this translates into opposing objectives. With "Instant Playwriting," you created your own objectives, and because you knew what they were, you were able to play them clearly and fully. But the dialogue in a well-crafted play is really no different.

Here is one final exercise you might try. Although, in my own early acting days, I used to do this one myself, I must give credit to Jeremy Whelan, author of the book *Instant Acting,* for bringing it back to my attention, and for refining it. Whelan claims that this exercise revolutionizes the whole acting process. An overstatement, perhaps, but there is no doubt that the exercise does force the actors to listen onstage. At the same time, the exercise helps the actors engage themselves physically in the scene by requiring them to make choices about movement, gesture, and business, the three elements of blocking (discussed in detail in Chapter 14). These are all big virtues, and I have witnessed the exercise work miracles on even the most recalcitrant of stage listeners, and, for that matter, stage movers.

EXERCISE 9-6

The procedure is simple. After familiarizing yourself with the scene you and your partner have begun working on, the two of you should read the scene into a tape recorder. The purpose is not to act the scene; it is merely to get the words onto tape. Once the scene is recorded, set up your rehearsal area with all of the props and set pieces the scene requires. Then rewind the tape to the beginning and play it. Oh, yes. And while the tape is running, act out the scene physically with each other while you are listening. But do nothing with the words you are hearing other than allowing them to provide all of the physicalization that should go along with the words. Before long, you will be listening with incredible specificity, and using your body with an expressiveness that will amaze you, your partner, and eventually your class.

Once again, the surprising results produced by "Instant Acting" are the by-product of good listening. Having the words of the scene coming from an inanimate, third-party source demands that your stage listening system realign itself to the new circumstances. That, in turn, results in some listening far superior to what you as an actor can usually get away with. The results, of course, are of the kind that all good actors require of themselves. As so many fine actors say, "Good acting is reacting." The secret is, you first have to listen before you can react.

Finally, remember this. It is your obligation as an actor to re-create with scripted material what you feel when you do the "Instant Acting" exercise. It is also your obligation to consistently find the compelling and clear physical actions, business, and gestures you will discover for yourself when you try "Instant Acting." You must always make clear each moment of your work and build those moments into a compelling story. You will do so by learning to translate the conflict you find in the scenes you select into playable objectives. But these essential results can only come if you learn to listen—in the same way you would in life. If you dedicate yourself to this goal, you will eventually be able to listen effectively onstage. It is part of the craft you must master—and craft can be learned. Just one last thing: Are you listening?

EXERCISE 9-7

Mirror Game

The mirror game is a game intended to fully connect you, at least externally, with your partner. The object is to get fully in synch with each other so that an outside observer would not be able to tell which of you is initiating the movement, and which of you, like a mirror, is simply copying or reflecting the movement of the initiator. There is no winner or loser in this exercise. Again, the purpose is to find a way to work together. Therefore, it is the obligation of the initiator to make movements that can be copied simultaneously, and it is the obligation of the reflector to observe, as closely as possible, all that the initiator is doing. If an outside observer can tell who is leading in the exercise, then it is a failure on the part of both you and your partner, since you were unable to find a way of giving the illusion of simultaneous action.

1. When you understand the rules, face your partner, standing about three feet apart with your hands at your sides. Once you are able to look at each other without resorting to any self-conscious behavior, you are ready to play.

2. When you are in synch, begin to explore space, height, and a variety of movement. Never allow your movement to destroy the sychronization. Without discussion, allow the initiator/reflector relationship to change.

EXERCISE 9-8

Whisper Down the Lane or Telephone

The party game known as "Whisper Down the Lane" or, more recently, "Telephone" provides another excellent way to work on your listening skills.

Sit with a group of individuals next to each other in a line. Someone will whisper a message to the first person in the line who must then repeat the message into the ear of the next person, and so on, until the message is repeated down the line to the last person. The final person must then repeat the message aloud so that everyone can hear it. The last person's message is then compared with that of the original message-giver—usually with hilarious results.

Discuss the results and draw conclusions.

Summary

In life, when we interact with others, we adjust everything we do and say in accordance with the input we are receiving. We listen to and interpret not only the words we hear but also the manner in which information is delivered and the body language of the speaker—his or her gestures, eye contact, and movement. We rely as much on our processing of this nonverbal information as on the words themselves. Believability onstage is created only when actors commit to the same level of listening. Actors must deal at every moment with the information communicated by the other actors who are sharing the stage with them and make adjustments according to the context, subtext, and visual cues they receive.

CHAPTER 10

Interpreting and Using Dialogue

Most young actors have read and studied plays for their high school English classes. The plays you have read were probably analyzed, synthesized, parsed, and, perhaps, even worshipped—as literature. If your teacher was a good one, you probably came to admire the words of Shakespeare, Shaw, and Williams for their poetic beauty. But unless you had a script analysis class, you probably never analyzed a play's dialogue for what it was intended—*as tools to help the characters who say those words get what they need.*

There are countless ways to say any line of dialogue. Yet it is up to the actor to choose one of those options and deliver the line so that it clearly reflects that choice. As I pointed out in the last chapter, if actors are really listening to each other, the way a line is said will affect the way the next speaking actor says his or her lines. This is how believability is maintained. But it is also one of the ways that the actors create the story's throughline and, more importantly, make it clear for the audience. Ultimately, if the lines are delivered without communicating this underlying meaning, the story is certainly altered, possibly muddied, and perhaps even destroyed completely.

In a number of recent films for television, for instance, the topic of date rape has provided the subject matter for thought-provoking story lines. The issue of whether the word "stop" means "stop" has often been at the dramatic center of these movies. What "stop" might actually mean also provided the subject for intensive and embarrassing media coverage at the trial of a well-known national sportscaster not so long ago. In situations like these, dramatic or actual, the question always seems to boil down to the speaker's contextual as well as subtextual meaning in saying the word "stop." The defense lawyers, both in television movies and in actual cases, invariably try to prove that "stop" meant something other than its literal meaning. Both the context in which a word is spoken and what the speaker actually intends to communicate can alter the word's surface meaning. The resulting nuance can spell the difference between freedom and a long jail sentence for the accused.

Contextual Meaning and Subtext

Contextual meaning refers to the circumstances within which a line of dialogue is spoken. Suppose in a date rape movie, the actor playing the accusing young woman had said "Stop" while willingly helping the actor playing her date unbutton her shirt. The meaning of her statement has been affected by the circumstances. Suppose she had said "Stop" and then continued to undress herself while knowingly allowing him to watch? Again the context has affected the meaning. I am not trying to create a political debate in my example; I am merely pointing out that meaning can be altered, subtly or dramatically, by the context in which words are spoken.

Subtext, or underlying objective, also alters meaning. Suppose the actress playing the young woman had said "Stop" as she was smiling and laughing? Suppose she was clearly saying it in order to tease her partner? Again, I am not arguing the rightness or the wrongness of the situation legally. I am merely pointing out that in life communication is seldom simply a matter of literal, or surface, meaning alone.

It is no different when actors convey meaning onstage or in film. Their responsibility is always to tell the story clearly, so they must make and execute choices—including choices about dialogue—that help further the audience's understanding as well as that of the other actors in the scene. Otherwise, the story will not be told effectively. The issue of the **literal meaning** of the words an actor uses versus their contextual and subtextual meanings is, therefore, a critical one.

So how does the actor select the appropriate way to say his or her lines? First of all, there is no single correct choice, any more than there is one single way to play Hamlet, Laura Wingfield, or Tarzan. In the end, if it works, it is a good choice—if it serves to convey the story of the play and the point behind that story. Of course, part of an actor's storytelling responsibility is to choose and deliver every line of dialogue in such a way that it reflects the context, or given circumstances, of each moment of the play as well as the character's subtext, or objective, at that moment. If you make choices that come from the given circumstances and reflect the manner in which the previous line was delivered, you will be well on your way to doing your job well. If, in addition, you make choices that help you get your objective or what you need, you have probably arrived.

EXERCISE 10-1

1. Examine the following two lines of dialogue.

   A: How do you feel?

   B: I feel just fine.

   On face value these lines are boring, if not clichéd. Their literal meaning offers up little in the way of drama. Were we to read these lines in an English class, we would probably move right along to some other more poetic or dramatic dialogue. But suppose we give these lines some context—a set of given circumstances that could help us find a specific and interesting way to deliver this dialogue.

2. From the following list select several "who's" that could help you play out the scene more specifically.

   Surgeon and patient
   Lovers
   Drug users
   Fighters
   Parent and child
   Prisoner of war and interrogator
   Astronauts
   Coach and athlete

   Once you have selected from the list, you will probably discover that knowing a little will force you into finding out a lot more. Provide yourselves with the other necessary circumstances that will let you play the little scene in step 1 specifically. You will likely need to deal with issues of time and place as well as other conditions affecting the scene.

3. When you have made decisions about all the given circumstances —the who, what, when, and where—you should have a working understanding of the context of the scene. You will then be ready to try reading the scene out loud.

4. Read the scene with a partner keeping in mind its context and subtext. Discuss the results.

5. Using the same procedure, try other choices from the list. Discuss the results.

Each of your readings was very different, right?

Every piece of information you added to the context surrounding the dialogue forced you to change the delivery of each line. In the case of the surgeon and patient, the way the question is asked in an operating room would need to be different from the way it is asked in the recovery room. How about several weeks later in a restaurant? How about in any of these locations if the surgeon had been drinking or if the patient had at first attempted to refuse treatment?

How about if in the lovers scenario the characters were kids? Suppose it was their first time. Suppose it happened in the backseat of a car. Or in the bed of one of their parents. Suppose the conversation took place as a phone conversation an hour later. Or after a pregnancy test. Suppose the conversation took place forty years ago, or a hundred. Notice how each add-on would affect the situation drastically.

What if the prisoner was about to be tortured? Suppose the prisoner knows he will be tortured the next day. Or in one hour. In five minutes, or in one. Suppose the prisoner and the interrogator have already been talking. Or try reversing the dialogue and discover a completely different scene.

The preceding examples should clearly demonstrate how dialogue means something very different to an actor than to a student in an English class. The way an actor uses dialogue to communicate and reflect the important ongoing story elements in a play is critical, whether the language itself is elevated poetry or seemingly banal chitchat. Of course, everything that happens onstage is important, because it all contributes to the successful telling of the story. But I cannot overstate the importance of a clear and specific context when telling the story through dialogue.

Dialogue is also one of the principal ways that actors convey the equally important subtext of their characters—their objective, or reason for doing what they do. Because of its power to communicate, dialogue is one of the most important tools actors use to get what they need onstage. Unlike in life, where most people seldom think about what they are saying and their reasons for saying it, the actor must know what his or her character needs and be pursuing the fulfillment of that need at all times. (See Chapters 6 and 7.)

With that in mind, let's take another look at the two-line scene above, and see what happens when we add subtext to those lines.

EXERCISE 10-2

1. After reading the subtext in parentheses, read the lines with a partner.

If the surgeon had been drunk and the patient is happy to be alive:

A: How do you feel? (I need to know I didn't kill you.)

B: I feel just fine. (I need you to know that I'm so glad you operated.)

Young lovers after a wonderful experience:

A: How do you feel? (I need to know that I pleased you.)

B: I feel just fine. (I need you to know that you were wonderful.)

Young lovers after a bad experience:

A: How do you feel? (I need to know you don't hate me.)

B: I feel just fine. (I need you to know that we made a mistake.)

Astronauts after leaving the earth's atmosphere:

A: How do you feel? (I need you to confirm my feeling of awe.)

B: I feel just fine. (I need you to know that I am awed too.)

Astronauts after a difficult take-off:

A: How do you feel? (I need to know you feel better than you look.)

B: I feel just fine. (I need you not to worry about me.)

Coach to athlete after athlete sets a new record:

A: How do feel? (I need you to enjoy your triumph.)

B: I feel just fine. (I need you to know I am enjoying it.)

Or:

   A: How do you feel? (I need to know why you're not enjoying your triumph.)

   B: I feel just fine. (I need you to know that I wanted to do even better.)

2. Try creating and playing your own given circumstances and objectives for the given lines. The possibilities are truly infinite and so are the opportunities to create believable, imaginative, and absolutely clear storytelling moments.

The Importance of Subtext and Context

Clearly, the speaker's subtext will change the literal or surface meaning of a line, as will the context in which a line is spoken. It is, therefore, essential that an actor be clear about both the given circumstances in the play at every moment, and about what he or she needs to convey through the dialogue. Only by establishing and continually playing both the situation at hand and the character's objective can you be certain to communicate the essential story elements to the audience.

When rehearsing a scene from a play, however, it is all too easy for actors to fall into the trap of simply delivering the surface meaning of the playwright's dialogue, falsely thinking that the storytelling responsibility lies solely with the writer. But an actor who does so is forgetting that the playwright writes knowing that what he or she creates is only the blueprint for the director and actors to follow and build upon. Even when the script is a good one, an enormous amount of information must be revealed through the imagination and problem-solving skills of the actors serving that script. Therefore, you must use your common sense and logic to make the right choices—choices that allow the story to unfold simply, clearly, and compellingly. It is only through dialogue and physical action, your primary storytelling tools, that the playwright's work can be revealed, and that will happen only when what the audience sees is governed by the appropriate context and subtext that you find in the script.

In the work of Harold Pinter, for instance, the playwright seldom tells you why his characters behave so strangely. In his early plays, Pinter provides only the vaguest hints at the given circumstances surrounding the action, yet the dialogue is filled with menace and conflict. Clearly, each character's words are affecting the others. It becomes the actors' job to determine the given circumstances that might justify the strange behavior of Pinter's characters, and from those circumstances figure out a subtext to make sense of the dialogue— both for themselves and for the audience. Why do the characters in *The Dumb Waiter* argue in a life-and-death manner over semantics, or run around frantically to please an upstairs phantom sending down orders via the eponymous dumbwaiter? Why, in *The Homecoming,* does Lenny suddenly ask his brother's wife if he can hold her hand and then tell her a story about how he nearly beat a woman to death? Things like this happen all the time in Pinter plays. If plays like these are to work, the actors must provide the story that the playwright has intentionally failed to provide. Context and subtext are the keys for making that happen.

In the play *Oleanna,* on the other hand, playwright David Mamet intentionally creates some ambiguity about what happens between a professor and his student. In the first scene of the play, the audience actually sees and hears the conference between the two that, in Scene 2, becomes a matter of interpretation for each of the characters and for the audience watching. At one point in the first scene, the professor touches the girl and tells her that he wants "to help her because he really likes her." In the second scene he finds out that he has been accused of misconduct and sexual harassment. If played well, only after the accusation is made does the audience think twice about the action of the first scene. A good production leaves the audience disagreeing about what they actually saw and heard, in spite of the fact that the entire audience shared that experience together.

Mamet wanted to create a play that pointed out that even objective reality is distilled through the subjective viewpoints of every individual. If the play is to work, however, the actors must play their subtexts very specifically through the dialogue and through what they choose to do physically, or the playwright's intentional ambiguity will seem like a self-conscious dramatic device intended only to manipulate the audience. But, when done well, the ambiguity is hidden by the acting choices, though the script never allows the ambiguity to disappear completely. The audience ends up judging what they saw by bringing their individual politics into their perception. Without the subtext and context of the play clearly accounted for by the actors, however, the play will make the audience feel manipulated rather than moved, and the results are far less affecting.

Analyzing a Script to Tell the Story

Analyzing a script always requires a lot of detective work. Some clues lie in the stage directions of the play, if the playwright chooses to provide them. But most of a play's storytelling clues are hidden in the dialogue. The literal and contextual meanings of the lines combine to suggest a dramatic throughline of action, or story. That story is based on conflict between the characters in the situation. Once the conflict is determined through the dialogue and the implied action, the subtext for the dialogue can be created and executed.

Read the following scene.

A: Look!

B: I am looking.

A: Do you believe it?

B: We're both seein' it, ain't we?

A: I guess so. How many can you count?

B: 'Bout a dozen, more or less.

A: It ain't like when you read about it.

B: Never is. I'm goin' now.

A: What? You ain't goin' nowhere.

B: Good-bye, (*name*).

A: Hey! Wait a minute. Wait a doggoned minute!

B: I been waitin' my whole life.

A: (*Name*)! Oh my God!

In a contextless scene like this one, an actor can't be lulled into thinking that the contextual clues are already provided by the playwright. To make sense of such a scene, you must use all the tools of your craft—but only after you have made your own preliminary decisions regarding the given circumstances. Doing so is essential for good work.

Here is a list of acting tools you will need to use before putting our contextless scene together. These are the basics that I've discussed in this and the previous five chapters, and a quick review of the terms follows. Be sure to develop a complete response to each item before attempting to rehearse the scene. Only after you have done so, will you be ready to read on.

- Find or invent given circumstances.
- Find the conflict.
- Create a dramatic throughline.
- Find and play an objective.
- Find or create risk, high stakes, and obstacles.
- Find and play the dramatic moments.
- Justify each line of dialogue.

Given Circumstances

Because our scene is contextless and provides no given circumstances, for the moment we'll skip over a discussion of context. Obviously, everything else you decide will be affected by the given circumstances you invent, but first we'll focus simply on the clues the dialogue provides regarding the possible story it tells. Remember, besides their contextual meaning, the lines also have literal and subtextual meaning that, when studied in sequence, can help shed light on the story being told.

Conflict

Scenes must have conflict, so it stands to reason that the conflict in the scene is between characters A and B. The conflict results from something they are seeing. After A and B see something very significant, B decides to go (somewhere). A tries to stop B, but fails to do so. B's going leads to something of major significance.

Throughline

The throughline consists of the events that occur chronologically in a scene. It is the map of the action, not unlike a musical score, that proceeds from beginning to end. Being aware of the action, event by event, can help actors tell the story clearly. Compare the throughline as I describe it with the actual lines of dialogue and see if you agree with my analysis.

The throughline in the scene starts in mid-action rather than at a clear-cut beginning. Both characters are witnessing something, and that something immediately becomes the catalyst for the action of the scene. A and B then discuss whether they believe what they are seeing. B counts the objects and determines that they number about a dozen. A is shocked by the difference between the reality of the objects and what he (or she) has read about them. B expresses less surprise. After the discussion B decides to go. A tries to stop B, but fails to do so. A sees something after B leaves that is shocking.

Objectives

Since objectives spring from conflict, the two characters in this scene have strong but simple objectives to play. Their first objectives are shared. Both are trying to make sense of what they are seeing. Once a decision is made about what they are witnessing, there is a transition. A's objective becomes to keep B from going; B's, to keep A from detaining him (or her).

Risk, High Stakes, and Obstacles

If the definition of good acting is "to be believable and tell the best possible story while serving the script," then whatever A and B see should be earth-shattering. As playwright/actors you and your partner need to invent something major for A and B to see—something life-and-death, something that the two characters can really have an intense discussion about. Obviously, the more at risk, the higher the stakes. The obstacle to obtaining each character's objective in this scene is the other character—since their objectives are in direct conflict.

Dramatic Moments

Good actors act every dramatic moment available to them. Dramatic moments are moments of victory, defeat, or discovery, or where new information changes the direction of a scene. The bigger an actor can make a moment, the more exciting the work.

A: Look!

B: I am looking.

The scene opens with a dramatic discovery. What is it the characters are seeing? Whatever has drawn A's attention has already also drawn B's. The lines suggest that the object is something that cannot be missed. It's big, so play it big.

A: How many can you count?

B: 'Bout a dozen, more or less.

A: It ain't like when you read about it.

B: Never is. I'm goin' now.

The dialogue in this section suggests action, and playing actions makes for good moments. The question about counting suggests that B is counting at that moment. If the objects being watched have already been established as major, then twelve of them make for a good storytelling sequence. The line, however, says "more or less." Why is the speaker not more specific? That line needs to be justified, and doing so can make another interesting moment to play. The subtext of "It ain't like when you read about it" suggests another discovery. Whatever they are seeing has been written about, yet the reality surpasses even the book description or explanation. It must, therefore, be shocking or awesome. "Never is" also suggests an interesting subtext. B must have thought about things like this before if he (or she) draws the conclusion that it "never is." The "Never is" is followed by a transitional moment: B must get from the line "Never is" to "I'm goin' now" in a believable and clear manner. Only by making a transition can B do so. Perhaps, the "Never is" triggers B to decide to go, but no matter what the ultimate acting choice, B's decision-making process is actable and must, therefore, be acted.

A: What? You ain't goin' nowhere.

B: Good-bye, (*name*).

A's "What?" also suggests a moment. Either A can't believe what B has said and needs clarification, or what B said did not sink in immediately. In either case, A has a moment to process the information. "You ain't goin' nowhere" is a strong statement, to say the least. Yet B does not respond to the statement with words. To ignore the command completely, however, would not be a good acting choice since good moments should be acted. At the least, B should take in what A has said, and then choose to ignore it. Is "Good-bye" just a formality or a meaningful moment? Which is a better choice? Obviously, a major "Good-bye" is the answer. What constitutes a meaningful good-bye in terms of physical action? Remember good actors always go for the big choice.

A: Hey! Wait a minute. Wait a doggoned minute!

B: I been waitin' my whole life.

A's "Hey!" also suggests action since the word "hey" usually comes as a response to something. Is it in response to B's good-bye, or has B already started to leave? If B is leaving, that "Hey" could be an attention-getter signaling that B should wait. A says "wait" two times. What does that suggest in terms of action between the two characters? A repeated phrase implies a dramatic progression. Good storytelling requires that the actors create one. B's "I been waitin' my whole life" suggests a subtext. If B has been waiting that long, B is probably impatient and wants to get on with it. Again, that suggests action in the scene.

A: Oh my God!

A's final line more than suggests a moment, it demands it. The phrase, the punctuation, and the placement of the line in sequence all scream out to the actor that a climactic big choice is needed. The good actor has no other option.

Justification

Justification means using the dialogue in such a way that everything in it makes sense for the audience. The problem of justifying the phrase "more or less" has already been discussed. But another justification problem arises from vernacular language the characters use. No one I am associated with says "doggoned" or "ain't" in the manner the characters in this piece do. What does their dialect suggest about who these characters are and where the story takes place? You cannot plan a set of given circumstances for the scene without heeding the clues found in the language, not to mention play out a scenario believably. For instance, a story that involves two professors, or two characters of noble birth, could not be justified or made believable using the vernacular of the scene. The question, then, becomes "What sort of people would use this kind of language?"

Once you start considering the kind of people who would use this kind of language and where they might be found, you have begun to explore the contextual elements of the script, and you are probably now ready to do so. By completing the who, what, when, and where, you will find yourself with plenty of context to surround your plotline. Clearly, the big choices suggested in the dialogue should allow your imagination to run free. The more outrageous the better. Big stakes and risk translate into good acting, as long as you keep it believable.

EXERCISE 10-3

Provide the necessary given circumstances for the contextless scene above, and then rehearse it with your partner. Perform it for an audience or your class. Discuss the work and revise it based on the feedback you get.

Wasn't it amazing how much useful material there was to be discovered and sifted from the script even before the context was added? Examining the literal and subtextual meaning of the lines in any play or scene can give the actor a remarkable amount of information to work with. By studying the dialogue through the filter of its emerging story, line by line, the conflict and the character objectives that support that conflict lead a skilled script reader to the heart of the drama—to the action it contains.

EXERCISE 10-4

Using the format established in the preceding discussion, analyze, rehearse, and perform the contextless scenes that follow. Discuss and critique the work performed. Make necessary changes using the feedback provided. Rehearse the revised scenes. Perform the revised scenes.

Scene 1

A: I'm over here.

B: Where?

A: Over here.

B: Oh. I see.

A: It's not what you think.

B: I hope not. Then what is it?

A: Can't you guess?

B: I'd prefer not to.

A: Suit yourself then.

B: I guess I'll have to. What's happening here?

A: Nothing' happening here. A format change, that's all.

B: That's all?!

A: You'll grow to like it. I did.

B: I'm not like you. I'm not like you at all.

A: Are you sure?

B: I'm sure.

A: So was I. But I was wrong.

B: You're still wrong. I'd better go.

A: If that's how you feel.

B: It is. Good-bye.

A: Good-bye.

Scene 2

A: Come out here.

B: Not now. I'm busy.

A: You'll be sorry. Better get out here. Now.

B: Okay. This better be good.

A: It is . . . or it was . . . no it is.

B: What's the big deal?

A: Look and ye shall see.

B: Oh . . . oh . . . my . . . yes. Thanks, you're right.

A: I told you.

B: Yes, you did, didn't you?

A: You believe me now?

B: Completely. Completely.

A: So, cough it up.

B: What? Oh, that.

A: Yes, that. That, that, that.

B: Here.

A: You're a good sport.

B: Thanks. I get a lot of practice.

Scene 3

A: Hello.

B: What do you want?

A: I just thought we could talk.

B: I have nothing to say.

A: Oh. Johnny saw you do it.

B: What did you say?

A: Johnny says he saw you do it.

B: Yeah? Screw Johnny.

A: Okay. Later.

B: Screw you too.

Summary

A line of dialogue can be said in an almost infinite number of ways. Which is the right one? It is up to the actor saying that line to communicate not only a line's literal meaning but its contextual and subtextual meaning as well. Only by determining and playing the given circumstances and the objective that a character is pursuing can an actor determine an appropriate delivery for any given line, and only by understanding the throughline of action of a particular scene will an actor's line delivery contribute fully to the unfolding story.

CHAPTER 11

Working with People, Places, and Things

From the previous chapters in this section, you have learned that actors must play actions that have beginnings, middles, and ends, and that each of these actions must tell a small story that serves the larger story the playwright has created. You have discovered that finding the conflicts in the play, in the scene, and at every moment will help you define the dramatic throughline of the piece you are working on. It will also lead you to an objective to play—the completion of which rests with the actor sharing the stage with you. The purposeful relationship between you and your partner, obviously, will serve the conflict and compellingly occupy your every moment of stage time—if you are listening to each other. In addition, by specifically determining the given circumstances of any acting situation and by asking yourself the "magic if," you will be able to choose tactics that will help you obtain your objectives. Together, these acting tools will ensure that your work is clear and believable for the audience as well as for yourself—even as they help make clear the overall story being told.

Now that you have begun to absorb all this, it is time to look more closely at some of the specifics that face you on your acting journey, and what dealing with these specifics might entail. Let's start with *things*.

Relating to Things

I once had an acting teacher whose approach to acting primarily consisted of using props. "No matter what's going on in the play," he would say, "you should have the appropriate props selected, and you should be using them. They will make your work seem real and that's what's important, being real." I didn't study with this guy for too long. I thought the premise for his work was simplistic, if not ridiculous. I knew even back then that acting involved a lot more than picking up a prop. But today, frankly, I'm not so sure that I didn't judge him too

112

harshly. Like many acting teachers, this one probably overstated his case, but I must now admit that there is much virtue in what he was saying. Using props or, more specifically, relating to the things you choose to use can both move the story forward and make it clearer. Further, the effective use of props can provide the audience with information about your character's inner life that the dialogue alone won't necessarily provide. The well-chosen prop can also enhance your ability to convey the emotional nuances of the acting situation to the audience, as well as to tap into your own emotions—even while you are propelling the story forward.

Don't panic. I know that I have used the nasty "e" word—*emotions*. But I am not suggesting that you throw away what I've said up to now. We are still talking about telling stories and playing actions. But it's impossible to deny that there are times onstage when characters are obviously feeling emotional. In those situations, it is important to be able to convey those feelings to the audience through what you choose to do, even if you as an actor don't necessarily have those feelings yourself. However, it is an interesting psychological phenomenon of human beings that physically engaging in a particular set of actions often stimulates emotional reactions.

Here are some examples of what I mean.

EXERCISE 11-1

1. Hug a pillow. Take a pillow from your bed or a throw pillow from a couch or sofa and hug it; really squeeze it like you mean it. Commit to the hug. What did you feel?

Surprising, huh? You probably felt something akin to an emotion as you hugged the pillow—an emotion not unlike what you might feel if you really hugged someone you care about.

2. Hug the pillow from your bed, and then hug a throw pillow from the couch. How were the experiences different? Why?

The one from your bed is probably softer and cozier. Did that one produce a stronger emotional reaction in you? Or, at least, a different one? If so, why do you think that was?

3. Pound a pillow. Make a fist and, while the pillow is resting on a bed or strong table, hit it. Really hit it. Hit the pillow several times. Hit the pillow like you hate it, like you really want to hurt it. Commit to the action.

Now survey your physical apparatus. Note your breathing, your heart rate. Can you feel the blood surging in your temples? Do you feel something emotionally? Is the feeling the same as the one you should be feeling as a pillow hater?

4. Caress your pillow. Pretend that your pillow is someone you'd like to caress, someone that you've fantasized about. Commit to the fantasy, and actually begin to gently stroke your pillow as if that pillow were the person you dream about. Stroke the pillow

in the way that you might stroke a face or an arm, or some other place your fantasy takes you. What happens?

5. Now go back and do to your pillow each of the actions listed above. Only this time, while doing the action, recite a favorite nursery rhyme as if you were saying it to the pillow. It can be any one that you know all the words to. Don't worry about the recitation. Focus on the action and your reason for doing the action.

Read on when you have completed the exercise.

Think about the experience you just had. Were your actions committed? Did you have appropriate emotional reactions? How did the different actions affect the nursery rhyme you recited? Did the words of the poem support the actions you were performing? Was the meaning of the nursery rhyme destroyed by the action, or was the meaning enhanced as a result of the committed actions you were carrying out?

The point of these pillow exercises was probably clear to you simply by your carrying out and committing to the instructions. But just in case, here are some conclusions you might have drawn from the exercise.

1. Committing to and carrying out a strong action on an object can produce an emotional response.

2. The emotional response feels almost identical to an actual emotional response. In fact, it may be an actual emotional response.

3. Physical actions carried out on an object help focus and clarify your behavior. In fact, doing the action to the object makes your acting experience more purposeful, more specific, and fuller. (Though you could not judge it, it probably made your work clearer as well.)

4. Saying dialogue while committed to an action directed at an object gives purpose to the words in a stronger and more specific way than when the words are simply spoken alone. Further, the literal meaning of the dialogue (provided by the content itself) is enriched when you add the meaning suggested by the given circumstances and by the purpose contained in the action.

This list provides some reasons why that former acting teacher of mine was not as far off base as I once thought so many years ago. All of the benefits of using props described here speak for themselves, but, more importantly, props also serve to enhance an actor's ability to tell the story clearly and compellingly. Therefore, there is a significant gain and no apparent loss from using props in your work. Remember, though, that every prop an actor uses while playing a character must have specific meaning for that character. It is up to you to make sure that each prop you use is *endowed* with that specific meaning. It is not enough to know intellectually that an object has meaning for your character. You must commit to choices that demonstrate that meaning as well. When you do so, the **endowment** of objects can be a powerful tool for you as an actor.

EXERCISE 11-2

Repeat the pillow exercise, yet another time. Provide yourself with given circumstances to work from.

Be sure to know who you are, where you are, and what has created the situation in which you find yourself acting out with a pillow. You will also need to ask yourself what your character would do in this situation. This is the "magic if." It is a given that for the exercise you must deal with the pillow, but who you are in this situation will affect the manner in which you carry out the exercise. You must consider how the character you are playing would deal with the pillow under this set of circumstances rather than simply relying on what your own personal reactions might be.

As you thought through the given circumstances and the "magic if," you might have come to realize that the pillow was really just a **substitution** for the real thing. Your hugging, punching, and caressing was not really about the pillow at all. You had to decide specifically whom or what the pillow was substituting for. You might have endowed the pillow with the qualities of the person or thing the pillow represented to you. Again, the more specific you were about that substitution, the more likely you were to find and commit to specific physical choices that clarified and strengthened your acting.

The pillow exercise, however, is just that. It is not meant to suggest that you should grab a pillow any time you want to enhance a moment or scene. The objects you choose must always be organic to the scene you are working on, and they should always add to the clarity of the overall story being told, rather than pulling focus from what is essential to the scene as written. In other words, the props you choose must help you tell the story you are supposed to tell. You must never make choices that are interesting for you or your character at the expense of the script. Further, what you choose to do with your props must be well thought out and executed. Relying on impulse or spontaneity is not enough. The actions you commit to and execute must reveal things that complement and add to the unfolding story.

To demonstrate what I mean, let's go back to the exercise in Chapter 5 in which you were asked to tell a story about finding something. Remember, the story you create must have a conflict; have a beginning, a middle, and an end; and use no dialogue. It should also be the best possible story you can come up with. In Chapter 5, I suggested telling a story about finding a penny. Now try the exercise using the objects in the list that follows.

Create a one-minute story using one of the following items:

A wad of cash	A letter
A doll baby	A piece of jewelry
A gun	A mirror
A snake	A piece of underwear

Immediately, your mind probably jumped to all kinds of things you could do with these items. But in order to do the best possible work, you must refine your ideas and make sure all the things you do add up to a logical and compelling whole—the best possible story told with clarity. That means you must create a set of given circumstances and think about the "magic if" before you begin.

Take the doll baby, for instance. You might want to use the doll literally as a doll, or you might want to have it represent a real baby for this exercise. If it's a doll, you will relate to it one way, if it's a real baby, then another. Who are you in this exercise? An adult or a child? If you're an adult, what are you doing with a doll? If the doll is meant to be a real baby, then whether you are an adult or a child will be significant to the actions you choose to carry out. Where does the scene take place? In the baby's bedroom, the living room, the kitchen? Where the scene occurs will influence the choices you make. When you enter the scene, where is the baby or the doll? On the floor, on the ground, in a crib?

What will you do in the scene? The answer depends on who you are in the scene, as well as where you are. If you are the baby's mother, you might act one way, if you're the father, another. How about if you're its sister, brother, or babysitter? If it's your first child, or third? The answers will affect the choices you make. Is the baby crying or asleep? If the doll is a doll, is it yours? Is it your mother's? Your sister's? Your best friend's? Your worst enemy's? What do you think of the doll? What does the owner of the doll think of the doll? How old are you?

Each of these questions raises many more additional questions that, once answered, will affect the way you choose to interact with the baby or the doll. Since the exercise is not scripted, you are responsible for creating the most interesting set of given circumstances you can, as well as carrying them out clearly. Now you begin to understand why I said that you can't rely on impulse or spontaneity alone when playing physical actions with a prop.

With each of the items on the list, you could come up with a tremendous number of scenarios by manipulating the given circumstances—the who, what, when, and where. With each scenario you could invent endless variations simply by changing the actions you choose to do with the prop; but even using the same actions, you could invent countless more variations, simply by changing the manner in which you execute the actions.

For instance, suppose you decide to stroke the baby doll along its head. Stroking slowly and gently will tell one story. Stroking rapidly will tell another. The same goes for rocking the baby. There are many ways to rock an infant. Each reveals something different about the character and situation to the audience. Each is likely to produce a different response in you as well. Which choices are the most effective for communicating the story you want to communicate?

Now, let's apply these concepts to some real plays in order to demonstrate further the point I'm making here.

EXERCISE 11-4

1. Following is a list of characters and props from some plays that you may be familiar with. Select one or more of the suggestions below and create a one-minute silent scene as the character using the listed prop. Be sure that your story is consistent with the given circumstances of the play, the scene, and the character. There is only one way you can be sure that it is. You must *read the play;* and you must read it very carefully.

   Laura, *The Glass Menagerie,* a glass animal
   Brick, *Cat on a Hot Tin Roof,* bottle of scotch and a glass
   Blanche, *A Streetcar Named Desire,* a diamond tiara
   Stella, *A Streetcar Named Desire,* Stanley's bowling shirt
   Juliet, *Romeo and Juliet,* a bottle of sleeping potion
   Romeo, *Romeo and Juliet,* a bottle of sleeping potion
   Macbeth, *Macbeth,* a dagger
   Lady Macbeth, *Macbeth,* her husband's letter
   Othello, *Othello,* a handkerchief
   Lenny, *Of Mice and Men,* a mouse or puppy
   George, *Of Mice and Men,* a mouse or puppy
   Lenny, *Of Mice and Men,* a can of beans with ketchup
   Lenny, *Of Mice and Men,* a can of beans without ketchup
   Joan, *Saint Joan,* a crucifix
   Jerry, *The Zoo Story,* a knife
   Peter, *The Zoo Story,* a knife
   Elizabeth, *The Crucible,* a poppet
   Abigail, *The Crucible,* a poppet
   Hedda, *Hedda Gabler,* one of her father's guns
   Eilert, *Hedda Gabler,* one of Hedda's father's guns
   Hedda, *Hedda Gabler,* Eilert's manuscript
   Eilert, *Hedda Gabler,* the manuscript

   You may, if you wish, use characters and props from other plays. Remember, whatever scene you create, whether actually in the play or imagined from it, it must be consistent with the play's action and given circumstances, and it must serve to complement and enhance what is already known about the character and situation. Write up a detailed physical action score as described in Chapter 6. This will help you build a piece of work that has a beginning, a middle, and an end—one that tells a clear and interesting story.

2. Perform the one-minute scene.

3. Discuss the results.

4. Redo the scene making adjustments based on what you learned during the discussion.

If the actions you selected and used—including those actions specific to the object—were consistent with the character being played, then those actions probably not only made the story clear, but revealed specific details about your character as well. As a result, your work was interesting, clear, and served to enhance the script. You fulfilled your job as an actor.

Remember, as human beings we possess five senses, each of which provides us with an enormous amount of sensory stimulation that can provide an actor with excellent storytelling possibilities. Most of us think first in terms of visual stimulation, but the fact is our other senses can be used to create exciting and believable acting choices. Our use of **sense memory** also tends to jog our emotional memories, which, in turn, stimulate emotional responses. The power of the sense of touch has already been demonstrated in the pillow exercise. But think about the possibilities of using the senses of smell, taste, and hearing in your work as well.

EXERCISE 11-5

1. Use the following to tell a story, with or without props, that involves one or more of your senses.

Drinking liquor
Drinking some other beverage
Eating a particular food
Eating a meal
Smelling something rotten
Smelling something delicious
Touching something that hurts
Touching something that feels good
Hearing something in the distance
Hearing something approaching

2. Repeat the exercise, after you have given yourself a complete set of given circumstances and specific details for using each sense.

   Remember, the more detail you provide yourself with, the more specific and clear your body of physical choices will be. You will be surprised at how specific you can be, and at how the discipline of getting so specific can remarkably improve the clarity of your work. You may also be surprised at the excitement your specificity can generate for yourself and for the audience.

You choose to eat an orange, for instance. Is it cold or warm? Is it big or small? Sweet or sour? Tasty or dull? Easy to peel or difficult? Does it come in sections or not? Is it with seeds or seedless? Do you love oranges, or don't you? Are you hungry or full? You get the idea. Whatever your choices, make sure that, together, they combine to tell an interesting story and that the story is the one that you want to tell.

By now you should realize that good acting requires more than just being believable. As I hope the previous exercises and examples make clear, good acting also requires an ability to make great acting choices—choices based on your reading of the script and your interpretation of it. But making the best possible choice when confronted with an enormous number of possibilities can be very daunting. How can you select the single right door when there are hundreds that can be opened? In the preceding exercises you learned that defining the given circumstances and using the "magic if" can help reduce the number of possibilities to choose from, but, even then, you may still be facing more choices than you can handle.

Categorizing

It is a fact that all of us act every day of our lives. The basic principles of this social acting are the same as the acting we do for the stage. As social actors, we are constantly defining our given circumstances and making behavioral choices that are socially acceptable for that set of particulars. We act differently at school and at church than we do at a bar or in the gym. We act differently with our fathers than we do with our boyfriends or girlfriends. We constantly offer up different aspects of our personalities according to the social requirements of the situation and what it is we need in those circumstances. In short, we act differently at different times and in different places with different people.

By using some of the categories that people automatically adjust to when acting socially, you can begin to separate your available acting possibilities into smaller units that will make them easier to choose from. In Chapter 8, for instance, I mentioned that objectives could be put into six broad categories to help you figure out what your character might be doing in a scene. A similar device might prove helpful when you are dealing with the setting of a play or with the other characters. By generally defining the setting of a scene or the relationship you have with the people sharing the stage with you, you can begin to narrow down the set of actions you might choose to employ.

Let's first take a look at the categories of location.

Defining and Using the Space

By specifically defining the "where" of a particular scene, you might find some excellent tangibles that you can use to color and shape your acting choices. For instance, an acting teacher I once had suggested that all locales for scenes could be divided into three categories: **public space, private space**, and **personal space.** Loosely defined, public space is any space where all people are free to come and go and to observe each other. A public library, a bus terminal, and a school yard fall into this category. Private space is space to which there is restricted access. Not everyone is permitted to go or be there, but it is space that may be expected to be shared. A work office or the living room or kitchen of a house would be examples. Personal space, on the other hand, is space in and over which a person has privacy and control. No one is permitted there without the owner's approval. A bedroom or private office would be examples.

Generally speaking, each of these environments produces a different set of behaviors, a different vocabulary of actions. A person's behavior would be far more restricted in the school library, for instance, than in his or her den watching a football game. By applying the "magic if" to a particular setting, you can narrow down the kinds of behavioral choices you might want to make for your character. This, in turn, can help color the story you are telling as well as make your character's personality clearer. It is also likely to make your work more believable than it otherwise might be.

EXERCISE 11-6

1. Say the line "I love you" aloud.

2. Now say it again as if you were sitting across from someone in a restaurant.

3. Say it as though you were sitting across from someone in a library.

4. Say it as though you were sitting next to someone in your living room.

5. Say it to someone in a crowded train station. At a football game. How was each different? Discuss.

Obviously, the location of a scene helps determine the kinds of choices that an actor can make. The good actor will, whenever possible, create the best physical setting he or she can for a particular scene to ensure its dramatic effectiveness

and believability, and also carefully consider the impact that any setting predetermined by a script will have on a particular scene.

1. Create a dramatic situation, and improvise a short scene with a
   partner. Discuss the results. Redo the scene after making adjustments based on what you learned.

   Possible Situations

   Giving an engagement ring
   Breaking up with someone
   Informing someone you are very ill
   Discovering you have won the lottery
   Having an itch
   Having an argument

2. Select a setting, either personal, private, or public, and play out
   the scene. Discuss the results. Redo the scene after making necessary adjustments.

   Possible Settings

   In a library
   In a restaurant
   At a train station
   In your office
   At a football stadium
   During an airplane attack

3. Discuss the resulting scenes. Which were the most successful?
   Why? How was each situation affected by the setting? What conclusions can you draw?

Defining and Using Relationships

Relationship is another tool that actors can use to help narrow down and make
more specific the choices available to them. In our everyday social acting, we recognize the need for a certain presentation of ourselves in specific situations. We
adjust the way we conduct ourselves in accordance with the unspoken rules of
social relationships. Part of this comes as a result of the social customs we come
to understand and accept, and part comes as a result of our experience and our
innate social intelligence. Whether or not you knowingly use this awareness in
life, as actors it can be an essential tool for making specific, interesting, and believable choices.

Here is a short list of possible relationships that can be used to help define
an acting situation:

Husband and wife	Boss and employee
Boyfriend and girlfriend	Grownup and child
Mother and daughter	Old person and young person
Father and son	Rich person and poor person
Teacher and student	Native and foreigner

The possibilities are endless, but by defining and narrowing down the relationship between characters onstage, it is possible to get some insights as to the dynamics that affect the way a scene might work.

EXERCISE 11-8

1. Make a list of other relationships that might be helpful in defining the way two characters relate in a play or scene. Discuss your choices.

2. Make a list of movies, books, plays, or television shows in which some of the relationships you have isolated are portrayed. What behaviors in those works come directly as a result of these relationships? Explain.

3. With a partner improvise a short scene based on a specific conflict. Then redo the scene using one of your listed relationships. How does the scene change? How is it more specific? How does defining a relationship help the scene?

4. Do the improvised scene several more times using a new relationship for each. Observe and discuss all changes. Draw conclusions.

Of course defining a relationship alone is not enough to complete your obligations when performing scripted material. It is merely scratching the surface. Every character relationship is unique. But, by isolating as many details as you can, you begin to build a network of choices that lead to exciting work. By working specifically with objects, space, and relationships at the beginning of your rehearsal process, you can rely less on intuition and inspiration alone, and allow those natural gifts to merge with the craft you are developing.

Summary

In this chapter you have learned about three additional tools an actor can use to make his or her work specific, interesting, and clear while serving the story being presented. By using and endowing props with specific emotional and sensory meaning, actors can achieve a reality in their work that generalized choices might never allow. By thinking about and defining space into personal, private, and public locales, the specifics of setting that result can help actors make choices that randomness or intuition might never allow them to discover. Finally, defining and making choices based on an understanding of relationships can also help an actor find exciting, compelling, and believable choices with an accuracy and an economy that non-categorization would never allow.

CHAPTER 12

Script Analysis: A Blueprint for Storytelling

In just about every introductory theatre text, the author will point out that the term "playwright" means "play maker" not "play writer," and that a play script is "wrought" or "built" rather than written as other genres of literature are. The author will go on to point out that scripts are the blueprints of the play. I am sure that few playwrights would disagree. Just as an architect's blueprints are two-dimensional renderings suggesting what a finished building might look like, so is a play script, consisting principally of dialogue and limited stage direction, a two-dimensional rendering of what a mounted production might be like. The finished production is the result of many hands working in collaboration, and if that finished work is an artistic and/or commercial success, the credit must be shared. The point is that, like an architectural blueprint, a script is merely a springboard for the imaginative efforts of the actors, the director, the designers, and the rest of the production team, who are all trying to tell a good story.

Too often actors, especially young actors, forget this very basic piece of information. They can't get over the idea that a play is not really just about the dialogue. After all, don't we study Shakespeare and Tennessee Williams in English class? Didn't Chekhov write short stories as well as plays? Wasn't Steinbeck's *Of Mice and Men* a novel before it became a stage play? We're talking literature here, and isn't literature about words? That's what dialogue is, right? Words, words, words!

Many fine plays are studied as literature, and they often contain a wealth of language and imagery worthy of such study. But the truth is that most plays are written in the hope that they will be produced for the stage. A playwright's reward is to see his or her work performed on a lit stage by living, breathing actors. To be paid for one's efforts is, certainly, a bonus. To have one's work live on in a published record, especially in a literary edition, is a dream come true.

The fact is, however, that playwrights, if they are going to be successful, must write good stories—stories that an audience will find entertaining, compelling, and enlightening. Dialogue alone does not guarantee this. In fact many fine plays, when examined for their dialogue alone, appear at first glance to be mediocre, or worse, boring. The character of Helen Keller in *The Miracle Worker,* for instance, speaks not a word until the end of the play, and even then her only dialogue consists of a valiant attempt to say the word "water." Nonetheless, it is one of the great roles in contemporary American theatre.

Shakespeare wrote lines and handed them to his actors. They were assembled as written plays later. But embedded within the poetry of his written lines are stories bursting with interesting characters ready to fill a stage with action. Every speech in a play by Shakespeare contains action. There is the physical action—often **implied action** suggested through the dialogue—and there is the psychological action provided by what the characters say about their problems, desires, conflicts, and confusion.

Implied Physical Action

She *speaks,* yet she *says nothing*

(Romeo in *Romeo and Juliet,* Act II, Scene 1)

Implied Physical and Psychological Action

This is most brave,
That I, the son of a dear father murdered,
Prompted to my revenge by heaven and hell,
Must like a whore unpack my heart with words
And *fall a cursing* like a very drab, . . .

(Hamlet in *Hamlet,* Act II, Scene 2)

These actions are the very things that help make a really good story. Shakespeare knew this. He was a consummate theatre professional. He just happened to be a literary genius as well. But Shakespeare's focus was always on a good story and making sure that the story was well told.

Reading for the Story

Telling the best possible story is the job of the actor as well as the playwright. The problem is that most actors, especially beginning actors, don't read a play for the story. They read a script in the same fashion that they read plays in a literature class. Unfortunately, most of us read literature passively. If we read actively at all, our focus is usually on the artistry of the language, imagery, or symbol. The story and character, for the most part, we intuit rather than analyze actively. If the writer is good, we get much of the story without heavy analysis.

But translating the story from the printed script onto the stage is a very difficult task. Before it can happen successfully, the actor must discover what that story is specifically, and then break it down into its working parts. This brain work is too often neglected by both trained and untrained actors. When this happens, the task of producing compelling, exciting theatre is made that much more difficult.

EXERCISE 12-1

Read several scenes from a volume of collected scenes, and do the following for each:
- Write a paragraph briefly outlining the story of each scene.
- Determine and write down the conflict(s) in each scene.
- Summarize in writing the events (specific things that happen) in each scene in chronological order.
- Write down the story of each scene from beginning to end focusing only on the dramatic throughline (the cause and effect journey the plot takes).
- Make a list of the big events in each scene and detail those moments.

When I first began to study acting seriously, I could never find a scene that I liked. I would scour play after play after play. The two-character scenes from the plays that had been suggested to me were always boring. I spent far more time trying to find that "perfect scene" than I ever did rehearsing it once I thought I had found it. And even when I did find the "perfect scene," it usually sank quickly in my esteem once I started rehearsing. It turned out to not be so exciting after all. I often wondered why the better actors in my class always seemed to find scenes that were far more interesting than my own. Then one day, two of the good actors in a class I was taking presented a scene I had just recently read and tossed into the boring pile. To my surprise and chagrin, the scene was not boring at all. In fact, it was a great scene, chock full of dramatic moments and interesting things to say and do. How could this be? How could I have missed all this? Then the answer rushed in upon me. It was the way I had been reading plays. In earlier days I had been an English major, and the literary way in which I had been trained to read simply did not work for me as an actor.

Asking the Right Questions

Whenever you begin your work on a scene, you must ask yourself a series of questions that will help you recognize and define the story. Until you begin asking these questions and finding answers to them, it is very likely your work will remain hit-or-miss. Nicely acted moments that don't connect and build will not make for good scenes, and actors completing these disconnected moments will never be consistently clear and compelling onstage.

Remember, choices about the actions you will play in a scene are critically important, but these choices cannot be made effectively until you have defined and broken down the story. It may also help you to keep in mind that all stories have beginnings, middles, and ends. If an audience is to get the story, each of its stages must be clearly presented. But that will only happen when each stage is clearly understood by the actors working on the play. First and foremost, that means that an actor must know and understand the entire play. Scenes will only make sense if they are seen in relation to the whole. It is imperative that you understand the overall play before you begin your work on a specific scene. We will take a closer look at play analysis in Chapter 19.

Here is a list of questions you might ask yourself before beginning to make choices about what you will do as your character in any given scene:

- *What are the given circumstances that set up the scene?* Who are the characters? Where are the characters? What is going on with the characters? When does this action take place? What are the characteristics of the society in which the play takes place?

- *What actually happens in the scene?* Literally, what are the story events, one by one?

- *What are the conflicts in the scene?*

- *What are the most dramatic moments in the scene?* What leads up to these moments of drama? Be specific.

- *What is the climax of the scene?* Why?

Once you can answer these questions, you have mapped out the shape of the story contained within the scene. It is important to remember that stories always start with conflict, and the more conflict you can find within a scene the more interesting the story you're telling will be. Most playwrights know this, even if they don't hit you over the head with the conflict in their written blueprint. A playwright who spells the conflict out for you too specifically is really narrowing down the dramatic possibilities. In some cases that can be helpful, especially to untrained actors, but often this results in constricting the dramatic choices that the imagination can provide. Many playwrights don't direct their own work for this reason. They prefer the input a director and actors can bring to it.

Once you have fully answered the preceding questions, you are ready to focus more specifically on your own character and how he or she will interact with the other character(s) sharing the stage. You are now ready to ask yourself the following questions:

- *How does your character contribute to the conflict in the scene?*

- *What does your character need in this scene from the other character(s)?*

- *What actions does your character perform in the scene?*

- *What stands in the way of getting what your character needs?*

- *What does your character do to get around these obstacles?*

- *How badly does your character need what is needed?*

- *What is your character willing to do to get what is needed?*

- *What discoveries does your character make during the scene?*

- *How does this new information affect your character?* Does it change your character's behavior, way of thinking, or needs?

- *Can you specifically identify the places in the script where your character receives new information?* Do so.

- *Does this information somehow change what your character thinks and/or feels?* Does this news signal a victory? A defeat? A reason for reevaluation?

- *What internal changes (changes in feeling, attitude, needs) does your character go through at these moments?*

- *Can you map a throughline of action for your character now that you have answered these questions?* Do so.

Once you have answered both sets of these questions specifically, you will be able to begin rehearsing the scene with a strong sense of what the story is. Because you know how it develops and where the dramatic moments are, the moments will connect and build toward some dramatic climax. If your choices are big enough, the scene will provide you with more than enough material to keep your work clear and dramatically interesting.

Dialogue Serving the Story

Even after answering all the preceding questions, however, the dialogue trap still remains. Don't let the dialogue make your choices for you. Use the dialogue to get what you need in the scene. As I pointed out in Chapter 10, "go away" can sometimes mean "come here and kiss me," and "I hate you" can mean "I love you." Most often, of course, you should interpret a character's lines as true unless you know the character to be a liar, but people don't always say what they mean or ask for what they desire directly. You will avoid any confusion if you make sure that your acting choices come out of your character's needs (reflected through the dialogue's context and subtext) rather than from what you think a specific line means. Never say a line in a manner inconsistent with the context of the situation as you have defined it.

Cold readings can provide an excellent way of developing your analytic skills. Whether or not you are familiar with the play from which you must read, you will need to make choices that are compelling, logical, and consistent with those of the other actor reading with you. It will be necessary to go through a process similar to the one provided in the earlier lists. If you do not do this, you will end up simply reading lines. There will be no story, no conflict, and no logic behind the moments you arbitrarily create. However, if you provide yourself with answers, even if they are not actual ones from the play, you will find your work to be clear, exciting, and logical. This appeals to directors casting plays, by the way. They will think you are reliable, that you might even make them look good if they cast you.

EXERCISE 12-2

Select a scene to read with a partner from a book of collected scenes. Each of you should read the scene independently. When each of you has read the scene, determine for yourselves the story, the conflict, and the given circumstances. Then, without discussion, read the scene together for the class. Discuss the results. Was the story clear? Why or why not? Reread the scene after making the necessary adjustments.

Suggested Plays

Absurd Person Singular, Alan Ayckbourn
Agnes of God, John Pielmeier
Ah, Wilderness!, Eugene O'Neill
Album, Robert Rimmer
All My Sons, Arthur Miller
Am I Blue?, Beth Henley
Amber Waves, James Still
And Miss Reardon Drinks a Little, Paul Zindel
Angels in America, Tony Kushner
Ascension Day, Timothy Mason
Aunt Dan and Lemon, Wallace Shawn
Awake and Sing, Clifford Odets
Baby With the Bathwater, Christopher Durang
The Bad Seed, Maxwell Anderson
The Baltimore Waltz, Paula Vogel
Barefoot in the Park, Neil Simon
Betrayal, Harold Pinter
Boesman and Lena, Athol Fugard
Beyond Therapy, Christopher Durang
Biloxi Blues, Neil Simon
Birdbath, Leonard Melfi
Bloodknot, Athol Fugard
Blue Window, Craig Lucas
Boy's Life, Howard Korder
Brighton Beach Memoirs, Neil Simon
Broadway Bound, Neil Simon
The Caretaker, Harold Pinter
Cat on a Hot Tin Roof, Tennessee Williams
The Children's Hour, Lillian Hellman
Coastal Disturbances, Tina Howe
The Collection, Harold Pinter
Come Back, Little Sheba, William Inge
Come Back to the Five and Dime, Jimmy Dean, Jimmy Dean,
    Ed Graczyk
Common Pursuit, Simon Gray
The Conduct of Life, Maria Irene Fornes
A Coupla of White Chicks . . . , John Ford Noonan
Crimes of the Heart, Beth Henley
The Crucible, Arthur Miller

The Curse of the Starving Class, Sam Shepard
The Dance and the Railroad, David Henry Hwang
Danny and the Deep Blue Sea, John Patrick Shanley
The Dark at the Top of the Stairs, William Inge
The Days and Nights of Beebee Fenstermaker, William Snyder
The Day They Shot John Lennon, James McLure
Death and the Maiden, Ariel Dorfman
Death of a Salesman, Arthur Miller
The Death of Bessie Smith, Edward Albee
The Dumb Waiter, Harold Pinter
Eastern Standard, Richard Greenberg
Educating Rita, Willie Russell
The Effect of Gamma Rays on Man-in-the-Moon Marigolds,
    Paul Zindel
Eleemosynary, Lee Blessing
Fen, Caryl Churchill
Fences, August Wilson
5th of July, Lanford Wilson
The Film Society, John Robin Baitz
Final Placement, Ara Watson
FOB, David Henry Hwang
The Food Chain, Nicky Silver
Fool for Love, Sam Shepard
For Colored Girls Who Have Considered Suicide . . . ,
    Ntozake Shange
Getting Out, Marsha Norman
The Gingerbread Lady, Neil Simon
The Glass Menagerie, Tennessee Williams
Greater Tuna, Jaston Williams
A Hatful of Rain, Michael V. Gazzo
Hello From Bertha, Tennessee Williams
The Homecoming, Harold Pinter
Hooters, Ted Tally
Hothouse, Megan Terry
The House of Blue Leaves, John Guare
I Remember Mama, John Van Druten
In the Boom Boom Room, David Rabe
The Indian Wants the Bronx, Israel Horowitz
Invisible Friends, Alan Ayckbourn
Isn't It Romantic, Wendy Wasserstein
Italian American Reconciliation, John Patrick Shanley
The Kentucky Cycle, Richard Schenkkan
Key Exchange, Bernard Wade
Ladies of the Alamo, Paul Zindel
Lakeboat, David Mamet
Later, Corrine Jackler
Laundry and Bourbon, James McLure
Lemon Sky, Lanford Wilson
A Lesson from Aloes, Athol Fugard

Life Under Water, Richard Greenberg
Lily Dale, Horton Foote
Lips Together, Teeth Apart, Terrence McNally
Lonely World, Steven Dietz
Loose Ends, Michael Weller
Lou Gehrig Did Not Die of Cancer, Jason Miller
The Lover, Harold Pinter
Ma Rainey's Black Bottom, August Wilson
Marvin's Room, Scott McPherson
"Master Harold" . . . and the Boys, Athol Fugard
The Middle Ages, A. R. Gurney
The Miss Firecracker Contest, Beth Henley
Moonchildren, Michael Weller
Nice People Dancin' to Country Music, Lee Blessing
'night, Mother, Marsha Norman
The Normal Heart, Larry Kramer
The Norman Conquests, Alan Ayckbourn
Of Mice and Men, John Steinbeck
Oh Dad, Poor Dad . . . , Arthur Kopit
Oleanna, David Mamet
On the Verge, Eric Overmeyer
Open Admissions, Shirley Lauro
Orphans, Lyle Kessler
Other People's Money, Jerry Sterner
Our Country's Good, Timberlake Wertenbaker
Our Town, Thornton Wilder
Out of Gas on Lovers' Leap, Marc St. Germaine
The Perfect Ganesh, Terrence McNally
The Piano Lesson, August Wilson
Picnic, William Inge
Pterodactyls, Nicky Silver
Raised in Captivity, Nicky Silver
A Raisin in the Sun, Lorraine Hansberry
Reckless, Craig Lucas
The Rimers of Eldritch, Lanford Wilson
The Rise and Rise of Daniel Rocket, Peter Parnell
The River Niger, Joseph A. Walker
Sarita, Maria Irene Fornes
Savage in Limbo, John Patrick Shanley
The Sea Horse, Edward J. Moore
Search and Destroy, Howard Korder
Seven Guitars, August Wilson
Shivaree, William Mastrosimone
Speed the Plow, David Mamet
Spike Heels, Teresa Rebeck
Spring Awakening, Edward Bond
Steaming, Nell Dunn
Steel Magnolias, Robert Harling
Streamers, David Rabe

A Streetcar Named Desire, Tennessee Williams
The Strong Breed, Wole Soyinka
The Substance of Fire, John Robin Baitz
The Sum of Us, David Stevens
A Taste of Honey, Shelagh Delaney
Top Girls, Caryl Churchhill
Uncommon Women and Others, Wendy Wasserstein
Vanishing Act, Richard Greenberg
The Wager, Mark Medoff
A Walk in the Woods, Lee Blessing
Watermelon Rinds, Regina Taylor
Wedding Band, Alice Childress
A Weekend Near Madison, Kathleen Tolan
Who's Afraid of Virginia Woolf?, Edward Albee
The Widow Claire, Horton Foote
Women and Wallace, Jonathan Marc Sherman
The Woolgatherers, William Mastrosimone
The Zoo Story, Edward Albee

In my own acting classes I often give a cold reading exercise using part of a scene from *Blue Denim,* a play by James Herlihy written in the 1950s. It is contained in many scene study collections, so you might want to take a look. The play is seldom produced nowadays because it seems so cliché-ridden, especially after so many movies centering on teenage angst have since been produced. After the class has read the assigned pages from the play to themselves, I always ask how they liked it. Invariably the more literary-minded students in the class tell me they hate it. "The characters and dialogue are so dated and stereotypical," they tell me. "Nothing happens." The dialogue, as a matter of fact, is often described as "boring." Then I have volunteers read from the scene between Arthur and Janet that comes early in the play. What is presented time after time is, indeed, a boring scene—one in which two kids, a boy and a girl, discuss their friends, their parents, and their dreams. There is no tension, little conflict, and zero story.

A careful reading of the scene fragment, however, strongly suggests the seduction that actually occurs by the end of the entire scene. It is amazing how students consistently get fooled by the dialogue. Because Arthur is nervous and unsure about his love-making abilities, he avoids Janet's advances, at first by ignoring them, then later by physically avoiding them. Here, Arthur is his own obstacle. His desire for Janet is overcome by his fear of embarrassment. Janet, however, pursues her need for Arthur moment by moment using tactic after tactic, until by the end of the scene, she has Arthur just where she wants him. Sounds like an exciting scene, a great one to work on, right? Well, it's just the kind of scene that I would, years ago, have thrown into the boring pile. You must learn to read for the story.

There is a wonderful storytelling moment midway or so through this *Blue Denim* scene, by the way—where Janet gets Arthur to dance. Janet pulls Arthur up, steps into him, and finally presses herself against him. Arthur's next piece of dialogue is described by the author as spoken "breathlessly." How could a reader miss this clue to the action of the scene? How could actors possibly, intentionally or unintentionally, fail to act out this moment, even in a cold reading? Playing out this wonderful little story within the story—where there is absolutely no dialogue—could get you the part! It gives a director or casting agent everything he or she needs to see in terms of your acting. It gives you the opportunity to do all you could wish for onstage. In fact, this little beat, fully realized, is worth more than pages of seemingly clichéd dialogue. It instantly turns cliché into universal truth.

This example clearly demonstrates why scripts are merely blueprints of the story we see onstage. Only action, imagination, and good sense can transform the dialogue of a script into a successful production. This is why you must learn to develop the same kind of vision that architects possess. You must learn to imagine the completed building even as you metaphorically draw that first blue-penciled line on your script!

EXERCISE 12-3

1. Analyze a play you are currently working on or have recently read. Use the detailed questions concerning the overall play found in this chapter to guide you in your analysis. Be sure to write your answers to make certain that you are really doing all the necessary work. Only by doing the head work first will you truly be prepared to analyze a scene.

2. Select a scene from the play and analyze it using the scene study questions found in this chapter. Put your answers in writing to ensure you have thought about the answers specifically.

3. Discuss your findings with your class.

Summary

Like an architectural blueprint, a script is a springboard for the imaginative efforts of actors, directors, and the rest of the production team, who are all trying to tell onstage the good story the playwright has provided. Focusing only on the dialogue is no guarantee that an actor will discover the story a script contains. Every piece of dialogue contains action—physical and psychological—that provides hints for unlocking that story. Actors must learn to read a play for that sometimes hidden story. It is their responsibility to discover what the story is specifically, and then break that story down into its working parts. This is head work and must never be neglected. When it is, the task of producing compelling, exciting theatre is made that much more difficult. Invariably, it is the story of the play that holds the audience.

CHAPTER 13

Rehearsing the Scene: Preparing for the First Read

In Shakespeare's *Hamlet* a group of traveling players, under Hamlet's direction, enact a play for the Court of Elsinore. In it the player-king is murdered—poisoned by his rival who desires the queen's hand. The scene is repeated twice, first as an exaggerated dumb show and then again with stodgy, poetic dialogue appropriate for the group of journeymen players who perform it. The dialogue of the play-within-a-play is overwritten and even boring. (Often this spoken part is cut altogether to shorten the play's running time.) Why, you might ask, would Shakespeare write such second-rate material? Probably because he didn't want any first-rate material standing in the way of the real story. The Bard knew that if this play-within-a-play scene were properly executed, the audience would ease forward in their seats, as a palpable tension filled the theatre. So why, if the play-within-the-play is so second-rate, has this scene worked so effectively for the past four hundred years or so?

The answer lies in the given circumstances of this scene and with the action for which those circumstances are the catalyst. This long-winded dialogue allows the audience plenty of time to observe King Claudius and his wife Gertrude as they watch "The Murder of Gonzago." The audience also has plenty of time to watch Hamlet as he studies his two prime suspects. Will the reactions of Claudius and Gertrude prove them guilty as they are forced to witness a fictional murder not unlike the one they themselves perpetrated?

This is an exciting scene because it is an exciting situation. Yet what makes it exciting is barely hinted at in the dialogue. It is not the turgid poetry of "The Murder of Gonzago" that makes the scene work, but rather the action of the characters who watch it. This is the metaphor at the heart of this chapter. As I pointed out in Chapter 12, plays are not about the dialogue. Plays *use* dialogue to tell the story of the play. Dialogue is a tool, not unlike blocking, physical actions, or playing objectives, that helps actors fulfill their task of telling the playwright's story clearly and compellingly onstage.

In his *Poetics* Aristotle states that action is the most important element in drama. The word "drama" itself comes from the Greek word meaning "to do." Directors and actors are hard pressed to make their productions work if they fail to deliver the action. How often have I seen idea plays bore an audience to death because their directors have forgotten that an audience comes to the theatre to see the story. The script analysis questions I listed in Chapter 12 focused heavily on the ingredients of the story. Many of these questions concern themselves with the conflict, with opposing objectives, and with spotting the dramatic high points in a scene. Once you have fully addressed these questions, you've found a basis for making a story unfold on the stage. It is time to translate your answers into playable actions that keep the story clear and exciting. A play consists of one or more large stories, but those stories can be subdivided into a series of smaller stories. Potentially there is a story in every scene, every beat, and every moment of a play. Ultimately, it is your job to discover and tell those stories. Following is a step-by-step approach that can help you make that happen. At the same time it may provide you with a reliable and efficient modus operandi for working with a scene partner.

Choosing a Scene

The purpose of doing scene work is to develop a process that will enable you to build solid work in a rehearsal situation—even when the director is not as helpful as you might wish. This is, unfortunately, the rule more often than the exception in the business. Particularly in film, the director may not have a background that will help the actors succeed. It is not unusual for the film director to be looking for the actors to make him look good rather than the reverse. Even in theatre, where the director invariably has more experience with the acting process, it is not unusual for actors to find themselves, more or less, on their own. It is, therefore, imperative that you not only learn how to analyze the material, but that you are also able to make choices based on that analysis—choices that make the play work dramatically and clearly. That, then, is the purpose of doing scene study.

I suggest to my classes that the scenes they select be no longer that five or six minutes. That may seen like a very short amount of material, but in fact this length of script can provide more than enough nutrition for actors who are rehearsing properly. (My use of the term "scene," by the way, refers to the "cutting" from the play that you are actually using. For class work it is not necessary to rehearse an entire "scene" from a play.) Selections longer than five or six minutes will often tempt you to skim through the scene, rather than explore each moment. Since you and your scene partner can rehearse for only a limited amount of time, you will probably settle for reading through it a couple of times and discussing it in a general way if the scene is too long. Scenes of five or six minutes, on the other hand, encourage actors to work moment by moment, a brick at a time. A scene is built on its moments, and each one leads to the next until the throughline is completed. When actors generalize, or "ice skate" through a scene, they seldom find the key to a satisfying piece of work. By starting at the beginning of a beat and working to an ending five minutes later, you will find ample bricks on which to build a scene and your technique.

Student actors often agonize over selecting a scene. Finding the perfect scene often becomes as important as the work eventually done on it. This should not be the case. What the actor should focus on instead is turning the scene, whether it is expository or climactic, into the most interesting piece of work possible for what it is. If you develop your ability to recognize where the story lies by finding the conflict, playing fully the most dramatic moments, and listening and reacting fully to your scene partner, then whatever scene you select will have served its purpose. A scene study class should not be about doing performances, but, rather, about developing your skills and a process that will eventually *lead to* good performances. I discussed the necessary homework that begins this process in Chapter 12.

EXERCISE 13-1

Repeat the process of selection and analysis laid out in Chapter 12. Either choose a new scene from the play you have been working on, or read and analyze a new play. Be sure to answer the play and scene questions thoroughly.

The First Read

I call the first presentation of the scene in class the **first read.** That does not mean it is a cold reading. A cold reading of a scene is one where the actors have barely had time to even look at the material. This is often the situation in commercial and screen auditions, where the script may not be completed yet or is simply unavailable. Auditions of this kind are often set up at the last moment, and it is not unusual that only sides (short cuttings of the script) are available for the reading. The actors are forced to make arbitrary choices based on what little they know about the material they have been asked to read. They must try to play the material knowing little or nothing about the given circumstances surrounding the dialogue. If the actors are smart, they will make strong, simple choices that will offer them some reason for saying the things that the script requires them to say. The purpose is to make the script and, more importantly, the actors themselves seem as interesting and clear as possible under these difficult circumstances. This is not what I mean by the first read.

The first read is a fully prepared reading, one that has been carefully rehearsed. Before any scene reading can take place, however, you must discuss with your partner the results of your homework. You must agree on the given circumstances of the play and scene. You must not assume that your individual "mental movies" of the scene are the same. That is very unlikely in light of the fact that a script is barely an outline for what eventually becomes a mounted production. It may be necessary for you and your partner to modify your individual choices a bit in order to have a unified vision of what the background information is. Acting is a **collaboration.** Actors have a shared stake in making sure that what the audience sees is compelling and believable. If actors are playing from two sets of assumptions about the scene, the likelihood of that happening is greatly diminished.

In addition to the given circumstances, you should discuss the shape of the scene you are working on. It is important to recognize how the story develops. What is the nature of the conflict, how does the story unfold (its beginning, its middle, and its end), what are the dramatic moments, and so forth? This shared vision will provide you with a map of the scene through which you will travel, which is far more efficient than wandering through the scene moment by moment without a clear destination. Perhaps a better metaphor for this shared vision of the scene is that of the skeleton on which to build up the dramatic muscle. Without the skeletal structure, your scene will have no dramatic shape.

The one thing you should not discuss with your partner, however, is your objectives. Playing an objective fully provides an actor with the engine for conflict in the scene. Reacting to your partner's tactics for obtaining his or her objective provides the spontaneity that makes the work onstage seem real and in the moment. When actors know each other's objectives, they often try to help each other achieve them at the expense of their own. This results in a loss of believability and conflict, and the dramatic tension suffers as a result. Responding in-the-moment to your partner's choices will keep your work fresh and exciting.

EXERCISE 13-2

Discuss the results of your analysis with your partner (except that part related to your objectives). Be willing to collaborate until the two of you find a shared vision of all the given circumstances of the play and the scene. Also agree on the story of the scene, its most dramatic moments, and where the beats change. Do the same with all other relevant matters. Be willing to give up your "mental movie" for a new one that you both can share. Be certain that the decisions you have agreed on are the best ones for making the scene work for the two of you.

Once you've established a shared vision, you are ready to begin rehearsing. You now know the shape of the scene and where the most dramatic moments lie, as well as your own objectives. What you don't know is what the actor/character sharing the space with you is like. You don't know how he or she will behave. As a matter of fact, you don't yet know how you will behave either. Only as you begin to read with each other will the answers to these questions begin to take form. Only by listening closely and observing what your partner says and does will compelling acting choices emerge from your rehearsal process.

Your obligations during this part of the rehearsal process are simple. Play your objective in a positive way and listen carefully to what your partner says to you. Since you have already made choices about everything else, that is really all that you have to do. Playing your objective fully and positively is not as easy as it sounds, however. Remember, acting is not life. It just seems like it if done well. In life our behavior is not always structured. Too often our actions are random and do not get us what we want. Too often we make choices to avoid confrontation, to evade the dramatic moment. Plays, on the other hand, are dramatic and they are structured. You have to focus on achieving your objective in order to maintain dramatic tension. You narrow your range of choices by using only dramatic ones. In short your work must be dramatically selective.

Playing your objective in a positive manner means focusing on what works rather than on what does not. Suppose, for instance, your objective is to get your partner to accept your love. In the scene you try to kiss him. He rejects your attempt. Your reaction is to sulk, and you do so for the next several beats. This is probably an example of playing the negative. Does playing your rejection get you what you want in the scene? If the answer is no, then this choice is not a good one. A better choice would be to acknowledge the rejection somehow, and then let it go. Find a new way to get your partner to accept your love. By doing this you avoid playing an emotional state, and you keep the scene going. If, however, you choose to sulk as a tactic and work it actively to make your partner feel guilty—*and* it makes sense in the context of the scene—then you are playing your objective in a positive manner. It is a choice that may get you what you need. If your choices are not getting you closer to what you need, then you must abandon them and find better choices. These are the things you should be discovering during your rehearsal process for the first read.

Keep in mind that you will only make these discoveries if you are really listening to your partner. Don't make the mistake of focusing on your own next line. Most good actors will tell you that the most important part of acting is reacting—that everything good an actor does comes from responding to what the other actor has just put on the table. You have to get away from the idea that playing a script is only about saying your lines. Remember, your job as an actor is creating and telling the story. What the characters do is as important as what they say. How they say what they say is as important as the words themselves. If you are not listening with both your ears and eyes, you will not be able to make the in-the-moment responses that allow you to get to the next step in the story. (If you find you are not listening to your partner, or not listening well enough, try some of the suggestions from Chapter 9.)

So make sure that when your partner is speaking, you are focused on your partner, not your script. Look at your partner. Listen to what he or she says, how the lines are spoken. Watch for physical clues as to what your partner is really thinking and feeling. Only when you are satisfied that you have received what your scene partner has tried to communicate should your eyes travel to your script for your next lines. Then deliver your next speech in response to the determinations you have just made. Play your objective with your line, but make sure you are playing it in a manner that is justified, given what you have just seen and heard. Do not rush your lines. Before you say them, clearly have in mind your reason for doing so. That reason should be strong and specific, so strong and so specific that neither you nor the audience nor your acting partner will have any doubt as to why you have said your lines. Do not feel compelled to say your next lines in real time if you have not found the reason for saying them. This is an early rehearsal. You are under no obligation to rehearse your work in performance time. The discoveries you make now will serve you throughout the rehearsal process and help you build a performance. But now is not the time to perform. Now is the time to discover the scene.

Taking the time is critically important at this stage of rehearsal. If you take the time to listen, you will be able to make the discoveries that you have previously recognized in the script. You will be able to make choices for shaping the dramatic moments you have recognized and discussed with your partner. You will be able to create and react to the physical actions required by the script even though you are not necessarily executing them yet. Here is an example of what I mean. Suppose the script tells you that during your conversation with your partner she hands you something to read. Suppose it is a love letter to her from your best friend. Almost invariably, because there are no lines, the actor reading the letter will pretend to read it and quickly jump right to his or her next line. The irony is that the reading of that letter is as interesting, as dramatically compelling, as any line of dialogue in the scene could ever be. Further, it is the reading of this letter that leads the story to its next beat. Yet the actor chooses to jump to the next piece of dialogue. This is not the way to work. The reading of the letter, both for the reader and for the actor who watches the reading, is critically important to the scene and dramatically compelling for the audience. Those moments must be sketched out during the first read rehearsals. A scene is constructed brick by brick, and each brick must be there or the story collapses before it is built. Make sure you take the time to go through all your actions and reactions, physically or mentally, as required by the script. This will help you build moments, and one good moment onstage is worth far more than a scene full of ice skating.

Just a word more on moments. For an actor, a moment is a little theatrical event. It is an opportunity to really "act." It is a point at which the actor has the green light to tell exactly what he or she is thinking and/or feeling. It is an opportunity that no money actor will ever pass up. Moments occur when big news is given or received, when a victory or defeat occurs, when new information is injected into the situation, or, to generalize, when something in the situation has changed. In life people are not obligated to respond to these moments. But acting is not life. If actors do not respond when these moments occur onstage, they are missing a wonderful acting opportunity—an opportunity to show their stuff and, more importantly, to provide the audience with essential information about the characters and the unfolding story. What you communicate physically or with the lines during these moments is critically important. The first read provides actors with their first chance at developing these storytelling nuggets.

EXERCISE 13-3

Rehearse your scene with your partner. Work moment by moment, one beat at a time. Focus on your objectives and tactics and play them fully. Be sure you are listening to your partner and adjusting at all times to the specific input you are getting. Stay in each moment, but feel free to stop if it is not going in a manner that supports the story. Keep in mind that your only obligation is to discover the active playing of the scene you have already analyzed. You are not obligated to perform the scene during your rehearsals. Don't worry about that until you put the scene up for the class. But, even then, it is only a work in progress. There are no paying customers to disappoint.

You are ready to present your first read to your class when you can fulfill the following acting tasks:

- You can play your objectives fully, using moment-to-moment tactics.

- You can listen to your partner fully, with both your eyes and ears.

- You can execute all the physical tasks that the scene requires of you (even if only mentally) with beginnings, middles, and ends.

- You can react fully and specifically to all the discovered moments provided to you in the scene.

These acting tasks provide the muscle of the scene. All of the in-the-moment acting choices that you have made with your partner while working together in rehearsal must support the story structure that you have previously agreed on. In other words, the most dramatic moment in the scene, according to your homework and discussion, should really be the most dramatic moment in the scene as you play it. If that is not the case, then somewhere along the line you have lost the shape of the overall story and some adjustments will have to be made. Realize that this is not a terrible problem. The overall structure of the scene is often easier to see from the outside than from the vantage point of the actors working. Your teacher will be able to offer suggestions that will help you adjust your choices to better shape the way you build the scene. This is part of the process, and you should take all suggestions and criticism of your work in class as a positive part of that process. The feedback you get will help you build a better scene the next time. It will also give you hints about what you need to emphasize when you put your scene on its feet for the first time.

Armed with feedback, you are now ready to begin the next step of your rehearsal process. You are now ready to begin **blocking** your scene.

Summary

Armed with the shared vision of the scene you and your partner have negotiated through collaboration and compromise, you are ready to begin rehearsing your scene. You will rehearse moment by moment, beat by beat, focusing and playing your objectives and tactics specifically and positively. You will be listening and adjusting to your partner's choices at every moment. Only when you are satisfied with a moment should you continue into the next one. Good work is built one brick at a time, brick on brick. You already know the story of the scene as well as its dramatic progression. Even as you work in each moment, you will be trying to fulfill the dramatic throughline you have discovered through your analysis. When you have satisfied the preceding checklist, you are ready to present the scene to your class.

CHAPTER 14

Rehearsing the Scene: Blocking and Working It

Actors with more than a few plays listed on their resumes have probably worked with a director obsessed with making beautiful pictures on the stage. Such directors are usually concerned more with how their productions look than with how their pictures help tell the unfolding story. More often than not, the actors working with such directors have a difficult time justifying the director's blocking choices and making them work in terms of what they are doing as actors. This can be a very scary and frustrating experience—unless actors know enough technique to solve independently the acting problems created by such a directorial approach and solve them, of course, without compromising their director's visual creations. Working out the blocking problems of the scene you are doing for class can help you develop the skills necessary to do this—if you approach the material properly.

Using Blocking to Tell the Story

Telling the story should be the motivation for any blocking choices you make in a studio situation. Beautiful pictures alone, whether in a production or in a scene study setting, will not make your acting look beautiful. But blocking choices that are justified can, even when the choices are not your own. They will help you look believable, fulfill your objectives, clarify a moment, or create dramatic tension, and they will allow you to tell exciting and satisfying stories onstage. Using physical action to tell the story of the play is an essential skill for the actor to master, but one that is, unfortunately, too often ignored altogether or not given enough attention, especially by beginning actors. Once you have satisfactorily completed your acting obligations in your first read, you are ready to add in the blocking that will help you tell the story of your scene clearly and powerfully.

You have three primary blocking tools available to you, and using each is essential if you are going to do the best work possible. These blocking tools are:

1. **movement**—when actors move from one place to another onstage.

2. **gesture**—a specific physical action that communicates emotion, information, or attitude.

3. **business**—any ongoing activity actors engage in while fulfilling their acting tasks onstage.

In addition, actors need to consider the **composition** of the scene they are acting in. Composition refers to the picture created when the set, props, and actors are all present in the scene. The composition changes whenever the relationship between any of these elements changes. Actors must keep in mind how these relationships can help or hinder the story being told at each moment. Actors who can effectively use their three primary blocking tools, within the context of the setting and composition they have created, are likely to present clear and compelling stories with their scene work.

Following is a diagram showing the primary locations on a stage. Since all stage directions use this notation, it is important that you get accustomed to the terminology. Remember, all stage directions refer to location from the point of view of the actor looking out at the audience.

Upstage Right	Upstage Center	Upstage Left
UR	UC	UL
Right Center	Center Center	Left Center
RC	CC	LC
Downstage Right	Downstage Center	Downstage Left
DR	DC	DL

AUDIENCE

EXERCISE 14-1

1. Move across the stage from stage right to stage left. Move from upstage center to downstage center. Move from downstage right to upstage left. Move from upstage right to downstage left.

2. Select three positions onstage. Move from one to the next and stop at the third destination. Repeat the movements, but this time justify your actions. In other words, create a reason for making these moves and execute them in such a way that those reasons are clear to those watching.

3. Pick a position upstage. Move downstage and look at the class. Do the movement again. This time find a way to justify your actions.

4. Repeat Steps 1 through 3. This time vary the speed and tempo of each movement. What things do you discover? How does varying the speed and tempo change the meaning of the movement for you? For those watching?

Playing in a Defined Space

Before you begin blocking any scene, you need to think about where the scene takes place and all the things that need to be in that place if your scene is to work. If, for instance, the scene takes place in a living room, you need to decide what specifically is in the living room. Your decisions should not be arbitrary, though. Anything you and your partner decide on should help to make the scene work. What pieces of furniture are in the living room? Is there a sofa or a chair? Would two chairs be better? One sofa? Are two chairs and no sofa more appropriate and helpful? Once you make these decisions, you need to carefully consider where to place the pieces of furniture. Placing furniture in a position that makes the actors feel comfortable but serves to block them from the audience is not a wise choice. Good acting that can't be seen by the audience is not good acting.

You also need to consider the characters' physical position in relation to each other. Their relative positions can give the audience important information, even before you start to work. The positioning of the characters can demonstrate the nature of their relationship or even suggest where the story is picking up. Keep in mind that you will need to change some of your decisions as you go along. You will make discoveries as you rehearse your scene that will make you rethink your choices. That is good. Rethink them. Your obligation as an actor is to solve the problems of the scene. Be practical. Use your common sense.

EXERCISE 14-2

1. Place three pieces of furniture in a playing space and create a physical action score using at least five specific physical actions. Be sure to involve the furniture. Execute the actions.

2. Repeat the physical action score after rearranging the furniture. What is changed? Why? Are the changes good or bad? Why?

3. Find the most effective arrangement of furniture for the story being told in the physical action score. Perform the story.

4. Create and perform a two-character, two-line scene. Something like:

   I hate you.
   I hate you too.

Perform the scene three times. Each time position yourselves differently. Discuss the resulting scenes with the class to determine how positioning affects the scene. What conclusions can you draw?

Movement

The movement you create for your scene should be **organic.** That is, it should come out of the situation you and your partner are creating. Unlike the director mounting a production, you need not concern yourself with pretty pictures per se. Your task is to tell your story clearly and create as much conflict as possible. Your objectives are clear to you at this point because of the work you have done in your first read. Your obligation now is to use your movements to support your attempt to obtain your objectives.

In discussing the first read, I emphasized the importance of looking at your partner as much as possible. This rule is just as important through the rest of your rehearsal process. The completion of a good, playable objective should somehow be connected with your scene partner. If you need something from your partner, then your blocking choices should be connected to him or her. You need to look at and move toward your partner as much as possible when he or she has something you need. Try to keep the heat on. That will create dramatic tension.

Too often beginning actors turn away from their scene partners thinking that speaking into space is somehow more dramatic or theatrical than addressing their partners directly. It isn't. In life when you are involved in an angry discussion, do you turn away in the middle of making a point? No, you stay focused on the other person, determining even as you speak what effect your words and actions are having. Let it be the responsibility of your partner to do the turning or moving away if you are accomplishing your mission. If your partner needs to move away, he or she will, because getting some distance from you has become your partner's objective. If your partner moves and you have more to do to accomplish your objective, you will follow during the retreat. Play your objective physically. If you have won, if your objective is completed, then you can play a moment of victory not necessarily connected with your partner. Your partner will then get his or her own moment of defeat to play. This transition will lead to a new beat and to a new set of actions to play physically and with words.

EXERCISE 14-3

1. Invent a two-line scene with a partner. Something like the following will do:

> A: Do you love me?
>
> B: I'm not sure.

2. Improvise the blocking of the scene, changing the movement each time. How do the changes affect the scene? Which movements work better? Why?

Now, here's the rub. Stage movement is not quite as simple as I've described it. The way you choose to move onstage is important not only for the audience, but also for you as an actor. If, for instance, you cross to your scene partner at the moment your heated argument begins, and the argument is a long one, do you really want to be in your partner's face the whole time? Is that dramatically effective? Will it be believable? Does it become boring to watch? These are all matters to consider as you rehearse your scene. Good acting does not necessarily happen spontaneously. As artists, you must go through a process of discovery and selection as you work. You must try out and weigh the options you find until you and your partner settle on choices that work effectively. The movements that you finally settle on should be the most dramatically interesting ones you can find. The movements should have beginnings, middles, and ends so that there is a sense of a story unfolding with every moment and to every beat.

In one of my scene study classes, two students were working on a scene from Michael Gazzo's *A Hatful of Rain,* a realistic play from the 1950s. In it a male and female character are alone with each other for the first time. They are in love, but have never acknowledged it because the woman is married—to the man's brother. The male character is a little bit drunk so his normal inhibitors are not working. His objective is to get her to admit her feelings for him. Hers is to keep from admitting those feelings. The built-in conflict is strong. The male character must use a series of tactics until he finds one that finally gets her to admit how she feels. Although the playwright offers little stage direction to help the actors, a few lines in the scene suggest that there is some physical contact. The first time the students put the scene on its feet, they either missed this or chose not to deal with it. The scene did not work.

After discussing and working the scene, the actors realized it was not about the small talk. Rather, it was about how the dialogue was used to hide what the two characters were really feeling. Once the male character finally chooses to pursue his feelings, he does so fully. When the scene was presented again, the male actor chose to move toward the woman, forcing her to move away from him. The actress began finding things to do in her kitchen to avoid getting too close to the man. Once the two came in close proximity, they touched and finally kissed. The script did not specifically call for this. But it certainly solved the problems of the dialogue. It also created a story that was told as much through physical movement as through the words. A dated scene from an old chestnut had suddenly become hot—with a sexual plot that contained a clear beginning, middle, and end. The audience was absolutely getting its money's worth, and the choices served the play.

Gestures

During your work for the first read, you identified the big moments in your scene. The most dramatic moments usually come at the climax of a scene. They grow logically out of the ongoing conflict that has been created. Transitional moments may be more subtle. They come at the end of an objective beat—a point in the script where your objective is won or lost, or where new information suddenly changes what you need. Big dramatic moments are seldom a problem for actors to recognize because the script usually points them out. Even though transitional moments can be far less obvious, actors must fully play these moments onstage as well as the bigger dramatic ones. Transitional moments are revealing for the audience and provide actors with wonderful opportunities to act. Unlike in life, where you are under no obligation to reveal what you are thinking and feeling, actors should always choose to convey this information unless there is a reason dramatically for not doing so. Some actors believe, however, that all reactions on the stage, particularly physical ones, should be natural and spontaneous—that if you are truly living in the moment something will happen inside you that will be communicated to the audience.

Unfortunately, this is not always the case. Even when actors are playing fully and reacting beautifully in the moment, what they are feeling is not necessarily getting out to the audience. It is sometimes necessary to physicalize what your character is thinking and feeling. How many times have you watched actors in class or in rehearsal react with disbelief when they are told that an important moment was not being played? After all, they felt it. It was even real for them. In fact it was their best moment. In film and TV, where the camera can get intimate, this situation happens less frequently than when playing onstage.

But in any case, doing something physical that communicates a specific thought or feeling can greatly enhance the effectiveness and clarity of your work. If you understand the point being made right now you could nod, for instance. That is a physical action that defines the moment. Perhaps you are not sold on this idea yet, and want to think about it a bit longer. You could put your bent index finger to your mouth and gently bite it as you turn away. Then you could remove it as you turn back—more rapidly than your initial turn. You've now thought about the usefulness of gesture and you get the point. You could slap your hands together crisply. You love this acting tool. You could slap your hand against your forehead. Why didn't you think of working this way before? Even when gestures do not feel comfortable at first, by working with them in the same way you work with lines, you will soon find they become as natural as physical choices that came to you spontaneously. Further, because you have chosen them consciously, they are helping you build a performance with acting moments that are clear and specific. Selecting the appropriate gestures will allow you to communicate the story in a manner that is repeatable and controllable as well.

1. Say a line of dialogue to your partner. Try to make it provocative. Your partner must react to the line by using any single gesture that comes to mind.

2. Repeat the line of dialogue several times to your partner. Each time he or she must respond with a new gesture.

3. Discuss which gestures worked best. Try to find the reason. Rehearse the one-line scene using the best gesture.

4. Exchange roles in the exercise and repeat.

5. Again, say provocative things to your partner but in rapid fire succession. Don't give your partner time to think. For each line, your partner must gesture in response. The gestures should be totally spontaneous. What happens? What did you learn?

Props and Business

In addition to movement and gestures, you must also think about the props that will help make your scene work. Too often beginning actors doing a realistic scene will focus only on the dialogue. If you and your partner don't think about the physical action going on while your story unfolds, you will be forced to stand around in the middle of your set for long periods of time with nothing to do except say your lines. This will not create a feeling of reality. How often do you stand in the middle of your kitchen talking dramatically for long periods of time? What are the given circumstances that bring you and your partner to the kitchen at this moment? Are you preparing the evening meal, cleaning up after dinner, or chatting while putting the newly cleaned dishes away? Whatever you decide on, make sure you have the props to support your choices. Remember, you are not there just to stand in the middle of the room and recite lines. Doing believable physical actions (having "business" to attend to) will help make your work seem real and believable. Dialogue will seem natural if it comes out of what you are doing physically. It is better to actually use props, by the way, than to mime them. Miming forces an additional burden on actors by making them create the illusion of reality. If actors have the props, the reality is already there.

Here is an example of what I mean. Two other actors in the same scene study class I mentioned earlier were rehearsing a scene from *Dark at the Top of the Stairs*, a realistic play by William Inge, also from the 1950s. In the scene two sisters are discussing their marital problems. One sister needs her sibling to take her and her children in since her own marriage is falling apart. While she is looking for a way to ask, she discovers that her sister's marriage is no better than her own. The other sister must keep finding new ways to refuse the request during the course of the scene. The scene takes place after dinner.

The actors simply could not make this scene work. They understood the conflict, the time and place, what their objectives were, and even where the big moments were. But they simply could not make the conversation sound real. The first time they put up their scene, it took place in the living room. One sister sat on a sofa, the other on a chair. They had nothing to do except talk. The dialogue seemed forced. The second time they put up the scene they relocated it into a dining area. They chose to put away the dinner dishes they had just washed and dried. The physical actions of handling the plates, glasses, and silverware provided them with just the business they needed to make the difficult conversation work. Their movements to shelves and cupboards to put away the dinner items gave them the perfect reasons for advancing toward and moving away from each other as their objectives required. Once they had added in this kind of organic movement and business, the scene took off.

EXERCISE 14-5

1. Say aloud a poem you know.

2. Provide a context for saying the poem and repeat the poem keeping in mind the context.

3. Create some business to do while saying the poem. Repeat the poem while doing that business using the context you created. Discuss the differences.

4. Repeat Steps 1 through 3 using a song instead of a poem. Discuss the results.

5. Improvise a scene with a partner. Repeat the improvisation using business.

6. Perform a monologue that you know for the class. Repeat the monologue using a piece of business. How does the monologue change because of the business? Try repeating the monologue while doing a different piece of business each time you do it. What happens? Discuss the results.

7. Improvise a two-line scene using movement, gestures, and business. Repeat the scene using different movements, gestures, and business. What do you learn?

Whether your blocking is imposed on you by a director in a rehearsal situation or your blocking is organically based, the key to making it work is justification. Actors are responsible for finding the reasons behind all movements and gestures. They are responsible for making sure that any business included in the context of the work makes sense in the situation and, whenever possible, contributes clarity and storytelling detail. If actors can find and communicate the reasons for any movements their characters make, their comfort level as actors will increase as will their ability to engage the audience. In all probability, a director will expect his or her actors to do just that. It is essential, then, that actors master this aspect of their acting work.

Working through the Scene

Although I've presented it as a separate step, the blocking stage of your scene work rehearsals is really a continuation of the work you began with your first read rehearsals. Remember, rehearsing your scene is not science. What I've presented here is meant to serve as a guideline for efficient, creative acting work. This sequence of steps is intended to help actors build work logically and economically. There are, however, no absolute rules. The bottom line is always "if it works, then it works."

Here then is a list of items that you need to consider or reconsider for every scene you work on.

- *Work moment to moment.* Your blocking decisions, like all acting choices, must come out of the moment being played. They must not be generalized. Like bricks being stacked one at a time to make a solid structure, each moment must lead to the next, or the work will lack shape, clarity, and believability. You will find, by the way, that if you approach your work in this manner, memorization will become much less burdensome. Because all your senses will be at work, they will reinforce each other and facilitate the memorizing process. By the time you have completed your blocking rehearsals, most of your lines will already be in your head without painful rote repetition.

- *Every movement and gesture must be complete and full.* Blocking moments, like all acting moments, must have beginnings, middles, and ends. Before they occur, the reason they occur should be clear for the actors playing them and for the audience watching them. Once the action is completed, its impact should register with the actors and with the audience. In addition, a physical action played without full commitment is a bad acting choice. It will lack dramatic impact and clarity. How often have you watched actors in your class kiss or hug half-heartedly onstage, causing the scene to quickly deflate? How often have you seen a supposed "telling glance" onstage disappear long before the moment registers? How often have you seen an actor grab another actor in order to stop him or her, yet with such little force the other actor was hardly grabbed at all? What effect does this kind of false movement have on the work?

- *Every journey onstage should have a purpose and destination.* When actors cross away from something or someone onstage, they must remember that they are also moving toward something or someone else. Even if an imposed blocking choice has an actor stop mid-journey, the original intention of the character had to have been to get somewhere. Make sure that when you execute a cross, you have in mind where you are going. It will help give purpose to your move, and it will help communicate that purpose to the audience.

1. Design a setting for the scene you have been working on. Be sure that the design functions in such a way that it will help the scene dramatically. It should be practical and fulfill the requirements of the script. Make sure the arrangement allows the action to be seen clearly and effectively by the audience.

2. Rehearse the scene focusing on objectives, working moment to moment. Use the set pieces in your scene in ways that help you get what you need at each moment. Keep in mind the previous guidelines. Be sure all movement choices take into consideration the audience's ability to see.

3. Be sure to use gestures to make the important moments of the scene clear for the audience and for yourself.

4. Incorporate business that will help make the work realistic for you and for the audience.

Final Notes

Remember that all the suggestions for rehearsing a scene in this chapter are predicated on the fact that you and your scene partner have done the essential actors' homework—before embarking on the rehearsal process. If you don't know the story of the play and scene, then you couldn't possibly have made acting choices that intelligently serve the play and the scene you are working on. If you haven't made the necessary specific decisions about what is going on in your scene dramatically, then your scene will probably lack those essential qualities. Good acting requires not only believability, but good storytelling as well. Good storytelling must be exciting and clear, and will usually not come as a result of chance. Your rehearsals must make it all happen—through planning, practice, and even trial and error. Along the way, the feedback you receive from your teacher after presenting the work in class will keep you focused on what still needs to be accomplished. Accept the criticism willingly, and use it to guide your next set of rehearsals. When you work on your scene, your obligation is to fulfill the requirements of the scene, not to do the entire play. Don't feel obligated to reveal information that is revealed elsewhere. In other words, work on the scene as though it is part of a greater whole. Finally, remember to focus on the action of the scene. The manner in which you execute your sequence of actions will go a long way toward creating the character you are playing. What a character does onstage is far more revealing than a library of regional dialects and peculiar mannerisms could ever be. Character is action. And so are all compelling theatrical works!

Summary

The story of a play is told as much by what the actors do as what they say. Actors must, therefore, concern themselves with the physical elements of their story-telling responsibility. It follows then that blocking is not the domain of directors only. Actors must not only be aware of the composition of the stage, they must also learn to incorporate the three basic elements of blocking into their work if their acting is to be effective. They must learn to use movement, gesture, and business, and mold those elements into the overall composition of the scene. The effective use of stage movement can help clarify and enhance the story-telling of each moment and in the overall scene. The effective use of gesture can reveal specifically what a character is thinking and feeling. The effective use of business can help a scene seem more real and believable for both the actor and for the audience. What the audience sees the actors do is every bit as important as what they hear the actors say.

CHAPTER 15

Using the Words: Discovering and Telling the Story

In the previous three chapters of this section, we have explored the manner in which a script can be analyzed and synthesized to tell the story of the play and its smaller units—the scene, the beat, and even the storytelling moment. But since a play consists almost exclusively of dialogue, it is with the spoken words of a play that any analysis must begin; it is there that the principal tools for communicating the story are found. Even the physical action of the play, the other great storytelling tool the actor can use, begins with the action suggested by the dialogue. It is, therefore, essential that actors not only interpret the layers of meaning to be found in the dialogue, but also find the right way to deliver the dialogue so that the story is clearly communicated.

It is not unusual for young actors to think that the words of a play will spring perfectly shaped and inflected from their mouths once they understand the general meaning of a line, the given circumstances surrounding the line, and the intent of the character speaking the line. This, unfortunately, is simply untrue for most actors most of the time. It is possible, of course, that some well-trained and talented actors can make a reasonable delivery of a line without consciously shaping it, but that is almost impossible to do successfully with language that is the least bit **elevated.**

Elevated Language

Most plays not written in this century employ dialogue that is elevated in some way. The language spoken in those plays can range from dialogue with at least some poetic devices—both structurally and figuratively—to dialogue that is poetry of the highest order. But no matter where on the poetic scale the dialogue falls, it is clear that the language spoken in these plays is a different brand of palaver than what we speak. Even in modern and contemporary works, it is not

153

unusual to find playwrights employing a writing style that is clearly not the way we speak in everyday life, even though it may reflect our speech patterns. These playwrights, like their predecessors from other centuries, use structure, rhythm, repetition, figurative language, and many other poetic devices that enrich and elevate the language they write. In spite of the fact that these playwrights may fool you into believing the dialogue is written as people actually talk, their dialogue will invariably require a good deal of actor preparation before it can be delivered effectively.

The rhythms established between the characters speaking in a play by David Mamet or Harold Pinter or Maria Irene Fornes, for instance, demand that the actors maintain a certain verbal energy as well as recognize the connecting words linking one speaker to the next. Those connecting words must be emphasized by each speaker to allow the other actor to interrupt without destroying the established rhythm and pace.

EXERCISE 15-1

Read the following scenes several times. Try to get a sense of the rhythm and pace the authors create in the dialogue. What specific things do the authors do to create that sense of tempo? Point out as many connecting words as you can from the three scenes. Describe how they work. The first scene is from David Mamet's *Speed the Plow;* the second from Harold Pinter's classic, *The Dumb Waiter;* the third from Maria Irene Fornes's *Sarita.*

Gould's office. Morning. Boxes and painting materials all around. Gould is sitting, reading, Fox enters.

GOULD: When the gods would make us mad, they answer our prayers.

Fox: Bob . . .

GOULD: I'm in the midst of the wilderness.

Fox: Bob . . .

GOULD: If it's not quite "Art" and it's not quite "Entertainment," it's here on my desk. I have inherited a monster.

Fox: . . . Bob . . .

GOULD: Listen to this . . . (*Reads:*) "How are things made round? Was there one thing which, originally, was round . . . ?"

Fox: Bob . . .

GOULD: (*leafing through the book he is reading, reads*) "A certain frankness came to it . . ." (*He leafs.*) "The man, downcast, then met the priest, under the bridge, beneath that bridge which stood for so much, where so much had transpired *since* the radiation."

Fox: . . . yeah, Bob, that's great . . .

GOULD: Listen to this: "and with it brought grace. But still the questions persisted . . . that of the Radiation. That of the growth of animalism, the decay of the soil. And it said, 'Beyond terror.

Beyond grace' . . . and caused a throbbing . . . machines in the void . . ." (*He offers the book to Fox.*) Here: take a page.

FOX: I have to talk to you.

GOULD: Chuck, Chuck, Chuck, *Charles:* you get too old, too busy to have "fun" in this business; then what are you . . . ?

FOX: . . . Bob . . .

GOULD: What are you?

FOX: What am I . . . ?

GOULD: Yes.

FOX: What am I when?

GOULD: What are you, I was saying, if you're just a slave to commerce?

FOX: If I'm just a slave to commerce?

GOULD: Yes.

FOX: I'm nothing.

GOULD: No.

FOX: You're absolutely right.

GOULD: You got to have fun. You know why?

FOX: Okay: Why?

GOULD: Because, or else you'll die, and people will say "he never had any fun."

FOX: How close are you to Ross?

GOULD: How close am I to Ross . . . ? I don't know. How close should I be?

(*Speed the Plow,* Act 1)

Gus takes the matches from pocket and looks at them.

GUS: Well, they'll come in handy.

BEN: Yes.

GUS: Won't they?

BEN: Yes, you're always running out, aren't you?

GUS: All the time.

BEN: Well, they'll come in handy then.

GUS: Yes.

BEN: Won't they?

GUS: Yes, I could do with them. I could do with them too.

BEN: You could, eh?

GUS: Yes.

BEN: Why?

GUS: We haven't any.

BEN: Well, you've got some now, haven't you?

GUS: I can light the kettle now.

BEN: Yes, you're always cadging matches. How many have you got there?

GUS: About a dozen.

BEN: Well, don't lose them. Red too. You don't even need a box.

Gus probes his ear with a match.

BEN: (*slapping his hand*) Don't waste them! Go on, go and light it.

GUS: Eh?

BEN: Go and light it.

GUS: Light what?

BEN: The kettle.

GUS: You mean the gas.

BEN: Who does?

GUS: You do.

BEN: (*his eyes narrowing*) What do you mean, I mean the gas?

GUS: Well, that's what you mean, don't you? The gas.

BEN: (*powerfully*) If I say go and light the kettle I mean go and light the kettle.

GUS: How can you light a kettle?

BEN: It's a figure of speech! Light the kettle. It's a figure of speech!

GUS: I've never heard it.

BEN: Light the kettle! It's common usage!

GUS: I think you got it wrong.

BEN: (*menacing*) What do you mean?

GUS: They say put on the kettle.

BEN: (*taut*) Who says?

They stare at each other, breathing hard.

(*The Dumb Waiter*)

Sarita's kitchen in a tenement building. Sarita is seventeen years old. She sits at the table and reads out loud from a letter she has just written. There is another chair facing the right side of the table. Sarita and Julio wear the same clothes as in the scene before.

SARITA: Julio, you left and here I am. You are a son of a bitch and did not appreciate my love. You did this too many times already and this is the last time. I don't care, I'm doing fine. It's you who will suffer. (*She writes as she speaks the following.*) I'm going to put a curse on you. (*She reads.*) You cannot treat me like this.—Sarita. (*She props the letter on the table. She looks at it and kisses it. She props the letter up. She turns it so it will face the door. She waits. A few seconds later footsteps are heard. She quickly exits left. There is a knock on the door. There is silence. There is another knock.*) Come in!

JULIO: (*Kicking.*) Open up!

SARITA: Come in!

JULIO: The door is locked! Open it! I don't have the key.

SARITA: (*Enters, tiptoes across, opens the door and returns to the left still on tiptoe.*) How come you don't have your key?

JULIO: (*Enters.*) I don't know how come I don't have my key. (*He goes over to Sarita and tries to kiss her. She scurries to the right corner. He turns the chair to face her and sits. He opens his fly and lowers his suspenders as he speaks.*) Come here, sit on my lap.

SARITA: No.

JULIO: Come here. I'm hot.

SARITA: No.

JULIO: Hey! How come you say no?

SARITA: Look behind you.

JULIO: (*Sees the note and takes it.*) What does it say?

SARITA: Read it.

JULIO: I can't read that. It's not clear. You don't write clear. Read it to me, but read it quick because I want to kiss you.

SARITA: You just read it.

JULIO: O.K. (*He starts to read. He sneaks looks in her direction.*) Hey, honey, you look cute.

SARITA: Did you read it?

JULIO: Hey, honey, look at me.

SARITA: What for?

JULIO: Give me a kiss.

SARITA: Never mind.

JULIO: Come here. Sit on my lap.

SARITA: What for?

JULIO: For nothing.

(*Sarita straddles him. They kiss. Her pelvis moves.*)

SARITA: Why are you the way you are? Why are you so sweet and so juicy and so bad?

(*Sarita,* Scene 7)

In a play by Tennessee Williams or Sam Shepard an actor must be able to shape the figurative language and its music in such a way that the dialogue does not seem affected, yet allows the poetry to come through.

EXERCISE 15-2

Read the following scene. Notice the cinematic quality of the language as Sam Shepard creates a verbal montage that uses rhythm, repetition, and tempo. The combination of language elements builds almost musically in this speech by Wesley from Shepard's *Curse of the Starving Class.* Study the speech to discover how the effect is created.

> I was lying there on my back. I could smell the avocado blossoms. I could hear the coyotes. I could hear stock cars squealing down the street. I could feel myself in my bed in my room in this house in this town in this state in this country. I could feel the presence of all the people outside, at night, in the dark. Even sleeping people I could feel. Even all the sleeping animals. Dogs. Peacocks. Bulls. Even tractors sitting in the wetness, waiting for the sun to come up. I was looking straight up at the ceiling at all my model airplanes hanging by all their thin metal wires. Floating. Swaying very quietly like they were being blown by someone's breath. Cobwebs moving with them. Dust laying on their wings. My P-39. My Messerschmitt. My Jap Zero. I could feel myself lying far below them on my bed like I was on the ocean and overhead they were on reconnaissance. Scouting me. Floating. Taking pictures of the enemy. Me, the enemy. I could feel the space around me like a big, black world. I listened like an animal. My listening was afraid. Afraid of sound. Tense. Like any second something could invade me. Some foreigner. Something undescribable. Then I heard the Packard coming up the hill.

Now study the following monologue. Notice the poetic use of imagery and rhythm, the standard devices of Tennessee Williams, in this speech by Tom from *The Glass Menagerie.*

> I didn't go to the moon, I went much further—for time is the longest distance between two places. Not long after that I was fired for writing a poem on the lid of a shoe-box. I left Saint Louis. I descended the steps of this fire escape for a last time and followed, from then on, in my father's footsteps, attempting to find in motion what was lost in space. I traveled around a great deal. The cities swept about me like dead leaves, leaves that were brightly colored but torn away from the branches. I would have stopped, but I was pursued by something. It always came upon me unawares, taking me altogether by surprise. Perhaps it was a familiar bit of music. Perhaps it was only a piece of transparent glass. Perhaps I am walking along a street at night, in some strange city, before I have found companions. I pass the lighted window of a shop where perfume is sold. The window is filled with pieces of colored glass, tiny transparent bottles in delicate colors, like bits of a shattered rainbow. Then all at once my sister touches my shoulder. I turn around and look into her eyes. Oh, Laura, Laura, I tried to leave you behind me, but I am more faithful than I intended to be! I reach for a cigarette, I cross the street, I run into the movies or a bar, I buy a drink, I speak to the nearest stranger —anything that can blow your candles out!

In a play by Eugene O'Neill or Arthur Miller there is often a formality of language and a surfeit of words requiring an actor to find a way to keep the story moving forward. This is not a simple task considering the density of the language these playwrights have chosen to use.

EXERCISE 15-3

Read the following passage from O'Neill's *Long Day's Journey into Night*. Notice the difficulty an actor faces in order to keep the forward thrust of the story in this speech by Mary Tyrone.

> That wedding gown was nearly the death of me and the dressmaker, too! I was so particular. It was never quite good enough. At last she said she refused to touch it any more or she might spoil it, and I made her leave so I could be alone to examine myself in the mirror. I was so pleased and vain. I thought to myself, "Even if your nose and mouth and ears are a trifle too large, your eyes and hair and figure, and your hands, make up for it. You're just as pretty as any actress he's ever met, and you don't have to use paint." Where is my wedding gown now, I wonder? I kept it wrapped up in tissue paper in my trunk. I used to hope I would have a daughter and when it came time for her to marry—She couldn't have bought a lovelier gown, and I knew, James, you'd never tell her, never mind the cost. You'd want her to pick up something at a bargain. It was made of soft, shimmering satin, trimmed with wonderful old duchesse lace, in tiny ruffles around the neck and sleeves, and worked in with the folds that were draped round in a bustle effect at the back. The basque was boned and very tight. I remember I held my breath when it was fitted, so my waist would be as small as possible. My father even let me have duchesse lace on my white satin slippers, and lace with the orange blossoms in my veil. Oh, how I loved that gown! It was so beautiful! Where is it now, I wonder? I used to take it out from time to time when I was lonely, but it always made me cry, so finally a long while ago—I wonder where I hid it? Probably in one of the old trunks in the attic. Some day I'll have to look.

It would take several volumes to cover the variety of challenges that face an actor when dealing with the elevated language supplied by the great dramatic wordsmiths. Suffice it to say that for our purposes here, you must never take the dialogue for granted. Your job as an actor is to tell the story of the play, and if that play has been written by a first-rate playwright, you will best serve its language by making it serve you. In other words, you must realize that the playwright is not writing his or her dialogue just to be poetic. The good playwright never forgets that the dialogue's principal purpose is to communicate the story. You must never forget that either. It is your responsibility as an actor to discover, by examining the dialogue, first, what the story is and, second, how that story is served by the dialogue. If, as in the previous examples, the language has special demands, it is your obligation to fulfill them. Once you have met those obligations, you will be able to make choices that tell the story clearly and compellingly.

Using Literal, Contextual, and Subtextual Meaning

In Chapter 10 I discussed the importance of understanding the dialogue of a script on its three basic levels—the literal, contextual, and subtextual. The **literal** meaning of the dialogue refers to the straightforward meaning of the words themselves—alone and in combination. The **contextual** meaning of the dialogue refers to how the words are used in regard to the given circumstances in which they are spoken. The **subtextual** meaning refers to how the words relate to the speaker's purpose in saying them. The literal meaning of the dialogue, of course, is altered completely by its contextual and subtextual meanings. That is why you must never assume that by simply knowing what the words themselves mean, you can deliver them effectively.

Look at this line, for instance.

This chapter makes a lot of sense!

Reading the line out of context, you might see it as either a positive or negative statement, depending on your opinion about this chapter so far. Notice that there is even an exclamation point to support your belief. But suppose the line is from a play, and it is said while vigorously ripping up this text. Then suppose it is said while highlighting a few profound lines from this same text. In each case the line would mean something very different.

Once you have established the context of the line, or determined your objective (the subtext) in saying it, you can shape the line by the way you inflect it. Notice how the meaning changes when you choose to emphasize a particular word or group of words.

This chapter makes a lot of *sense!*
This chapter makes a *lot* of sense!
This chapter *makes* a lot of sense!
This *chapter* makes a lot of sense!
This chapter makes a lot of sense!

Did you notice how each inflection choice strongly affects either the contextual or subtextual meaning of the line? Words that, when stressed, give a line a particular meaning are called **operative words,** and your ability to find and use them can help make your acting clearer and more effective. Particularly when using elevated or poetic language—language that will not be taken for granted by the listening ear—an effective use of operative words can quickly turn the dialogue you deliver from vague to crystal clear.

EXERCISE 15-4

1. Read several short passages from speeches that you are already familiar with. Try inflecting the words differently than you normally would. How do these changes affect what you are saying? Did you discover anything new and useful? Discuss.

2. Circle or underline the operative words in the passages you have selected. Read the passages, emphasizing the operative words. How does this affect the meaning of the passage? Its effectiveness? What have you learned? Discuss your observations.

Now try reading the poem that follows. Be warned that at first it might seem somewhat difficult. You will notice that it is in the form of a dramatic monologue. There is a single speaker in the poem, and through this speaker's words, the entire story can be discerned. It will probably take several careful readings before the story hidden in the monologue becomes clear to you. But the process for uncovering the poem's meaning is no different than the process you would use in analyzing a play script. The first time through, read the poem for its literal meaning. Be sure that you understand the definitions of all the words. Keep a list of all the words that are new to you, and be sure to look them up. Try also to discover as much about the given circumstances of the poem as you possibly can. The dialogue contains myriad clues—if you are willing to hunt for them. Keep a list of given circumstances as well. Be sure to write them down as you discover them, and note for yourself where in the text of the poem the clues appear. There is a good deal of detective work involved in all this. But it is important to remember that everything in a good script is there for a reason. This fact should prove helpful with this exercise—and with all the scripts you read in the future.

Only when you have completed several careful readings of "My Last Duchess," and compiled your notes, should you read beyond the poem.

> Ferrara
> That's my last Duchess painted on the wall,
>   Looking as if she were alive. I call
> That piece a wonder, now: Fra Pandolf's hands
>   Worked busily a day, and there she stands.
>   Will't please you sit and look at her? I said
> "Fra Pandolf" by design, for never read
> Strangers like you that pictured countenance,
>   The depth and passion of its earnest glance,
> But to myself they turned (since none puts by
>   The curtain I have drawn for you, but I)
> And seemed as they would ask me, if they durst,
> How such a glance came there; so, not the first
>   Are you to turn and ask thus. Sir, 'twas not
> Her husband's presence only, called that spot
>   Of joy into the Duchess' cheek; perhaps
> Fra Pandolf chanced to say, "Her mantle laps
>   Over my lady's wrist too much," or "Paint
>   Must never hope to reproduce the faint
> Half-flush that dies along her throat": such stuff
> Was courtesy, she thought, and cause enough
>   For calling up that spot of joy. She had

A heart—how shall I say?—too soon made glad,
Too easily impressed: she liked what'er
She looked on, and her looks went everywhere.
Sir, 'twas all one! My favor at her breast,
The dropping of the daylight in the West,
The bough of cherries some officious fool
Broke in the orchard for her, the white mule
She rode with round the terrace—all and each
Would draw from her alike the approving speech,
Or blush, at least. She thanked men,—good! but thanked
Somehow—I know not how—as if she ranked
My gift of a nine-hundred-years-old name
With anybody's gift. Who'd stoop to blame
This sort of trifling? Even had you skill
In speech—(which I have not)—to make your will
Quite clear to such an one, and say, "Just this
Or that in you disgusts me; here you miss,
Or there exceed the mark"—and if she let
Herself be lessoned so, nor plainly set
Her wits to yours, forsooth, and made excuse,
—E'en then would be some stooping; and I choose
Never to stoop. Oh sir, she smiled, no doubt,
Whene'er I passed her; but who passed without
Much the same smile? This grew; I gave commands;
Then all smiles stopped together. There she stands
As if alive. Will't please you rise? We'll meet
The company below, then. I repeat,
The Count your master's known munificence
Is ample warrant that no just pretense
Of mine for dowry will be disallowed;
Though his fair daughter's self, as I avowed
At starting, is my object. Nay, we'll go
Together down, sir. Notice Neptune, though,
Taming a sea-horse, thought a rarity,
Which Claus of Innsbruck cast in bronze for me!

(Robert Browning—My Last Duchess)

It is probably time here to mention one of the underlying themes of this text—the importance of **head-first acting.** It is particularly worth alluding to if you had to struggle with the text of "My Last Duchess." Too many actors are aliterate, that is, not really much interested in close reading. Many talented young actors hide behind the false premise that they need only to behave, not to read, think, analyze, and synthesize, in order to become successful in their craft. Much of this book, I hope, makes the case for just the opposite premise.

Actors must know a lot about a lot of things because, eventually, just about every topic under the sun becomes the subject for a playwright's imagination.

But, more importantly, actors must be willing and able to use their brains to do the necessary actor homework. First of all, you must understand the subjects your character refers to. Then you must find a way to use the playwright's words and the actions they imply to articulate the story and its meaning (which, by the way, are always related to the subject). Without being able to read, analyze, and synthesize, this obligation to the playwright's text is probably impossible to live up to.

Following is a list of words and phrases from the Browning poem whose literal meanings might have been unfamiliar to you, or at least fuzzy. If these words, or others not included on the list, fall into either of those categories, it is your acting obligation to change their status—by making yourself do the necessary work. If you don't do the work, then ultimately, you will be saying the lines with no understanding of what they mean to the story. How can you *behave believably* as a character if you are blindly saying things without understanding them? In real life people know what they are saying, unless they are drunk, in a trance, or sleepwalking. The characters you play also know what they are saying, so you must as well, if you have any intention of playing those characters effectively.

Words to Check for Literal Meaning

Ferrara	chanced	excuse
Duchess	mantle	e'en
piece	laps	Count
Fra	courtesy	munificence
by design	favor at her breast	dowry
pictured	officious	disallowed
countenance	approving speech	avowed
earnest glance	stoop to blame	object
puts by (the curtain)	trifling	Neptune
durst	miss, exceed the mark	Claus of Innsbruck
husband's presence	lessoned	
spot of joy	forsooth	

Now, on the assumption that you have found the literal meanings of these words and phrases, we are ready to examine the text for clues that lead to the given circumstances. Here is the list I have compiled, along with my explanations of the clues. There may be more items than I have found. Compare your list with my own.

Contextual Clues

Ferrara—An Italian city-state known for its support of the arts in the Middle Ages and the Renaissance.

last Duchess—The wife of a duke and, by implication, a former wife of the speaker who is showing a painting of her. "Last" suggests previous rather than final, which in turn suggests there have been other wives before this "last" one. It also implies, perhaps, possibilities about the future.

sit and look at her—There must be a chair or seat that permits the character spoken to in the monologue to study the painting of the Duchess.

none puts by the curtain I have drawn—The painting is revealed only when the curtain surrounding it is pulled back by the Duke, and he does so rarely.

how such a glance came there—The other character has asked about the expression on the face in the painting.

so not the first are you to turn and ask thus—Others have asked about that same expression; it, therefore, must be a significant or unusual expression.

spot of joy—The woman in the painting is blushing.

'twas not her husband's presence only—Others were able to make her blush, suggesting she flirted, to say the least.

list of her described activities—She engaged in many things in public which the Duke found inappropriate.

nine-hundred-years-old name—The Duke comes from a long line of nobles, and, by implication, is not one to trifle with.

if she let herself be lessoned so—By implication, the Duchess would not accept the Duke's criticism.

set her wits to yours, forsooth, and made excuse—She had the audacity to argue with her husband.

gave commands; / Then all smiles stopped together—The Duke gave orders to have his wife killed.

meet the company below—There is a social gathering going on downstairs.

The Count your master's—The listener in the piece is an emissary of a Count.

dowry—The Count's emissary is with the Duke to discuss a marriage arrangement.

fair daughter's self—The marriage is to be between the Count's daughter and the Duke.

Claus of Innsbruck—A famous sculptor of the time; to own his work must have been a status symbol.

Following you will find the list of acting tools I first mentioned in Chapter 10 on finding and using dialogue. Using these tools will be critical in your analysis and synthesis of the story contained in "My Last Duchess." Before attempting to put this dramatic monologue on its feet effectively, you will need to consider each of these items. Together, they incorporate the basics you will need to tell the story of the poem clearly and dramatically.

- Find the given circumstances.
- Find the conflict.
- Create a dramatic throughline.
- Find and play an objective.
- Find or create risk, high stakes, and obstacles.
- Find and play the dramatic moments.
- Justify each line of dialogue.

Now here is a brief discussion of each of the items for analysis, based only on the words themselves—literally, contextually, and subtextually. Note how when analyzed in that manner, the words can turn the poem into an actable story.

Given Circumstances

A powerful and wealthy duke in Renaissance Italy has pulled away from a social gathering at his palace to discuss his impending wedding with an emissary from the Count. The two are discussing the dowry arrangements that will seal a marriage between the Duke and the Count's daughter. As the monologue opens, the Duke pulls back a curtain that reveals a painting in the likeness of his last wife. The picture, painted by Fra Pandolf, has captured a most unusual expression on the face of the late Duchess, an expression that shows her in full blush.

Conflict

There appears to be no overt or obvious conflict in the poem. Yet, by now, you know that every good dramatic work must have conflict. So then, what is it? Remember, for starters, that this is not really a monologue. The speaker is speaking to someone. That someone is an emissary from the Count who is there to negotiate terms for an impending marriage. Both sides want to do well in this business arrangement. How much should the Count pay to a Duke who has been a rather difficult husband in the past? The Count's daughter will be stepping up by marrying a duke, but will her life be in the same kind of jeopardy as the "last duchess"? Will the Duke, with his reputation, be able to negotiate an arrangement? There is much potential conflict here.

Dramatic Throughline

The story begins as the Duke pulls back the curtain, revealing the painting of his last duchess—a work that bears a strong resemblance to the actual person. The Count's emissary is much taken by the expression on the woman's face. The Duke sees his reaction, though he is not surprised by it. The Duke explains that the expression represents the inappropriate forwardness that the Duchess demonstrated toward everyone and everything. The Duke offers many specifics about his wife's unseemly behavior, and becomes surprisingly personal about his feelings regarding that behavior. The Duke further explains that he was unable to get his wife to change her demeanor, even though he was, admittedly, unwilling to argue with her about it. His position in society prevented him from "stooping" that low. Finally, when he could take it no more, he put his wife to death. The Duke then asks the emissary to rejoin the guests below, but, almost as an afterthought, assures the emissary that any proper dowry offer will be accepted by him. On the way back to the others, the Duke proudly points out a piece of sculpture that he had personally commissioned from a famous artist of the time.

Objective

Based simply on the possible conflicts and dramatic throughline I've described, it is an obvious jump that the speaker wants to complete the marriage arrangements. In other words, he wants to make the emissary agree to terms. This is a simple and strong objective to play. Its completion relies on the other character in the scene and is completely consistent with the contents of the poem. However, there is more. The Duke shows the painting of his last wife during the negotiation. What is his objective in doing this? Could he be trying to make the emissary understand that his future wife's conduct is more important to him than the dowry being negotiated? The text certainly supports this idea. The Duke, then, must make the emissary understand that, for him, a wife's behavior is far more important than a well-negotiated dowry.

Risk, Stakes, Obstacles

The stakes are implied in the previous discussion, and they are high. Marriage is obviously no small issue, especially in a Catholic country at a time when Popes had political and military as well as spiritual power. The future duchess's life is also at stake for reasons already explained. A failure to understand each other at this meeting could have life-and-death consequences, particularly for the Count's daughter, and for the emissary as well, if he does not accurately report his findings to his master. All this is good for heightening the power of the story.

Dramatic Moments

Based on the throughline, the first big dramatic moment is the Duke's reaction to the emissary when the latter sees the painting. Remember, moments of victory, defeat, discovery, and the arrival of new information all cause transitional moments. Those moments are always actable.

EXERCISE 15-5

In the following reprinting of "My Last Duchess," I have inserted slashes in the text in places where possible dramatic moments occur.

Try to determine why the notations have been placed there. You may disagree. You may also find other dramatic moments to act that I have not noted. Be sure that you understand fully why you are making the choices you decide on.

For my part, I noted a new beat each time the purpose, or the direction, of the Duke's words changed—sometimes by his own initiation, and sometimes as a result of the reaction I imagined the emissary would have. In a monologue, it is necessary to create what the listener is doing if you are going to play each moment clearly and fully.

> That's my last Duchess painted on the wall,
> Looking as if she were alive. I call
> That piece a <u>wonder</u>, *now*:/ Fra Pandolf's <u>hands</u>
> Worked <u>busily</u> a day, and there she <u>stands</u>./
> Will't please you <u>sit</u> and <u>look</u> at her? / I said
> "Fra Pandolf" by *design*, for never read
> Strangers like you that <u>pictured countenance</u>,
> The <u>depth</u> and <u>passion</u> of its <u>earnest glance</u>,
> But to myself they turned (since *none* <u>puts</u> by
> The curtain I have drawn for you, but *I*)
> And <u>seemed</u> as they would <u>ask</u> me, if they *durst*,
> How <u>such</u> a <u>glance came</u> there; so, <u>not</u> the <u>first</u>
> Are you to <u>turn</u> and <u>ask</u> thus./ Sir, 'twas <u>not</u>
> Her <u>husband's presence</u> *only*, called <u>that spot</u>
> <u>Of joy</u> into the Duchess' <u>cheek</u>;/ perhaps
> Fra Pandolf *chanced* to say, "Her <u>mantle laps</u>
> Over my lady's <u>wrist</u> too much," or "Paint
> Must never hope to reproduce the <u>faint</u>
> <u>Half-flush</u> that <u>dies</u> along her <u>throat</u>": /such <u>stuff</u>
> Was <u>courtesy</u>, *she* <u>thought</u>, and cause <u>enough</u>
> For <u>calling up that spot of joy</u>. / She had
> A heart—how shall I say?—<u>too soon</u> made <u>glad</u>,
> Too <u>easily impressed</u>: she <u>liked what'er</u>
> She <u>looked</u> on, and <u>her looks *went everywhere*</u>./
> Sir, 'twas <u>all one</u>! <u>My favor</u> at her <u>breast</u>,
> The <u>dropping</u> of the daylight in the <u>West</u>,
> The bough of cherries some <u>officious fool</u>
> <u>Broke</u> in the orchard for her, the white <u>mule</u>
> She <u>rode</u> with round the terrace—all and each
> Would <u>draw</u> from her <u>alike</u> the <u>approving</u> speech,
> Or <u>blush</u>, at least./ She <u>thanked</u> men,—<u>good</u>! but thanked
> <u>Somehow</u>—I <u>know not</u> how—as *if* she <u>ranked</u>
> <u>My gift</u> of a *nine-hundred*-years-old name
> With *anybody's* <u>gift</u>. / Who'd <u>stoop</u> to <u>blame</u>
> This sort of <u>trifling</u>? Even had you <u>skill</u>
> In <u>speech</u>—(which <u>I</u> have <u>not</u>)—to make your <u>will</u>
> <u>Quite clear</u> to such an one, and say, "Just <u>this</u>
> Or <u>that</u> in you *disgusts* me; here you <u>miss</u>,
> Or there <u>exceed</u> the mark"—and if she <u>let</u>
> <u>Herself</u> be <u>lessoned</u> so, nor plainly <u>set</u>
> Her wits to <u>yours</u>, <u>forsooth</u>, and <u>made excuse</u>,
> —<u>E'en</u> *then* would be some <u>stooping</u>; and I <u>choose</u>

Never to <u>stoop</u>. / <u>Oh</u> sir, she <u>smiled</u>, no doubt,
Whene'er *I* <u>passed</u> her; but *who* <u>passed</u> without
Much the *same* smile?/ <u>This grew</u>;/ I *gave commands*;/
Then <u>all smiles *stopped*</u> together./ There <u>she stands</u>
As if <u>alive</u>/. Will't <u>please</u> you <u>rise</u>? / We'll <u>meet</u>
The <u>company below</u>, then./ I <u>repeat</u>,
The <u>Count</u> your <u>master's known *munificence*</u>
Is <u>ample warrant</u> that no <u>just</u> pretence
Of mine for <u>dowry</u> will be <u>disallowed</u>;
Though his *fair daughter's self*, as I <u>avowed</u>
At <u>starting</u>, is my <u>object</u>. / <u>Nay</u>, we'll go
<u>Together</u> down, sir./ <u>Notice Neptune</u>, though,
<u>Taming</u> a <u>sea-horse</u>, thought a <u>rarity</u>,
Which *Claus of Innsbruck* cast in <u>bronze</u> for <u>me</u>!

Justifying the Lines

Every word and line a good playwright writes has purpose and meaning. The actor must discover that purpose and meaning and then pursue an objective that will support and clarify the purpose and meaning. If as I stated earlier, the Duke's objective is to make the emissary understand how important he considers propriety to be in a new duchess, then the actor's obligation is to maximize that objective through his use of the dialogue. Notice, by the way, the underlined and italicized words in the second printing of the poem. In my opinion, by emphasizing these words, the Duke will better make the points that will help him attain his objective, and the actor's primary obligation—to tell the story—will be accomplished.

EXERCISE 15-6

Explain why you think I have underlined and italicized the particular words in the poem. (*Hint:* Words that are both underlined and italicized are ones I find especially important.) If you disagree with my choices, explain why. What other words would you underline or italicize? Explain why.

Notice the number of verbs that are highlighted. This should not really be surprising. Verbs are action words, and, remember, stories are always about action. It follows that emphasizing action words will help you to better tell the story. Many non-verbs are also highlighted, however. Were you able to discover how those words enhance the story? A closer examination reveals that those words serve to make clear both the context and subtext of the story. Also, did you notice how the poet often uses alliteration (a repetition of sounds in close proximity) to emphasize the importance of those particular words? Once again, the importance of becoming a literate actor should be clear.

EXERCISE 15-7

1. Find a narrative poem or dramatic monologue that you like. Analyze the poem using the same process described earlier. Read the poem aloud before and after the work. Discuss the differences.

2. Following you will find another dramatic monologue by Robert Browning, "Soliloquy of the Spanish Cloister." Do the necessary work.

> Gr-r-r—there go, my heart's abhorrence!
>> Water your damned flower-pots, do!
> If hate killed men, Brother Lawrence,
>> God's blood, would not mine kill you!
> What? your myrtle-bush wants trimming?
>> Oh, that rose has prior claims—
> Needs its leaden vase filled brimming?
>> Hell dry you up with its flames!
>
> At the meal we sit together:
>> *Salve tibi!* I must hear
> Wise talk of the kind of weather,
>> Sort of season, time of year:
> *Not a plenteous cork-crop; scarcely*
>> *Dare we hope oak-galls, I doubt;*
> *What's the Latin name for "parsley"?*
>> What's the Greek name for Swines Snout?
>
> Whew! We'll have our platter burnished,
>> Laid with care on our own shelf!
> With a fire-new spoon we're furnished,
>> And a goblet for ourself,
> Rinsed like something sacrificial
>> Ere 'tis fit to touch our chaps—
> Marked with L for our initial.
>> (He-he! There his lily snaps!)
>
> *Saint*, forsooth! While brown Delores
>> Squats outside the Convent bank
> With Sanchicha telling stories,
>> Steeping tresses in the tank,
> Blue-black, lustrous, thick like horsehairs
>> —Can't I see his dead eye glow,
> Bright as 'twere a Barbary corsair's?
>> (That is, if he'd let it show!)
>
> When he finishes refection,
>> Knife and fork he never lays
> Cross-wise, to my recollection,
>> As do I, in Jesu's praise.
> I the Trinity illustrate,
>> Drinking watered orange-pulp—
> In three sips the Arian frustrate;
>> While he drains his at one gulp.
>
> Oh, those melons! If he's able
>> We're to have a feast! so nice!

One goes to the Abbot's table,
  All of us get each a slice.
How go on your flowers? None double?
  Not one fruit-sort can you spy?
Strange!—And I, too, at such trouble
  Keep them close-nipped on the sly!

There's a great text in Galatians,
  Once you trip on it, entails
Twenty-nine distinct damnations,
  One sure, if another fails:
If I trip him just a-dying,
  Sure of heaven as sure can be,
Spin him round and send him flying
  Off to hell, a Manichee?

Or, my scrofulous French novel
  On gray paper with blunt type!
Simply glance at it, you grovel
  Hand and foot in Belial's gripe;
If I double down its pages
  At the woeful sixteenth print,
When he gathers his greengages,
  Ope a sieve and slip it in 't?

Or, there's Satan!—one might venture
  Pledge one's soul to him, yet leave
Such a flaw in the indenture
  As he'd miss till, past retrieve,
Blasted lay that rose-acacia
  We're so proud of! *Hy, Zy, Hine* . . .
"St., there's Vespers! *Plena gratia,*
  Ave, Virgo! Gr-r-r—you swine!

EXERCISE 15-8

Following you will find a short scene from William Shakespeare's
Romeo and Juliet.

1. Read the scene. What do you understand from this simple reading? Is it enough to rehearse and play the scene? The answer
   should be "no." Why?

2. Read the entire play.

3. Answer the questions about the overall play found in Chapter 12
   on script analysis.

4. Reread the excerpt below. Analyze the cutting using the questions found in Chapter 12 on script analysis and in Chapter 13 on
   the first reading.

5. Analyze the language in the manner you did for "My Last
   Duchess" earlier in this chapter.

Enter Romeo and Juliet aloft (at the window)

JULIET: Wilt thou be gone? It is not yet near day.
  It was the nightingale, and not the lark,
  That pierced the fearful hollow of thine ear.
  Nightly she sings on yond pomegranate tree.
  Believe me, love, it was the nightingale.

ROMEO: It was the lark, the herald of the morn;
  No nightingale. Look, love, what envious streaks
  Do lace the severing clouds in yonder East.
  Night's candles are burnt out, and jocund day
  Stands tiptoe on the misty mountain tops.
  I must be gone and live, or stay and die.

JULIET: Yond light is not daylight; I know it, I.
  It is some meteor that the sun exhales
  To be to thee this night a torchbearer
  And light thee on thy way to Mantua.
  Therefore stay yet; thou need'st not to be gone.

ROMEO: Let me be ta'en, let me be put to death.
  I am content, so thou wilt have it so.
  I'll say yon grey is not the morning's eye,
  'Tis but the pale reflex of Cynthia's brow;
  Nor that is not the lark whose notes do beat
  The vaulty heaven so high above our heads.
  I have more care to stay than will to go.
  Come, death, and welcome! Juliet wills it so.
  How is't, my soul? Let's talk; it is not day.

JULIET: It is, it is! Hie hence, be gone, away!
  It is the lark that sings so out of tune,
  Straining harsh discords and unpleasing sharps.
  Some say the lark makes sweet division;
  This doth not so, for she divideth us.
  Some say the lark and loathed toad change eyes;
  O, now I would they had changed voices too,
  Since arm from arm that voice doth us affray,
  Hunting thee hence with hunt's-up to the day.
  O, now be gone! More light and light it grows.

ROMEO: More light and light—more dark and dark our woes.

Enter *Nurse* (*hastily*).

NURSE: Madam!

JULIET: Nurse?

NURSE: Your lady mother is coming to your chamber.
  The day is broke; be wary, look about. (*Exit.*)

JULIET: Then, window, let day in, and let life out.

ROMEO: Farewell, farewell! One kiss, and I'll descend.

(*He goeth down.*)

JULIET: Art thou gone so, love-lord, ay husband-friend?
  I must hear from thee every day in the hour,
  For in a minute there are many days.
  O, by this count I shall be much in years
  Ere I again behold my Romeo!

ROMEO: Farewell!
I will omit no opportunity
That may convey my greetings, love, to thee.

JULIET: O, think'st thou we shall ever meet again?

ROMEO: I doubt it not; and all these woes shall serve
For sweet discourses in our times to come.

JULIET: O God, I have an ill-divining soul!
Methinks I see thee, now thou art so low,
As one dead in the bottom of a tomb.
Either my eyesight fails, or thou lookest pale.

ROMEO: And trust me, love, in my eye so do you.
Dry sorrow drinks our blood. Adieu, Adieu! (*Exit.*)

(Act III, Scene 5)

The work required to prepare this scene may seem enormous to you, but, by doing the work, you will find that the scene becomes far clearer to you than when you first read it. You will probably find that you are able to begin making strong, well thought-out acting and dialogue choices based on your completed preliminary analysis. That, in turn, will mean that you are starting to get the hang of doing the actor's homework. You are also beginning to meet the requirements of good acting—telling the best possible story while serving the script. Remember, meeting the requirements of good acting requires head-first acting. Inspiration comes later.

Summary

Any analysis begins with the spoken words of the play. Actors must interpret the layers of meaning to be found in the dialogue before they can expect to find the right way to deliver the lines. Whether the language is elevated or not, the preparation necessary to say the words effectively will invariably require a good deal of thought. It is the actor's responsibility to examine the dialogue to discover what the story is and how that story is served by that dialogue. Once you have established the context of the line and have determined its subtext, you can shape the line by the way you inflect it. Stressing operative words can give a line a particular meaning and can help make your acting work clearer and more effective. Without being able to read, analyze, and synthesize the language of a play, an actor's obligation to the playwright's text is probably impossible to fulfill.

CHAPTER 16

Theatrical Conventions and Style

My introduction to theatre came as a young child through the magic of marionettes. Several times a year my favorite aunt would ritually take me to our sacred place—a musty old vaudevillian theatre. Its shiny planked floors and its smell of decaying plaster are still vivid in my memory. The old theatre had been lovingly converted to accommodate the special world of stringed puppets, and by the age of six, I knew what it meant when the lights began to dim. I was about to enter a unique world—a world with laws different from the ones that regulated my everyday life. This, then, was my introduction to the **conventions** of theatre.

I learned that theatre was a place where time could jump forward and back or accelerate with a simple fading of an overhead lamp. It was a place where a single tree, with the willing help of my imagination, could transform itself into an entire forest. It was a place where a piece of wood could come to life for an hour or two and mean as much to me as family and friends, a place where my emotions flowed freely and were no less real than those I produced in life. Even though I knew the characters I met were made of wood and cloth and glue, for the time those magical lights were dimmed, I decided wholeheartedly not to know. I chose to forget that living people were responsible for the illusion of life onstage. I, along with an auditorium full of children and their parents, had chosen to suspend our disbelief.

EXERCISE 16-1

1. Discuss your own first experience in theatre. What about theatre particularly struck you? What were the theatrical conventions you became aware of? What effect did they have on you?

2. What is your first memory of suspending your disbelief theatrically? Describe the experience.

3. Think about the six elements of drama as defined by Aristotle—action, character, dialogue, idea, spectacle, and music—and apply them to a play or movie you have seen. What theatrical conventions can you think of that apply to each of these elements? In other words, where, and how, are you asked to use your imagination? Make a list to share with your class. How do these conventions require you to suspend your disbelief? Why are you willing to do so? Compare and discuss your list with the lists of your classmates.

By the time a few years had passed, my interests had expanded to include movies. All kinds of movies. Movies from every **genre** (a term referring to a particular type or category of film or play). War pictures, for example, were exciting and patriotic, and like the puppet theatre of my earlier years, had a whole series of conventions which, when consistently applied, permitted me to believe in them. In World War II movies, for instance, everyone usually spoke English, even the Nazis. I understood that they had to in order for me to understand what they were saying. Sometimes the Germans spoke with English accents, so I could tell there was a difference. I accepted the convention. Nazis usually spoke with German accents, however—to make it absolutely clear to me that it was German they were speaking. Sometimes the Nazis spoke in actual German too, but only in the parts of the film where it was unnecessary that I understand them.

Then there were science fiction and fantasy films. In *The Wizard of Oz*, I willingly accepted that animals could talk and that people wearing costumes should be considered real lions, scarecrows, and tin men. I believed in flying monkeys even though, if I allowed myself, I could see the strings permitting them to fly. I accepted the convention. In movies about outer space, every kind of creature understood and used English. Is that possible? When traveling back in time, people in the Stone Age or in King Arthur's court spoke English too. No problem, I willingly accepted the convention. I even believed that superimposed garden lizards were giant dinosaurs, though I really knew they weren't.

EXERCISE 16-2

1. Watch some movies from the various genres in the following list. After you have carefully watched several movies, list the characteristics and conventions that seem common to that particular type or genre of film. Were the conventions of the particular genre made clear? Were they consistently applied? Explain.

   Adventure—*Raiders of the Lost Ark, King Solomon's Mines, Congo, Gunga Din, Romancing the Stone*
   Animal film—*Lassie, Flipper, Andre, Babe, Black Beauty, Free Willy, Paulie*

Buddy movie—*Thelma and Louise, Midnight Run, Lethal Weapon, 48 Hours*

Concept comedy—*The Mask, The Nutty Professor, Dumb and Dumber, Kindergarten Cop*

Cops and robbers—*The Rock, Con Air, Serpico, The Fugitive, The French Connection*

Costume drama—*Braveheart, Les Miserables, Rob Roy, First Knight, The Man in the Iron Mask*

Family film—*The Little Princess, The Secret Garden, The Borrowers, The Parent Trap*

Film noir—*The Big Sleep, The Maltese Falcon, The Postman Always Rings Twice, Double Indemnity, L. A. Confidential*

Gangster—*Public Enemy, Little Caesar, The Godfather, Bonnie and Clyde*

Horror—*Dracula, The Wolfman, American Werewolf in London, Frankenstein*

Invasion from space—*Independence Day, Invasion of the Body Snatchers, The X Files*

Monster—*King Kong, Godzilla, Tremors, Alien, Jurassic Park*

Musical—*My Fair Lady, Evita, The Sound of Music, Singin' in the Rain*

Romance—*Sabrina, Sleepless in Seattle, An Affair to Remember, Ghost, City of Angels*

Slasher—*Halloween, Scream, Friday the 13th, Nightmare on Elm Street*

Space patrol—*Star Wars, Star Trek, Starship Troopers, Lost in Space*

Tearjerker—*Imitation of Life, When a Man Loves a Woman, Terms of Endearment*

Teen comedy—*Ferris Bueller's Day Off, Heathers, Ted and Bill's Excellent Adventure*

Thriller—*Silence of the Lambs, Fatal Attraction, Seven, Psycho, Cape Fear*

War picture—*Platoon, Sands of Iwo Jima, The Green Berets, Saving Private Ryan*

Western—*Lonesome Dove, Silverado, A Fistful of Dollars, Stagecoach, The Searchers, The Unforgiven*

2. For each genre, compare your list of characteristics with the lists of your classmates. What characteristics in each genre require a suspension of disbelief? Why were you willing to do so? What movies left you unable to? Why?

3. Think of some hybrid genres of movies—movies that combine the characteristics of two or more of the genres above. Discuss your list and the characteristics of the new categories you discovered.

4. Make a list of play genres. Isolate the characteristics of each genre. Try to think of plays that fit the characteristics of each genre on your list. Support your placement of each play.

5. Define and discuss the play genres of tragedy, comedy, melo-drama, drama, and farce (see the Glossary for definitions of these terms). What other genres are on your list? Discuss examples that might fit into those categories.

Conventions and Believability

When the conventions, or rules, of a particular theatrical or movie world are established and then maintained, we will accept things as real and believable in order to better let the story come across. The worlds of theatre and film depend on the audience's willingness to do just that—to suspend its disbelief. In the movies I saw as a child, I wanted to believe in the established conventions. When Nazis spoke, it was more convenient to listen to English rather than having to read subtitles and to accept that everyone spoke the same language rather than having to watch the characters try to find ways to communicate. Science fiction was produced on the cheap so I accepted the imitation dinosaurs that a limited amount of money could buy, just as I accepted strings on puppets and flying monkeys. The conventions were used in a consistent manner and, therefore, I could and wanted to believe.

At about the same time I was absorbing science fiction and war pictures, I saw a movie called *The Vikings* with a cast that included Kirk Douglas, Tony Curtis, and Ernest Borgnine. The Vikings were all American actors; the more civilized English nobles were played, for the most part, by British actors. I had no problem accepting this convention—American accents for barbarians, English accents for civilized races. Even Tony Curtis's Bronx accent didn't bother me since it seemed to have been spawned from some unspecific slave gene pool. Only at the end of the film, when Curtis had to say the classic line "Prepeh a fewneral fohr a Viking!" did his accent suddenly become apparent and, therefore, ridiculous to me. We had only just found out that Tony, the former slave, was really the brother of Kirk and the son of Ernie. So how come only he had the Bronx accent? Suspension of disbelief had evaporated because the conventions were not consistent.

In an earlier movie, *The Black Shield of Falworth,* also set in the Middle Ages, I found Curtis was completely unconvincing as a young squire. His accent was literally laughable. Why unacceptable here yet okay for most of *The Vikings*? The answer was the presence of the always superb James Mason. As the evil nemesis of the young knight, the impeccably accented Mason created a believable illusion of medieval England that made the Bronxian Curtis simply unbelievable. The two accents within the same noble class would not allow me to suspend my disbelief. No consistent convention of dialect was created or maintained. In short there was a clash of **styles.** *The American Heritage Dictionary of the English Language* defines *style* this way:

1. The way in which something is said, done, expressed, or performed: *a style of speech and writing.* 2. The combination of distinctive features of literary or artistic

expression, execution, or performance characterizing a particular person, group, school, or era.

We will consider the meaning and uses of style in more detail shortly. But for now, suffice it to say that the problem was not that Tony Curtis was a bad actor; he simply had a bad accent for all those costume dramas he found himself in. Language and how it is used is an important part of performing a particular style convincingly.

EXERCISE 16-3

1. Compare the acting styles of Kevin Costner and Alan Rickman in the film *Robin Hood, Prince of Thieves.* What does this tell you about style?

2. Compare the 1938 Errol Flynn version of the story, *The Adventures of Robin Hood,* with the more recent Kevin Costner version. What conclusions can you draw about acting styles and about overall style in these films?

3. Is the 1993 remake of *The Three Musketeers* believable? Why or why not? Compare the movie to an earlier version (1973 or 1948).

4. Compare the original *King Kong* with its 1976 remake. Discuss their styles. How about the two *Mighty Joe Young* movies?

5. Compare two sitcoms, *Frasier* and *Seinfeld* for instance. How are they different in overall style? Are the acting styles different? Are the acting styles consistent with the kind of material of each show? Are the acting styles of the actors in each show consistent with each other? Explain.

6. Watch two gangster movies from the 1930s. Are their styles consistent with each other? Compare a recent gangster movie with one from the 1930s. Compare the styles.

7. Define the style of daytime soap opera. Compare it to nighttime soap opera. To a more serious drama. Discuss the characteristics of each.

8. Read a short scene with a partner in the soap opera style. Get feedback from your class and discuss your conclusions.

Language and the Playwright's Style

Unlike in movies where the audience might forgive a Viking from the Bronx, in theatre, from Shakespeare to Tennessee Williams, the language of a play demands that the actor think about its style. Disregarding a play's language can result in an audience disbelieving the world being created or its characters. The world of Shakespeare is not the world we know. Its characters dress differently, behave differently, and believe in things that are very different from the beliefs we hold to today. But most obviously, the characters in a Shakespearean play speak in a language very foreign to the contemporary ear, even though that language is recognizably English.

The language of Shakespeare is elevated and poetic. It is a language that can contain and support emotions and passions that are larger than the English we use today. Its words, familiar though they may be, often have different meanings, while its **figurative language**, rhythm, and tempo all require a special set of conventions, or a particular style, to make them work. If actors ignore this fact, their work might not be accepted by an audience, in spite of the fact that the same acting choices might work in a contemporary play.

The worlds created by Tennessee Williams, Maria Irene Fornes, Sam Shepard, or David Mamet operate in the same way. Each of these playwrights has a style of writing dialogue that differs from the language of the everyday contemporary world. (See the examples in Chapter 15.) It is important to keep in mind that *the style of a particular playwright also includes the characteristics and conventions found in the world of the play or plays he or she creates.* A close examination of the body of work by the four playwrights mentioned earlier would clearly reveal the distinctive style and voice of each. The actor must learn to recognize and understand how an author's style works, and be able to use this knowledge to serve the action of the story as well as the character being played. Using a stylized kind of language onstage, for instance, without giving it the special regard it requires, can lead to a failure to make the audience believe in and understand the story being told.

The importance of recognizing and playing within a particular style was made clear to me not long ago while I watched a college production of an old Cole Porter musical, *Anything Goes*. The book of this play is thin and written in a recognizably 1930s style. The dialogue is full of period slang and requires a rapid and staccato delivery. (You can see this style clearly when you watch movies from the era.) The overall success of the production was hindered by the inconsistent handling of this style by the actors onstage. Some characters seemed to belong in the world of the play. Others seemed to have been beamed down from our own time and place. This inconsistency kept many in the audience from believing in the world of the play or in its characters. We couldn't suspend our disbelief.

EXERCISE 16-4

1. Read as many plays as you can to develop your sense of a playwright's style. Considering works by the following playwrights, all of whom have their own distinctive styles, will help you cultivate your ability to do so.

Edward Albee	Bertolt Brecht	Anna Deavere
Jean Anouilh	Anton Chekhov	Smith
Alan Ayckbourn	Caryl Churchill	Christopher Durang
Samuel Beckett	Noel Coward	Lonnie Elder

Euripides	Charles Ludlam	George Bernard
Maria Irene Fornes	Edward Machado	Shaw
Pam Gems	David Mamet	Sam Shepard
Jean Genêt	Terrence McNally	Sophocles
A. R. Gurney	Marsha Norman	Tom Stoppard
Lillian Hellman	Eugene O'Neill	Paula Vogel
Beth Henley	Joe Orton	Wendy Wasserstein
Tina Howe	Eric Overmeyer	Oscar Wilde
David Henry Hwang	Suzan-Lori Parks	Tennessee Williams
Henrik Ibsen	Harold Pinter	August Wilson
Eugène Ionesco	David Rabe	Lanford Wilson
Frederico Garcia	José Ribera	
Lorca	Ntozake Shange	

2. Read aloud with your class a number of monologues from the works of various playwrights. After each reading, discuss the monologues for characteristics you discovered specific to that author's writing.

Note: This chapter is not intended to provide the skills necessary to do justice to the language of Shakespeare, or to any other poetic playwright for that matter. Nor is this chapter intended to provide the reader with a complete and detailed understanding of the complexities of style. It is intended, rather, to make the reader aware of the kinds of problems an actor must face when confronting a play requiring "style." To start a more detailed study in this area, consult the Suggested Readings found at the end of the text.

Types of Style

Everybody uses the term *style,* but defining the concept specifically is difficult because we use the term in so many different ways. It can apply to an individual. Cary Grant had style. So did Bette Davis and Katherine Hepburn. James Cagney and Humphrey Bogart had style too. Jack Nicholson has it. So do Sean Connery and Glenn Close. A particular playwright often has his or her own recognizable writing style—Christopher Durang, Wendy Wasserstein, Beth Henley, and Nicky Silver, to name a few. Plays can be written in a particular stylistic mode. There is the style of **realism** or **naturalism.** There is the **expressionism** sometimes found in the plays of Eugene O'Neill and Tennessee Williams. There is the **absurdism** of Beckett or Pinter, and the **magical realism** of Sam Shepard, Maria Irene Fornes, and José Ribera. Each writing style has its own conventions for creating the particular world of the play. Finally, the director of a play sometimes employs a particular style in order to make the script work effectively onstage.

Whether a play is **classical, modern,** or **contemporary**, once its style is understood, it then becomes a matter of selecting the right choices to reflect that style. This is not as hard as it sounds when we realize that all of us play out our own lives using different styles of behavior. In fact, some of us adopt several styles every single day. Observe the way you behave around your parents, for instance. Compare your behavior with them with your behavior when you're with your friends. If you're like most people, your vocabulary, manner of speaking, and physicalization are vastly different in those two universes. Yet you have little trouble playing the two styles. Now think about the variety of styles you take on in school. Are you different from class to class? When you compete in a sporting event in gym class? Between classes? Have you ever belonged to an organized group like the scouts or a church group? Think about the styles of behavior you successfully execute in those situations. Yet in all these situations, you are still you. What you do in every situation is to select a particular body of choices appropriate for each of the environments in which you find yourself. This ability—to select from a huge but specific vocabulary of acceptable choices —is no different from what is required of you when you act in a period play or in a play requiring a specific style.

EXERCISE 16-5

1. Improvise a scene in which you are discussing a movie with someone. Be sure to define the relationship between you and your scene partner. Are you a mother and daughter, a teacher and student, or what? Set the conversation in a specific place (a gym, a cafeteria, an English class, a church, and so forth). Pay particular attention to how you would behave in these circumstances. Redo the scene several times changing the relationships and locale. How do these changes affect the content of the scene? Discuss the work with your class. What behaviors were specific to the situation being played out? Which choices worked? Why? Which choices did not work as well? Why? How do these questions relate to the issue of style?

2. Improvise a scene in which you ask someone out on a date. Make the scene contemporary (set in the world of today). Redo the scene set in another time and place. Be sure to think about the differences time and place have on the scene. Discuss the work presented. What worked? What didn't? Why? How did the differences in time and place affect the work? How do these questions relate to the issue of style?

3. Choose a situation that you would find fun to do an improvisation based on. Rehearse the scene with a partner after selecting a specific time and place in which the scene occurs. Choose a time and place other than the here and now. Perform your scenes for the class. Was the class able to determine the time and locale of the scene, based on your choices? Why or why not? What choices in your work allowed them to do so? What choices kept them from doing so? Why? Rework your scene using the input provided by your class. Repeat the process.

4. Select several people from class and watch them play a familiar game such as Musical Chairs. Set the game in the Old West; in

the Middle Ages; in Elizabethan England; in a Three Stooges movie; in a silent picture; and so forth. What body of choices defined each game played and made it believable to watch? What characteristics of the individual players made them believable to watch? Which failed to do so? Draw conclusions.

On its most basic level, every time you accept a theatrical or dramatic convention as part of the world of the play, you have begun the process of playing a style. Think about acting in a musical, for instance. Though many actors take it for granted, the conventions that allow an audience to continue to believe in what they are seeing when characters suddenly burst into song is really quite a suspension of disbelief. Breaking into song and dance is a far cry from realism. In spite of that fact, the young actors in the film and television show *Fame* somehow managed to convey a sense of reality while doing so. The actors in a musical must fully believe that people do break into song on cue, and, when the song is finished, return to normal everyday behavior. Once they can do so, they have begun to master the style. If they couldn't make this look believable, musicals would seem ridiculous to the watching audience.

But even musicals have a tremendous variation in style. Musicals from the 1930s require a very different style of acting than those from the 1950s or 1960s. And what about Stephen Sondheim musicals? Every one is stylistically different from its predecessor. Imagine doing *Sweeney Todd* in the same style as *Into the Woods*. Then imagine doing *Assassins* in the same style as a Rogers and Hammerstein musical such as *The Sound of Music*. In musicals, as in period plays, every production requires a commitment to a unique world—one that has been especially created to serve the play.

EXERCISE 16-6

1. Improvise a scene in which you and/or your partner suddenly break into song. Try to make your class believe that this is really happening. You will only be successful if you first make yourself believe in it. Discuss the results with your class.

2. Improvise a scene in which you and/or your scene partner suddenly break into song while playing in a particular movie genre. You may select from the list in Exercise 16-2. How did the particular genre affect your ability to "go musical"? What style choices was it necessary to make? How did the exercise work, or not work? Why? Discuss the results with your class.

The particular genre of a play often requires a particular style to make it work in production. The style used in playing tragedy, for instance, will probably not work with a farce, and you'd probably want to avoid the slapstick style of the

Three Stooges when mounting a comedy of manners such as those by Noel Coward or Oscar Wilde. A frantic slapstick style is likely to get in the way of the beautifully crafted wit that pours from the dialogue in this kind of play—the wellspring of its humor.

EXERCISE 16-7

1. Using the list of play genres and examples you composed for Exercise 16-2, select a style of performance for each that you think would help make the play work for an audience. Be sure to be able to justify your choices. Discuss your choices with your class.

2. Take a very short piece of material that you know (it could be a poem, a nursery rhyme, or a short monologue) and perform it employing several different styles. How was each different? Which ones worked? Why? Which ones did not? Why?

3. Perform a short contemporary monologue using a soap opera style, an Elizabethan style, a naturalistic style, a theatrical style, a slapstick style. Discuss your work with the class, and draw conclusions.

Specifically defining style in regard to acting is a difficult task. For many actors and directors, defining style in acting is not unlike the famous remark about pornography once put forth by Supreme Court Justice Potter Stewart: "Perhaps I could never succeed in [defining it], but I know it when I see it." John Gielgud defined style in acting by saying, "It's knowing what kind of play you're in." Using the same kind of thinking, perhaps the following definition will work: *Style is the result of recognizing and using a set of characteristics and conventions shared by a set of characters in a play.* It often reflects the society about which the play was written or the world of the author who wrote it.

The Roots of Style

Conveying meaning, character, action, humor, and so on requires a specific understanding of time and place. *Oedipus Rex, Macbeth, The Importance of Being Earnest, The Cherry Orchard,* and *Hedda Gabler* are set in very different worlds—each requiring a particular knowledge about its history and society. To understand the work of Sophocles, we need to know, for instance, that to the ancient Greeks destiny was predetermined, and that attempting to avoid one's fate was tragically futile. When performing Shakespeare's *Macbeth,* we need to know that Elizabethans found the question of destiny not so clear and, because of that fact, Macbeth's tragic decision to kill King Duncan was, ironically, either predetermined or completely unnecessary. We need to understand Victorian attitudes about class and society to fully appreciate and convey the wit found in Oscar

Wilde's *The Importance of Being Earnest.* A Chekhov play requires an understanding of the social system of late nineteenth century Russia if we are to appreciate the gentle finger-pointing humor and sympathy the author felt for his characters. Finally, if we are to see her as more than a manipulating villain, Ibsen's Hedda Gabler must be understood in light of the powerful social restraints women were subject to in late nineteenth century Europe.

But in order to play a style effectively and believably, our understanding has to go far beyond these individual examples. Every play, whether consciously or not, is a reflection of the time and culture in which it was written. It is up to the actors, directors, and designers to think about its characters' beliefs about religion, politics, science, economics, ethics and morality, social customs, and so on. Further, as the preceding examples suggest, every play has its own logic, its own set of rules by which its characters operate. In short, every play is set in its own unique world, and every time an actor begins working on a new play he or she must buy into that world. It is essential that all the actors in a play share its rules or conventions and believe in them fully, if the audience is to be expected to do the same. After all, the rules that govern the world of the play work in the same way that our own contemporary rules hold together the world in which we live.

Take Shakespeare's *Measure for Measure,* for instance. In this play, the character of Isabella, a novitiate in a convent, is asked to sacrifice her virginity in order to save her brother's life. She refuses to do so. For an Elizabethan audience this decision would be seen as heroic. In an age where premarital sex was considered a venial sin or worse, a novitiate's unwillingness to trade her chastity for the brother she dearly loved would have been seen as a brave and painful sacrifice. To a contemporary audience, however, this same decision might seem heartless and selfish. In an age where sexual activity, even among the young, is neither uncommon nor particularly sinful, Isabella's conflict might appear almost trivial. If that is the case, it becomes the job of the actress playing Isabella to make her character's conflict and values clear through her acting choices. The audience must see her internal conflict and pain clearly. They must understand the reasons for her choice even though these are not necessarily made clear through a script that is reflective of its own time. Thus, it is the actor's job to tell the story of the play by emphasizing through his or her own actions and acting choices what is important for the audience to know.

EXERCISE 16-8

1. Select a character from a play by one of the authors on the following list. Write a description of the character based on our contemporary value system. Then write a description of the character based on what you know about the religious, political, moral, ethical, scientific, and social beliefs of the times when that character lived. Compare the descriptions and draw conclusions. Discuss your work with your class.

Chekhov	Forbes	Ionesco
Coward	Ibsen	Mamet

Pinter   Shange   Sophocles
Shakespeare   Shaw

2. With the help of your teacher, find three very short monologues to work on. Select from three different authors on the preceding list. Try to develop a style of delivery that works effectively with each piece of material. Be sure to do your homework before tackling the material directly.

The World of "Realism"

In spite of the difficulty of defining style, the argument about style and American acting training has raged on for at least two generations now. The most famous brand of acting training in America has long been the "Method" introduced by Lee Strasberg and based on Stanislavski's early work. Proponents of this emotion-based training for a long time claimed the market on "realistic" acting. At the same time, they ceded classical acting and other styles of performance to the outside-in technique of the British-trained theatrical actor. But implicit in this concession was the message that realism is the realer, truer, more artistic brand of acting, one in which actors use inner truth rather than external tricks to make the audience believe.

Today we have entered a new era of acting—an era in which the classically trained Anthony Hopkins can win an Academy Award for playing the horrifying serial killer, Hannibal Lecter; where Natasha Richardson can brilliantly play Anna Christie or Sally Bowles onstage and heiress/bank robber, Patty Hearst, on film; and where method-trained Al Pacino can keep trying to get the kinks out of his stage interpretation of Richard III. So what is this realism all about anyway, and what does it have to do with style in acting?

The contemporary world is most often reflected onstage through the style known as realism. When we view a play we consider realistic, we tell ourselves, "Yes, that's right, that's how we speak, that's how we move, that situation that I'm watching I can identify with!" The world of the play seems very like the world we live in. But, contrary to what some method actors might suggest, realism is a style, not unlike other styles of theatre. It is simply a style more familiar to us because it employs many of the conventions we use in our daily life. The vocabulary of choices an actor makes in a realistic play is dictated by the conventions of behavior currently popular in our society.

The fact that realism is a style can be demonstrated by examining some plays once considered prime examples of realism. In their time, for instance, the plays of Clifford Odets or William Inge were considered to be the essence of the realistic form. When read today, however, they often seem awkward and self-conscious. The working-class, immigrant English spoken by the characters in *Awake and Sing,* for instance, is alien both to our tongue and to our ears. The hidden desires, passions, and secret longings of the characters from *Dark at the Top of the Stairs* strike us today as almost neurotically inhibited if we don't consider the mores prevalent two or more generations ago. Making a successful production from the work of either of these realistic playwrights requires a selectivity of choice, both physically and vocally, not at all unlike the stylized plays of centuries past.

EXERCISE 16-9

1. Find and prepare some short realistic monologues to read to your class. A list of realistic playwrights follows to help you make your selections. Make your monologues as absolutely "real" as you can. Read the prepared monologues to your class. Get feedback for your work. Discuss the results.

Lee Blessing	Israel Horowitz	Marsha Norman
Richard Greenberg	Tina Howe	Teresa Rebeck
A. R. Gurney	Shirley Lauro	Neil Simon
Beth Henley	James McLure	Wendy Wasserstein

2. Did the class find your work "realistic"? What made it so? Were your readings dramatically interesting and clear as well? Why or why not?

3. Rework your readings so that your work is "realistic" and also meets the definition of good acting.

Some Concluding Thoughts about Style

Theatrical conventions and style choices can allow both the actors in a play and the audience watching it to believe in the world being created. The making of a successful production depends more on creating a consistent fictional reality on the stage than on reflecting the reality we know in life. Here is what I mean. Not long ago, I did an exercise with a freshman acting class in which I asked them to pass around an imaginary ten-pound ball. The first six students passed an imaginary ball that consistently had the same shape and weight, although the weight seemed far less than ten pounds. The seventh student took possession of an imaginary ball that, in real terms, did seem to weigh ten pounds, but by changing the established weight of the imaginary ball, the student destroyed the illusion created by the six previous handlers. In the world of the theatre, the six who maintained the illusion believably, inaccurate though they might have been, were the better actors—for they shared a fictional theatrical world with a consistent set of conventions and made that world seem real to the audience.

A shared world of theatrical conventions produces a recognizable style that, in turn, creates for the audience a believable though sometimes alien universe. The world of soap opera has its own style. In life we do not act as soap opera characters do, yet there is a consistency of style in their universe and so we believe. The comedy style of *Frasier* is far different from that of *Mad About You* or *Seinfeld*. Yet we have no trouble suspending our disbelief to enjoy each of them. The styles of the gangster films *Public Enemy* with James Cagney and Coppola's *Godfather* series are very different. When we watch *Public Enemy* today, its style is clearly over the top. But, in its time, like the more recent *Godfather* films, it was praised for its ultra-realism. We can still enjoy both films equally, for each creates a consistent interesting universe, though, clearly, *Public Enemy* is one very unlike the world in which we live.

In conclusion then, a theatre audience will suspend its disbelief and accept the world of a play as long as it understands that world's conventions, values, and customs. Unlike movies, which usually reflect values and customs that we know and understand (since they have been written mostly in our own time), many period plays are motivated by needs and customs that are no longer valued and understood. It becomes the actor's responsibility not only to understand those needs and customs, but also to convey them to the audience in such a way that the story and character motivations come through. This was not the actor's responsibility when these plays were first written. Their original audiences already understood them, in the same way a contemporary audience understands the conventions of a play centered in contemporary realism.

Summary

Theatre has its own set of conventions that require an audience to suspend its disbelief. An audience will be willing to do so when a convention is made clear to them and is consistently presented during the course of a play. Period pieces, musicals, and plays from various genres each have their own particular set of conventions that must be established onstage and maintained. An actor who has done his or her homework, and who understands the social customs, history, politics, and language characteristic of a play from another period, can begin to commit to its style. The actor must learn enough to understand the world of the play and to create the illusion that he or she actually inhabits that world with the other actors onstage. Through rehearsals, a particular style comes to seem no less real than that of a realistic play from our own time. Every style requires a specific kind of physicalization, a specific attention to and use of language, as well as selectivity about what is important to occupants of the particular world of the play.

When doing a play set in Elizabethan England, for instance, an actor must learn to move based on the etiquette of that time. He or she must also know the reasons governing that etiquette in order to convert those conventional gestures into readable actions communicating the story. But once the actor is prepared to commit to the world of the play, non-realistic styles and the style known as realism are not as different as they first appear to be.

CHAPTER 17

Criticism

Not long ago I directed a production of *SubUrbia,* by Eric Bogosian. The play offers a harsh look at a group of directionless and amoral Generation Xers. The play's language is rough, its inhabitants unlikable, and its themes critical of both the characters themselves and the audience watching. At the very least, the play is potentially offensive. Race, gender, religion, art, morals, parenting, and even American society itself are all put under the playwright's microscope, and what he shows us is not pretty to watch or listen to. But when I read the play, I said to myself, "Now this is good theatre!"

I knew when I set out to direct this play that it would not be easy to mount a "successful" production. (For me, *a successful production is one that brings the script to life in such a way that the audience can see the remarkable things about the play that I saw when I read it.* In short a successful production must serve the script and satisfy the audience.) I knew this would be difficult. The characters of *SubUrbia* are not easy to like, so I asked myself how, directorially, I could get the audience to care about them. I decided that I would somehow have to reveal the characters' vulnerable interiors to the audience. I would have to get the audience inside the souls of these characters so they could see the wounded, sensitive, and basically good people those nasty exteriors hid. But I needed to do all this without giving up the mean-spirited edge that makes the play theatrically worthwhile. For the entire rehearsal period, I worked very hard to achieve these seemingly opposing ends. By opening night I was very proud of what my actors and I had been able to accomplish.

At the first scene change on opening night, there was a mass exodus of audience members, mostly the ones with gray hair. At the second scene change, many middle-agers followed suit, and when the lights began to dim after intermission, I even noticed some empty seats that had been occupied by student-aged audience members.

The ultimate reaction to our production of *SubUrbia* was mixed. Some people, including a critic for our major newspaper, thought it was the best production they had seen at my school in years. Many others wrote angry letters to the president of the university, my college dean, and the manager of our theatre, several strongly suggesting that I be fired. Others liked the production itself, but thought the play "garbage" and unworthy of being produced, particularly in a university setting. Personally, I felt that I had fallen short in one of my most important personal goals as the director. I had been unable to get the audience as a whole to identify with *SubUrbia*'s characters. This failure, I felt, ultimately prevented them from appreciating the play.

For at least a week after the production was over, I was able to cover an aching depression only because I had obligations to fulfill and because, as a supposedly mature adult, I have come to realize that life must go on. Though intellectually I knew I had done a fine job with the play—everyone, even those angered by the production, acknowledged the fine acting and directorial touches —emotionally I felt like a failure, and it hurt—badly. In short, I suffered over the way my play and, indirectly, I myself had been received.

In recent years I have not often felt the way I did after the production of *SubUrbia* closed, but those feelings were not at all unfamiliar from my earlier days as an acting student, and as a professional actor. The reemergence of those feelings, along with the observations I had made regarding audience and student reaction to *SubUrbia*, led me to the following important realization. No book on acting should be complete without a section on **criticism**, which, to my knowledge, few acting texts have. As my *SubUrbia* story suggests, criticism clearly plays an important role not only in understanding and appreciating theatre, but also in how a theatre artist functions, survives, and continues to grow artistically.

There are at least three areas of criticism that actors must learn to master. The first of the three I'll deal with here concerns the development of a strong critical eye for the work you experience as an audience member. The importance of being able to intelligently and objectively judge theatre, film, and other kinds of dramatic productions cannot be underestimated. In simplest terms, you must be able to analyze and evaluate the overall work you see as well as the specific ingredients that make up that work. The second area concerns the development of your ability to judge the studio work of your peers and to be able to articulate criticism of that work in a way that is supportive, specific, and useful—for your fellow students as well as yourself. Finally, the third and, perhaps, most important area of criticism I'll deal with in this chapter concerns the development of your ability to receive criticism in a positive and helpful manner. Only through the criticism you receive from others can true artistic growth occur. Those who are unable to receive criticism objectively will not only fail to grow as artists, but they will also end up as victims of the very criticism that was intended to foster growth.

Critiquing a Production

Being able to analyze and objectively evaluate the work you see others perform will ultimately help you analyze and make choices in your own work. As a student training in an art form, it is important for you to realize that there can be a difference between your personal taste (what you like) and what is good. Since it is your obligation as a critical artist to focus primarily on the question of "what is good," you must be able to put aside your personal tastes when making qualitative judgments. Here is an example of what I mean.

The other night I was catching up with a colleague when the conversation turned to favorite television shows. I reported that though I don't watch a lot of television, my favorite by far was the show *ER*. I supported my view by saying that the show had excellent production values along with the best acting, writing, and directing on the little screen. My colleague responded by saying he hated the show. When asked why, he declared that the show was too frenetic, that the action and pace made him nervous. The show was simply too upsetting to him.

Was my colleague's opinion of *ER* valid? Of course it was—in terms of his personal tastes. He is entitled to think and feel whatever he thinks and feels. But in terms of answering the question "Is *ER* good?", my friend failed completely. As a student of acting, *you have the responsibility to analyze and critique the work you read or see on the basis of what it is trying to do or say, not on whether you personally like the content.* Remember, in your professional life, you may have to work in many plays or films that you do not like personally, but, nonetheless, these projects may afford you the opportunity to do valid, worthwhile work; or they may simply help you pay the rent for the month. In either case, it will be your responsibility to get past any questions of personal taste so that you can analyze the material to make it work.

Going to plays or movies or watching any work you are not involved in can provide you with the opportunity to develop your skills in **analysis and synthesis,** if you go about it in the right way. As you have learned earlier in this book, your ability to make good choices that serve the script is as important as being believable when you deliver those choices onstage. There is no better way, other than working onstage yourself, to develop your ability to make the right choices than by watching the work of others. From the neutral position of the audience, you have the opportunity to observe, to weigh, and to evaluate what works and what doesn't, and you have the luxury of answering the question of why it does or does not in your own time. You can do so without the pressure of meeting performance obligations and without worrying about being judged yourself. In other words, you can hone your skills without having anything at stake.

And so, back to the question of what is "good." Obviously, all value judgments are somewhat subjective, but there has to be some kind of standard by which we make those judgments. When you refer to someone as a good person, for instance, you are bringing your personal definition to the evaluation. Does "good" mean kind, ethical, caring, generous, or some, or all of the above? Does "good" mean worthwhile, talented, smart, useful, or even boring? It depends on your definition subtextually, to use actor talk. So how does this apply to theatre and acting?

In order to evaluate the work we see onstage, it is useful to ask a series of questions. These questions were first posed by the German playwright and critic Goethe centuries ago, but the questions he invented to evaluate a piece of theatre are as valid today as they were then. The questions are:

- What was the work attempting to do?
- Did it succeed in its attempt?
- Was it worth the attempt?

What Was the Work Intending to Do?

Let's begin with the first question, keeping in mind that all theatre is meant to be watched by an audience. Since that is the case, the first question becomes "What was the work attempting to do in terms of the audience watching?" Was it simply trying to be entertaining? Entertaining and enlightening? Was it trying to make a particular statement, or put a new slant on the subject? What elements in the production led you to think about the work in the particular way you are approaching it? You will recall that these are the same questions that performers must ask themselves when trying to put together a performance (see Chapter 2). By asking these questions from the perspective of an audience member, you are in a position to make fairer judgments of the works you view, certainly fairer than those you would make by simply relying on your emotional responses. You also have a better perspective from which to analyze the work presented.

Before you make judgments about a production, however, you might also want to consider its source material. Suppose, for instance, that the play itself is bad. Would it be fair to evaluate a production of a weak play as bad simply because of its source material? There is no perfect answer here because any production has to be, at least in part, a reflection of the source material, but your ultimate evaluation must certainly take the source material into consideration.

If you decide that the source material itself is bad, however, you once again run the risk of making a judgment that is more facile than fair. Are you, perhaps, relying on pure emotion again? If so, you might need to ask yourself, "What was it trying to do?" of the scripted work as well. If you have not read the play or film script before you see the work produced, this can be a difficult evaluation to make. However, by going through the process of asking the questions, your evaluation will probably be much fairer than if you didn't ask the questions at all.

Let's see how this all works in practice. Suppose you went to see my production of *SubUrbia,* and it is now hours later. Before you start critiquing the work, you should first ask yourself, "Was I able to view the production as an impartial audience member?" Remember, theatre is done for a general audience, not for a house full of harshly critical acting students or a house full of friends and supporters who bend over backwards to like everything they see and hear. It is important that as a student of theatre you maintain a balance between these two, viewing a production with the same aesthetic distance that an ordinary member of an audience would. And an audience is made up of people willing to suspend their disbelief while being told a story that entertains them even while it comments on the humanness we all share.

So, while sitting over coffee hours later, perhaps with a friend, you are trying to determine whether or not you saw a good production. In this case "good" might be considered synonymous with "successful," since we don't really know whether the play itself is a good play. What you do know is that the evening disturbed and upset you. You know that, though uncomfortable, you simply cannot dismiss the production from your mind. You ask yourself, "What was the production trying to do?" You had not read the play before you went to see it, but there were three striking production elements that you suspect were not from the script. First of all, there were two dances in the production, one before the action of the play began, and another during a scene change. They stood out because, stylistically, the dances were in sharp contrast to the extremely realistic feel of the rest of the production. You ask yourself, "Why were those dances there and what purpose did they serve?" You decide that in both cases the dances provided a mechanism for the characters to reveal sides of their personalities not shown during the scripted part of the play—in every case a softer, more vulnerable side. Huh! Second, projections of song lyrics appeared on the convenience store sign every time music was inserted into the production. These lyrics paralleled the action of the play while suggesting the pain and vulnerability the characters might have been feeling, but did not express. Huh again! Finally, the way the lighting at the end of the play closed in on one of the central characters made eminently clear his self-disgust with his own attitudes and way of life. The combination of these three production choices lead you to believe that the production was trying to highlight the softer, more vulnerable sides of *SubUrbia*'s rather unlikable cast of characters. Ultimately, you decide the production was trying to show how a group of contemporary suburban kids have been affected by their upbringing, by their environment, and by the values prevalent in society today. And the picture painted is not a pretty one.

Did the Production Succeed in Its Attempt?

Now that you have addressed the question of what the production was trying to do, you are ready to ask yourself the second critical question: "Was the production successful in its attempt?" You decide over your second cup of coffee that in spite of the dances and the lyrics projected on the convenience store sign, the production failed in its attempt. The characters, in spite of some interesting production choices, were still repugnant to you and the themes of the play were overstated in the extreme. The production offered an unfair view of today's youth because there were no well-adjusted characters to balance the picture being presented. The characters were simply too nasty to care about. Furthermore, the dances and lyrics detracted from the production's main strength—its ability to create a totally believable reality onstage. So the answer to the question "Was it successful in its attempt?" is "No," or at the least, "Not completely."

Was the Production Worth the Effort?

The third question to ask yourself is "Was it worth the time, effort, and expense to mount this production in the first place?" Obviously, to those who walked out, it was not. But you, on the other hand, have already admitted that the production troubled you. You have been unable to get it out of your mind. You keep thinking about those nasty characters, about their desires, their frustrations, their attitudes; and you can't help but admit to yourself that there is a part of you that shares some of what they think and feel, or that you know people that do. Such thoughts and attitudes are seldom expressed aloud or directly, but you know they are there. This play puts those nasty thoughts and feelings out in the open. There's something good in that.

You might conclude, then, that the effort to put on a production of *SubUrbia* was worthwhile. Though, in your opinion, it could hardly be called entertaining, it was certainly well done. The acting and production values were first-rate. The pacing and direction were excellent. You certainly weren't bored, the biggest crime in theatre. In spite of the fact that at times you were shocked and even a bit repulsed, the play forced you to think about, evaluate, and reexamine many opinions and feelings that, before seeing this play, had remained unexplored. In short the production was enlightening in spite of its flaws.

This example demonstrates how objective critical thinking can provide you with a means of exercising the muscles you should use whenever you explore a script or watch the work of others in class. It is part of your responsibility as an actor to think through all the choices that contribute to the work you produce. You will get better at it only through practice. Viewing the work of others critically is an excellent way to do so.

In terms of your reaction to *SubUrbia,* however, there is one more critical task to engage in, one that will also lend itself to the development of your own analytic process as an actor. You should ask yourself, *"What could the production have done differently that would have improved its overall success?"* You could begin by focusing on the acting, first in terms of its believability, and then in terms of its storytelling journey and the way it served the overall script. You could examine the effectiveness of its dramatic progression, its making the big moments, and so forth. Once you have completed that task, you could explore the other aspects of the production by tackling Aristotle's six dramatic elements one at a time. By the time you finish, your intellectual acting muscles would be well exercised, and your opinion of the work you saw would certainly be a fair one.

EXERCISE 17-1

1. The words you use for critiquing purposes must have specific, consistent meanings. Define for yourself what you mean when you "like" something, when you "love" something, and when you think that something is "good." In the context of this discussion, articulate the differences.

2. List your ten favorite movies, books, and plays. Justify your choices and your ordering of them.

3. Pick five favorite plays. Arrange them from favorite to least favorite. Evaluate them in terms of why you "like" them. Now evaluate them in terms of why you think they are "good." Arrange them from best to worst. What are the differences between your two arrangements? Why has your opinion changed?

4. Select a recent movie that you really enjoyed. Read some reviews. Compare your response to the reviews.

5. Select three genre movies. Critique them according to Goethe's questions.

6. Read and critique a play. See a production of that play. Evaluate the production according to Goethe's questions.

Critiquing Work in Class

It is a fact that I am a smarter actor now than I was before I began teaching acting. I am not afraid to add that I believe that my "technique" as an actor is also much improved now that acting is a sideline rather than my principal focus. How is that possible, you might be wondering, especially since my acting skills, for the most part, are lying rusty and dormant? The answer is really quite simple. In the years since I began teaching acting, directing, and script analysis, I have had to learn two very important skills that before then I had not really taken seriously. First, I have had to learn to articulate my thoughts about the work far more specifically and clearly than I had to when I was an actor. Second, I have had to learn methods of quickly analyzing an acting situation, so that what I say is immediately helpful to the actors I am working with. What I might say to an actor in a play I'm directing is different, of course, from what I would say to a student I am teaching. In the former situation I am interested more in product (having the actor do it the way I want), in the latter more in process (allowing the actor to find a way to make something work). But in either case, it is essential that what I try to communicate be clear, specific, and directly to the point. And the point is always about how the choices the actor is making serve the story of the play. It is a bit ironic, then, that those same qualities—clarity, specificity, and directness—are the qualities most important to a performing actor, yet until I had to teach the stuff myself, I paid more lip service than actual homage to this fact.

I guess that what I am admitting here is the fact that, as an actor and as an acting student, I too often settled on a generalized definition of what I thought I was doing at any given moment onstage. Like many of you, perhaps, I was willing to make a fuzzy choice and go with it. When pressed by some teacher to be more specific, or to articulate what it was I thought I was doing, I tried to accommodate the teacher more to stay out of trouble than because I truly believed that an articulated specificity would improve my acting. Yet, now, all these years later, I am here to tell you it wasn't just some silly semantic game. Good acting, as I hope you have learned by now, consists of a series of well-thought-out and executed choices. These choices are made, not on the basis of how you feel in any given moment of inspiration, but on how they communicate the story of the play, the scene, the beat, and the moment. Learning to make these well-thought-out and executed choices does not happen by magic. It happens through hard work and practice.

In an earlier chapter, I pointed out that an audience is invariably smarter than the actors onstage for several reasons, including the audience's ability to watch the story objectively and to listen. Students watching their peers work in an acting class possess the same qualities as an audience. Yet, too often, class members watching the work of others become passive or ignore altogether the work being presented. This is a tremendous waste of classroom time if you think about it. Probably at best, your own presented work takes up about one-eighth of the total time you spend in class. That means seven-eighths of your time goes down the drain—if you are not observing, analyzing, and synthesizing the work that others put up. Even if you are initially unfamiliar with the presented work, you are in a position to ask yourself all the basic questions that an audience might ask and that the actors onstage need to be answering through their choices.

Putting yourself in the audience's position allows you the same neutral view that you should bring to your first reading of a script. You cannot decide what your own character should be doing in a scene until you understand what is going on in the scene overall. Too often actors forget that fact. By watching others try to solve the problems of a scene, you can develop your own ability to see how all parts of the script must be integrated to make the story work. Through concentrated studio observation, you can figure out what necessary storytelling questions the actors on the stage have not addressed, or you can see how the choices they have made serve to tell the story clearly, specifically, and dynamically. It all boils down to watching actively, so that you can build intellectually on the basic architecture of the script. This skill is the same one necessary when you actively read a script while preparing your own work. Watching the work of others and reading a script yourself can reinforce each other very nicely.

The *test* of your mastery of watching actively, however, is in your ability to articulate your observations and analysis clearly and effectively out loud. If you are in a class where your teacher allows you to make comments about the work you see (and many teachers do not, or do so very sparingly), to some extent your teacher is taking a risk. He or she is taking a chance that comments you offer will not confuse the actors working because they seem to contradict other comments being offered. But your teacher allows such comments because he or she also recognizes the importance of your being able to articulate what you observe. Only when you can do so clearly and effectively, will those skills translate into your own work. You, therefore, have a tremendous responsibility to make comments that are clear, to the point, and helpful.

You must remember, however, that when others are working, they must be the principal focus of the teacher and class. Therefore, your comments should not be self-serving. They should not be about how smart you are, they should not be about what choices you would rather see, they should not be about what the working actors should do better. The critiquing you offer should reflect what was not clear to you and why, where you feel the story could be better told and why, but never should you offer solutions to the problems you see. That would be directing, and offering a solution seldom helps an actor find his or her own solution the next time.

A director is interested in product. He or she wants to solve the problems of the script quickly and efficiently. If possible, then, a director will provide an actor with solutions. Acting teachers, on the other hand, want their actors to learn how to solve problems and find solutions on their own. They will not give solutions unless they absolutely need to. They try instead to critique the work in such a way that their actors develop the necessary skills for finding those solutions. That should be your purpose when offering your comments in class as well. Through your own observation and analysis, you should be developing those skills, so be sure to allow others to develop them too. You can do so by shaping your comments in such a way that the solutions to the increasingly sophisticated questions you raise remain for the working actors to find. Further, if you can articulate some connection between difficulties you have in your own work and the work you are responding to, you are likely to soften any critical comment you make to others. Always try to connect with some empathy, so that the essence of your comment can get through to your fellow actor.

EXERCISE 17-2

1. Monitor and write down at least twenty comments made in class over the course of a few sessions. When you have collected them, analyze and evaluate them in terms of the criteria mentioned in this section of the chapter.

2. Separate your list into directorial comments and solid critical comments. Justify and explain your arrangement.

3. Which of the comments made were self-serving in your opinion? Why?

4. Critique in writing a scene you saw in class. Be specific and justify your comments. Repeat the exercise making directorial commentary. Compare the two critiques. Draw conclusions.

Receiving Criticism Effectively

I wonder if the story of my reaction to the criticism of *SubUrbia* rang any bells with you? If it did, then you should pay very close attention to this section. If you are like me, and sometimes respond too personally to criticism of your work, then it's time to start making a change. Learning to take criticism in a positive way is as important to your development as an actor as learning the craft, perhaps even more so. I have known people in the business who have never come close to mastering their craft; nevertheless, they have managed to earn a living as actors for their entire careers. Yet I don't think I have known any actors who were unable to take criticism who stayed in the business for the long haul. They just found it too painful.

At the beginning of almost every school year, at least one new student from one of my acting classes will nervously ask to see me privately in my office. When we are alone, that student will either angrily accuse me of being the meanest, cruelest acting teacher in the world, or break into a heap of sobs and tears because the student has suddenly realized that he or she had been deceived by acting teachers in high school. "You," they tell me, "honestly and fairly *shred* my work apart, while those former high school teachers shamefully misled me into thinking I had talent."

The truth, of course, is that I am neither the meanest, cruelest acting teacher in the universe, nor am I interested in exposing the talentless and talent-challenged to the world. As a matter of fact, if anything, I am a supportive, positive-oriented acting teacher who believes that almost anyone can learn to act reasonably well—if the person is available and receptive to the criticism that will let him or her grow as an actor. Further, I am happy to work with anyone who is willing to work hard to improve his or her craft. So how in the world do students at the beginning of every school year perceive me to be some evil ogre out to destroy both their confidence and their artistic futures?

The answer is simple really. Many of my students are unused to hearing criticism. In their high schools they may have been the stars of their drama classes and their high school productions. They were probably continually praised for their talent and for their performance charisma, and, compared to many of their peers, they no doubt seemed the embodiment of theatrical perfection. Their directors were probably happy to focus their energies on the scores of major problems plaguing their productions elsewhere. And now, suddenly, perhaps for the first time, these former stars are being told that not everything they do is flaw-less. For many students, this sudden turnaround can be shocking, and even painful.

It is unfortunate in some ways that actors are synonymous with the instru-ments they play, but it is, nonetheless, a fact of their existence. It is the actor who is out of tune, not his violin; it is the actor, not her painting, who demon-strates no sense of color or perspective. For the actor, there are no places to hide, no scapegoats to blame, no rationalizations to make. When the actor's work is faulted, it is the actor who must absorb the criticism directly. That is not always easy. But it is absolutely necessary.

As artists we learn only through our mistakes. What have you ever learned when your teacher simply told you that your work was great? Did the praise help you get better the next time? Did it give you a new perspective, a new tool to use, a new color to add to your acting palette? The truth is that compliments may make you feel good, but they offer up nothing useful in terms of your craft. Only constructive criticism does. Therefore, you must learn to take it. You need to be able to listen to criticism objectively, remember its essence until you have a chance to fix what is not working, and ultimately translate the criticism into ac-tive things you can do to improve the work you put up before. You will only be able to do all this if your attention is on the criticism, not on how you feel about the criticism at the time it is given. Learn not to respond to or defend yourself from the comments you are hearing. Learn to simply listen. Your only obligation is to try the comment on and see if it fits.

As an acting teacher, I focus primarily on what is not happening that should be happening in the work presented. That is my job. However, because of my own sensitivity, and the memory of what criticism felt like to me when I first heard it as an acting student, I am always careful to start my critiques with a pos-itive overview of what I saw. I might note the improvement over the previous presentation of the material, I might praise particular moments that worked well, or I might comment on the growth I am seeing in a particular student's work in general. But the bulk of my comments focus on what is not working rather than on what is, and when my general comments are over, I will work with the actors to help them find their way for the next time.

When students are unable to handle criticism, however, they are not avail-able for receiving this new information, nor are they prepared to work with their teacher and scene partner. Their focus is on their own emotions. Because they are defensive, they process every comment in terms of what it says about how good or bad they are, not in terms of what objective information is being offered. They are busy evaluating where they stand in the pecking order of the class now that they have been perceived as imperfect, or they are busy trying to figure out what the teacher and class may be thinking about their talent or their ability as students. All of this is a waste of time and energy, of course, and is probably very destructive as well. A student's misdirected focus invariably leads to a failure to understand the notes clearly, or to remember them accurately later when they are needed to rework the scene. In addition, the emotional residue of all this psychic effort usually leads to an inability to work the scene after the notes are given. Students who have been busy judging themselves, rather than listening objectively, have probably become too inhibited to work moment to moment and are likely to be unable to listen and react to their scene partners—because they are still living inside their own heads. In short, out of eight cylinders, such students are running very bumpily on one.

All of this is terribly sad and ironic, since a good teacher's focus is invariably on the work itself, not on any evaluation of the individuals doing the work. A good teacher respects the classroom or studio as a laboratory where mistakes can and should be made. That teacher knows that students must have the freedom to try and fail in a climate that is supportive and fertile. Any evaluative process is long term, ongoing, and separate from the work in the classroom. In short, good teachers put their energies into helping students grow, not into evaluating how good a particular student is at a particular moment in his or her development.

So, if you can identify with some of the characteristics of the defensive actor I've described here, know that those characteristics can stand in the way of your development. It is up to you to take responsibility for them and train yourself to compartmentalize them when you are working. And you *can* train yourself to do so, if you approach the problem as though it is a part of the craft you need to master. If, like me, you are a bit thin-skinned and sensitive, you can develop the ability to intellectualize the feedback you get. You can learn to recircuit your emotional system so that when you are working you are available and in the moment. You *will* be able to do so—*if* you accept the fact that it is *necessary* for you to do so. That is the key.

EXERCISE 17-3

1. Observe and draw conclusions about a student in your class during the time he or she is being critiqued by your teacher on the work just performed. Include in your analysis body language, verbal responses, and any other relevant factors.

2. Take specific notes at the time your work is being critiqued. Look at them later in the day. Do you still know specifically what each note means? Do the notes seem helpful? More or less so than when you heard them during the day? Account for the difference. If they no longer seem useful or clear, account for their loss of meaning. Explain the notes in relation to the work you performed. Be specific. What adjustments will you make in the next round of rehearsals to improve the work?

3. Think about how you were feeling during your critique. Write about how you felt and what you did physically. Draw conclusions.

4. Tape record the notes you are given. Listen to them only after a day or more has passed. Compare what you heard to what you thought you heard at the time. Draw conclusions.

5. Monitor how you felt after your scene presentation. How long did the feeling last? How did the notes affect your ego, your mood, your ability to continue normally through life? Draw conclusions.

6. Monitor how you react to positive and negative criticism. Which affects you more? Explain and draw conclusions.

7. Compare your reaction to criticism of your acting work with the way you react to criticism in other areas. Draw conclusions.

Your ability to accept and use criticism effectively, whether natural or learned, is closely related to your ability to accept rejection. Even the most talented and successful actors in the business must learn to withstand a mountainful of both. All you need to do is read a review from a sharp-tongued New York theatre critic like John Simon of *New York* magazine to know exactly what I mean. No one in show business is immune to rejection and criticism that is harsh and sometimes even cruel. Remember when Andrew Lloyd Webber fired Patty Lupone and replaced her with Glenn Close for the New York production of *Sunset Boulevard?* In the scheme of things, a little constructive criticism in the classroom is small potatoes indeed. Right?

Summary

Every actor must learn to use and deal with criticism. Viewing theatre from the perspective of an audience can help actors develop their sense of what is good and what is not as well as their technique for analysis and synthesis. In the classroom or studio, learning how to watch the work of others actively is an important skill to develop as well. Possessing an eye for what works, what doesn't work, and why is a skill that invariably helps actors to make better choices in their own acting. Finally, learning to accept and effectively translate the criticism they are offered helps actors quickly improve their current work as well as their ability to consistently produce good work on their own. Most importantly, it will serve to improve their staying power in the business.

CHAPTER 18

Auditioning

Most actors hate to **audition**. After all, they are being examined, evaluated, and all too often, rejected. Even after years of experience, most actors continue to find the audition process one of the most unpleasant parts of the acting business. But, hate auditioning or love it, learning *how* to audition is among the most important skills an actor needs to master. Do it right, it gets you work; do it badly, and you have to do it again as the price you pay for not getting the last job. Ironically, the more work you get, the more you'll also have to audition, because getting an acting job opens the door to more acting opportunities for which you'll still have to prove yourself—by auditioning. The bottom line is, whether you like it or not, it is essential that you learn to audition well.

Casting

An old cliché says "Casting the play well is 80 percent of the director's job," and as with most clichés, there is a lot of truth there. A director who casts a play well will be able to use the time available more efficiently to realize his or her directorial vision. Having cast a play badly, the director will spend too much time fixing problems that better casting might have bypassed altogether. *Any director will be looking to cast the actors that can best perform their roles believably and tell the story of the play in the clearest, most exciting way possible.*

The term "believable" has two important meanings to a director. First, he or she wants the audience watching the production to believe the moment-to-moment acting work of those who were cast. Second, the director wants the audience to believe the actors as the characters they are playing. These two concepts are not the same thing. How often in reviews have you read or heard the phrase "The actor was miscast in his role . . ."? For instance, Danny DeVito is a fine character actor, but what if he had been cast as Batman instead of the

Penguin in the film version of the comic book? What about Dustin Hoffman, one of our finest film actors? Had he been cast as Batman, you would probably have spent all your time in the audience thinking that Dustin Hoffman is no Batman, rather than suspending your disbelief.

EXERCISE 18-1

1. What films can you think of that were adversely affected by miscasting? Explain.

2. What films can you think of that were made better than they might have been because of casting? Explain.

3. Cast a play you have read with well-known actors. Support your casting choices.

4. Improve a film or play you have seen by recasting it. Support your choices.

5. Cite examples of bad pairing in films you have seen. Explain.

Directors want to cast actors who, by their very presence, suggest the characters being portrayed, because when they do so, they have already made great strides toward solving the directing problems they face. However, it is obviously not quite as simple as that. It is possible that the actor who seems most physically right for the role can't act, or can't act as well as another actor who isn't quite as right for the role. This dilemma is always a challenge for directors, and there is no simple solution to making the best decision. However, makeup, costume, and a lot of work can help a good actor satisfy the specific demands of a role, but no amount of help will compensate for the bad work of a hopeless actor. On the other hand, Danny DeVito and Dustin Hoffman will never cut it, no matter how well their Batsuits are made to fit them.

"What does all this mean to you as an actor?" you're probably asking.

What it means is this: As an actor, your most important consideration during the audition process should be about how to get cast—in a good role if possible, maybe even in the role you most desire. But you should avoid auditioning for a role for which you would not be considered. That would be like betting on the horse with one leg. If acting is going to be your job, keep in mind that learning how to get work and actually getting it are vitally important parts of the job. You should always focus on getting the roles you are capable of getting. This, in turn, means that before you audition for a role in a play, you should know the roles you are best suited for.

Of course it is true that if you are a really good actor, then you should be able to use your craft and talent to succeed with any role in which you are cast, but the reality is that you are not likely to be given that chance. So make choices that are designed to get you the work. By all means, use your studio and class time to stretch, to explore, and to develop your range, but when it comes time to get a job, work on your ability to do so. Do everything necessary to get the work.

You'll learn more from the work experience itself, if your audition gets it for you, than from almost anything else you can do as an actor. So why risk not being cast at all by going for an inappropriate role?

The way to know which roles in a particular play are right for you comes primarily from two sources:

1. From an understanding of the script in terms of both action and character; and

2. From an understanding of who you are and (more importantly) how you are perceived by those around you.

Both of these issues will be covered in detail in the following three chapters. But, for now, understand that the director of any play you'll be auditioning for already has ideas about the characters in the play—regarding both their *internal* and *external* makeup. Therefore, knowing how you appear to the world on first impression and how that appearance relates to the characters in a play is essential. But equally essential is your ability to convey the internals of the characters you are most right for. First, you must recognize what those internals are, and second, you must translate them into **tangible** external actions that those casting you can see.

Here's an example. Suppose you are Danny DeVito auditioning for a production of *The Taming of the Shrew*. You might decide as a result of your script analysis that Petrucchio is strong and domineering. You can do strong and domineering. However, your research tells you that traditionally Petrucchio is played by someone physically imposing—someone, perhaps, who is handsome, tall, and muscular. That, of course, is a valid choice. But *Shrew* is a comedy, and you know that in this particular production the director is going for broad humor. Your shortness might normally put you out of the running, but in this case, the director must choose between you and Arnold Schwarzenegger. Arnold would certainly use his stature to good effect. But you know that comedy is your strong suit, and you know that a strong, domineering, but very short Petrucchio would make a funny visual contrast played against a taller Kate. And Arnie's ability with comedy, not to mention language, is not so strong as yours. Who would be the better choice? Obviously the director can see the possibilities in each, so how will he or she decide between you? Ultimately, by the audition each of you gives, of course. You have made a solid decision in this case to try out for the lead because you understand both the script and the intent of the production. You also know how your appearance will strike an audience, and you use that knowledge to good effect. Now what do you do?

EXERCISE 18-2

1. Cast yourself in a play the class has recently read. Justify your choice. Cast other class members in the other roles. Justify your choices.

2. Recast a recent film you have seen using the members of your class. Justify your choices. Be sure to be consistent with the style of the movie.

3. Based on type and personality, recast a TV show with members of your class.

4. Select four popular television shows and assign a role to each member of your class. You may, if necessary, place more than one person in a role. Compare your answers with those of the other members of your class.

Auditioning with a Scene

When casting a play, most directors rely on scene readings, either at a first audition or during the callback process. At an audition in which you will be reading from a scene, you will likely be given sides (small sections of script) to read with a partner or in small groupings. You will usually be given time beforehand to familiarize yourself with the material. Before preparing for your reading, be sure to ask the director any questions about the script not provided. You may get very helpful information. At worst, you will be told not to be a bother. But it is to the director's advantage to see you at your best, armed with useful information, so don't be afraid to ask.

If your audition is scheduled for a particular time, be sure to get there early. Use the extra time to prepare after you have gotten your sides. Don't audition before your assigned time, unless you are fully ready to do so. If the play is one that is available, you should have read it in its entirety and done all the basic analytical work before you showed up for your audition. Your analysis with the sides should focus on the scene itself, but you will be able to use what you know about the rest of the play to guide you in the choices you make.

Sometimes you will be partnered up in advance of your audition. If that is the case, be sure to use the time with your partner to agree on the basics of the scene and to actually read together. If you do not have a chance to read with a partner before the audition, then spend your time making specific choices for the scene and for the words you will be saying. If you audition having already made some decisions about the scene, you will be letting the director see that you are able to make valid choices on your own. Remember, the more actors can do for themselves, the more time the director has to spend on other problems. Although you don't need to memorize the scene beforehand (remember, it is a reading), you should be as familiar with the text as you can be so that you can focus on your partner rather than the script during your audition. Make sure you are well acquainted with the words of the scene so the director won't mistake your bad reading for bad acting.

At some auditions, you will be asked what role you would like to read for. If that is the case, then ask to read for the roles right for you or the roles you think you could be cast in using the criteria identified earlier. At other auditions, you will be asked to read for a specific part. Try to anticipate how your auditors will perceive you, so you can go into the audition as prepared as possible. Anticipate well, and you will have already made some preliminary choices before you even get there. If, on the other hand, you are asked to read for a specific part or parts at the time you get your sides, try to figure out why. Obviously, there is something about you that those auditioning you are seeing. If you know what that is, you will be better able to play on that information to sell what it is you have. Never try to "act the character." It is far better to use yourself fully. Trying to play the character will only distance you from the work. Instead, make the choices your character would make, and use yourself completely to execute those choices.

Most of the time you will be reading with a single partner. This allows the director to see how well you act and react from moment to moment. It is critically important that you do so. In return, working with a single partner allows you to keep your focus simple and direct. If you stay connected with your partner and listen carefully, you will be able to find and make the moments any director wants to see. Every victory, defeat, discovery, and change of tactic you can go through is money in the bank at an audition, especially if you do them well.

Learning how to keep as much eye contact with your reading partner as much as possible was discussed in Chapter 13. When you have to audition with a reading, you'll be glad you have already developed your ability to work in this fashion. Remember, in a reading it is not necessary to do everything in real time. It is better to look at your script, take in as much of your dialogue as you can remember, and then deliver it to your partner while looking at him or her. Then, by staying focused on your partner, you will be able to react to what he or she does and says back to you. Do not return to your script until you need to go back for the next words you say. Working in this fashion, you are more likely to be listening well and reacting at every moment—two characteristics that are sure to impress your auditors. Don't worry if it takes a moment to find your place. Your auditors will suspend their disbelief.

If you have already made some good choices before your audition, chances are that most of what you do during your reading will be specific, clear, and exciting. If you have been diligent, and if you are right for a particular role or roles, then you have done all that you can do. Your chances for getting the role will have been seriously improved by your proper preparation and execution.

EXERCISE 18-3

1. Read *Rules of Love* (found in the back of this text). Select one of the characters and prepare for an audition. Discuss your choices in class.

2. Read a section of *Rules of Love* in class with a partner as though it were an audition situation. Focus on the actions you are playing. Do not worry about "playing the character." Discuss the results in class.

3. Select a character from a play previously assigned in class. Be sure that the character is one you'd be right for. Prepare a scene from the play to read with a partner. Present the scene to the class as though it were an audition situation. Get feedback and discuss the results.

Cold Readings

Occasionally, you will have to audition without having had time to prepare by reading the play—a last-minute call, perhaps, or a new play that is not available for advance reading. This is called a **cold reading.** Under these circumstances, the director will not expect you to have made choices in the scenes that are connected to the bigger picture of the play. But the director will still expect to see a reading that is clear, believable, and exciting. As with all good acting, that will probably happen only if you properly prepare, and it is possible to be well prepared—even when you have only the sides to work with.

The best complete source for learning about how to audition remains Michael Shurtleff's wonderful book titled *Audition.* In it you will find a galaxy of suggestions for approaching material in an audition situation. Ironically, many of his suggestions—the result of studying countless auditions over a long career as a casting agent and teacher—reflect the same basic principals explained here. They are the basics that apply to all scene work. They will serve you beautifully at an audition as well—if you know which tools to use, and how to use them.

Here is a checklist that you can use in getting ready for any audition, cold or prepared. You will notice that the essentials remain the basic tools we have explored from the beginning of this book.

1. *Figure out the story.* Develop a way to play through the scene in terms of its beginning, its middle, and its end. Invent a throughline of action to play.

2. *Find and play the conflict.* Find the basic engine that propels the scene, and from that information choose positive objectives to play. If you draw a blank, remember the six basic objectives:
   - To give information
   - To get information
   - To make someone do something
   - To keep someone from doing something
   - To make someone feel good
   - To make someone feel bad

Find as many ways as possible to get your objective from the other actor. Try actively to make your partner give you what you need.

3. *Determine your relationship with the other character.* What are the given circumstances of your relationship? How do these circumstances translate into actions you can play?

4. *Make the stakes as high as you can make them*—life and death if possible.

5. *Remember what happened the moment before* and use it to bring something to the scene.

6. *Play all discoveries, victories, defeats, and new information.*

7. *Find ways to use the setting actively in your reading.*

8. *Listen.* Respond to what is given, whether you agree with it or not, and react to it.

In addition, Michael Shurtleff instructs his readers to use the following three tools at an audition. They are wonderful suggestions, so I will add them to the list.

9. *Think in terms of competition.* In order to make your work exciting, think in terms of "I am right, you are wrong" while playing with your scene partner. It will help you keep the conflict strong. Do what you can to make your partner know he or she is wrong and to change.

10. *Use opposites.* If you can find logical, believable ways of going from one extreme to another, you can't help but be exciting to watch.

11. *Use humor and love.* People in real life have a sense of humor and use that sense of humor to get what they need. Too often actors as characters don't. You should, because actors who use humor are not only fun to watch, they are also appealing—to directors and to audiences. The same is true for "love." Actors like to be angry, but whenever possible, try instead to play the love you feel for your partner. The results can have a surprisingly positive effect on you, your partner, and on those watching you work.

Finally, one more thing before concluding this section. Always remember that how you come off as a person is an extremely important element in the audition process. There are many fine actors. If a director has a choice between working with someone who seems difficult or unpleasant and someone who is not, who will be chosen? During the entire audition process, you must remain flexible, nondefensive, and open to suggestions, and, most importantly, you must look like you are having fun. Keep in mind that the more fun you are actually having, the easier it will be to convey that impression. In time auditioning may actually become fun if it isn't right now, but with practice, it will certainly become easier. In the meantime, use your acting skills to make it seem as though it already is fun.

EXERCISE 18-4

1. Read some very brief plays with your class. There are many wonderful collections available. Have your teacher give you a limited amount of time to prepare and then read a scene with a partner. Get feedback.

2. Do an improvisation with a partner in which you are interviewed by a director or casting agent. Be yourself, but know that your objective is to make a good impression. Get feedback from your class.

Auditioning with a Monologue

Auditioning with a **monologue** is a standard part of the actor's life, and whether you are a professional actor or a novice, sooner or later you're going to need to prepare one. Monologues are standard procedure for many general auditions and first-round auditions for a season in regional theatre. Most professional actors have mastered a variety of monologues so that they are never caught unprepared when that audition suddenly appears on the scene. They have learned that the more prepared they are, the less nerve-racking the time spent before the audition will be. They are also sure to have a diversity of material prepared—comedy and drama, classical and contemporary—so that what they show at an audition is exactly what the auditor needs to see.

EXERCISE 18-5

Begin a collection of potential one- to two-minute monologues that seem right for you. Include selections from the following areas: contemporary, classical, comedy, and drama.

Auditioning with a monologue is very different from other forms of acting. First of all, its purpose is different. Unlike your responsibility when acting in a production, *your responsibility when performing a monologue is to serve yourself, not the play.* There is no play; there is only your one to two minutes onstage. You've got only that amount of time to make it the best show the auditors will see. And you will best do that by making your acting absolutely compelling as well as believable. In the minute or two of stage time allowed to you, you must convince your auditors of the following:

• That you are exciting, versatile, intelligent, charming, and easy to work with

• That you know how, when, and where to move

- That you know where the dramatic moments are
- That you can make the dramatic moments happen clearly and convincingly for an audience

In other words you need to show them that you can act and convince them that they'll like working with you as well. No small accomplishment in a minute or two, right?

The acting you do for a monologue audition is different from other acting in another very important way—a way that makes the acting task very difficult. Most acting situations involve two actors dealing with each other. In most cases, the **fourth wall** (the imaginary line that keeps the audience separate from the action on stage) is not broken. This separation allows actors to concentrate and to focus on an imagined reality far away from judging eyes in the audience. Each actor reacts to what the other feeds him or her, fueling the actor's own next line or moment. It is through this interplay that the most interesting dramatic things happen.

In the monologue audition, however, the actor has no one with whom to react. He or she may have to deal directly with an audience of hostile, judging eyes or pretend to talk to someone who isn't really there. To be successful, such an auditioner must compensate for that other missing actor and find ways to ignore his or her acting enemy, the auditors. Doing this successfully often determines the difference between a good and bad presentation.

The monologue audition, however, really begins long before you get to deliver your well-prepared speech. Proper selection and preparation of your work are equally important components to a successful process. It is absolutely essential that the material you select will allow you to demonstrate to the auditor that you can do what they need you to do. It is up to you to select material that possesses that potential. Then it is up to you to make choices in your preparation and rehearsal that bring out that potential. Finally, it is up to you to make sure that you can deliver when called upon to audition.

Finding a Monologue

Many acting teachers and books covering the subject of auditioning emphasize the need for actors to find material that is appropriate for their age and personality. That is, you should find material that is close to you, that is like you, that allows you to use the you that you are. All too often, however, student actors take that to mean that they must find material that is not only age appropriate, but so close to them that it jumps off the page screaming, "This is you, idiot! Use me!" For most young actors this monologue does not exist. Hours and hours of a student's time end up getting spent searching for the "perfect fit" monologue that may not actually be out there. What the suggestion really means is that you should find material that you can identify with and understand—material that will make sense to you, but also to the auditor when you deliver it. Your choice of material shouldn't have the auditor distractedly thinking, "Why is that actor doing that material?"

It is far more difficult, for instance, for the young actor to successfully deliver one of Blanche Dubois's speeches from *A Streetcar Named Desire* than a speech from, say, Timothy Mason's *Ascension Day*. In order to handle Blanche Dubois, the actor must understand the troubled psyche of a middle-aged, neurotic Southern woman who is out of place and time even fifty years ago when the play was set. Further, the role is so well known that the young actor's work can't help but be compared to other, more familiar interpretations by fine actors who are appropriate in age. For a nineteen-year-old to play a famous, poetic, middle-aged character that she might find difficult to understand and identify with is simply not a good bet.

On the other hand, a monologue from *Ascension Day*, a play about teenagers trying to discover the meaning of life and how to find their place in a confusing world, is probably a much wiser choice. Although the play takes place in roughly the same time period as *Streetcar*, the issues its central characters face are issues that today's young adults are still familiar with, issues that will have resonance for the young actor and can be communicated strongly and clearly to the watching auditors. The character you select to interpret may not *be* you, but the issues he or she speaks of will probably be issues not unfamiliar to you. You will be able to color and interpret the character's words and thoughts because you can understand what they mean and where they are coming from. Besides, your auditors will probably not know by heart the piece you select from *Ascension Day*. If you choose to do *Streetcar*, they just might!

EXERCISE 18-6

1. Reexamine the list of monologues you have begun to collect. Which of the characters do you best connect with? Why? Be specific. Draw parallels in writing between the character and yourself. Continue to add to your list and test the fit.

2. Start a new list that includes only the best-fit monologues from your first list. Continue to build your list. Before long, you will have your own specific source of material to draw from.

An equally important question to ask yourself while searching for material is "Does this material have a throughline?" In other words, does this piece tell a story, or can you make choices with this material that will give you a throughline to play? Your two minutes onstage, like any good theatrical performance, must take the audience on a journey. You cannot be at the same place emotionally or objectively when you finish your piece as you were when you began it, or it will simply be boring. Remember, acting is about doing, not being.

If, at an audition, for instance, you come out and cry at the beginning, the auditor may be impressed by your emotional availability. But once you have established that you can cry, what then? We've seen it. What are you going to do now? Keep in mind that actors must interpret the story going on through their selected actions. If there is no throughline in the piece, or none that you recognize, find some other material. A monologue that has a beginning, a middle, and an end will provide you with a strong reason to be telling the story and give you several solid moments to demonstrate to the auditor that you can act. If the piece goes somewhere, so can you. A couple of well-acted transitional moments will go a long way toward giving the auditors what they need to see.

A word of warning. Character pieces, where an actor demonstrates a character type, are very dangerous for a general audition. Suppose, for instance, that you have selected a piece about a loser in which you perform a few funny comic bits that cleverly demonstrate your geekiness. Either the selected piece has no storyline, or you have chosen to focus so heavily on the bits that any potential story is left undeveloped. The piece may be cute or funny, and you may perform the required geeky bits humorously, but the piece does not allow you to demonstrate that you can act. In fact, the auditor may not be certain whether you are acting or if you really are a loser saying the words of the monologue. When casting a play, I can get a good actor to act geeky. It is more difficult to get the loser to act like he or she is not. This kind of audition choice suggests limitation more than it suggests range. Not a good idea.

Many student actors think that they must find material that is unfamiliar to the auditors, or they will be at a great disadvantage. They think that if auditors have heard their piece before, the likelihood of their falling asleep during the audition is greatly strengthened. Students end up spending a great deal of time searching for that undiscovered gem, and often ignore pieces that would fit them perfectly. The irony is that most student actors use the same set of audition books available at your local bookstore. The likelihood of finding virgin material is nonexistent when almost everybody is using the same source material. It is always good to use fresh material, but it is more important to do the material well, whatever it is.

In some audition situations, it is not unusual for me to see well over a hundred auditions in a day. In that time I might see a particular piece three or four times. Audition monologues go in and out of fashion just as show tunes do. They get overused and disappear only to be discovered again after an appropriate exile. But a repeated piece never seems quite the same because of the difference in the skill level of the actors and the acting choices they make. There is no negative bias on my part seeing a piece several times unless, of course, the piece is done badly. When it is, I quickly forget both it and the actor; when it is done well, it makes me appreciate the actor doing it all the more. It is the actor's job to make sure he or she is the one who does it extremely well.

EXERCISE 18-7

Return to your best-fit list of monologues. Read one monologue carefully, looking to find the story contained within it. Write down a summary of the story you find there. Then rewrite the story in more detail, focusing on what happens (the events the monologue contains). Be sure to focus on the monologue in terms of its action.

Do not think in terms of how the character is feeling. Reread your summary. If you do not hear a story, attempt the exercise again. Is there now a throughline? Has your character made a journey? Describe the journey.

Preparing the Monologue

Before you start putting your monologue on its feet, it is important that you do the actor brain work it requires. Remind yourself that your purpose is to demonstrate your excellent acting ability. Since good acting is acting that is believable and tells the best possible story, you need to make the stakes as high as possible in your monologue. That means you need to create as much conflict as you can and give yourself the longest, clearest, most exciting throughline to play. Plan out the journey you will take us on.

You also need to keep in mind that the dialogue you use in your audition is only one tool for telling the story. What you do physically in your one to two minutes can be as compelling as what you say. Your silences, changes of focus, and transitions can speak as loudly as the words you use. The physical choices you make can reveal your inner struggle as clearly as any verbal description. Besides, auditors want to see how you move, behave physically, gesture, and do business. Physicalization is a major component of the acting work you will be called upon to do in a stage performance. Sitting and talking for an entire monologue is a bad choice. So is failing to act the nonverbal moments that cause the dialogue to be spoken.

Never forget that a good story always starts with conflict. When you deliver a monologue, you are either thinking aloud or speaking to another character. If you are talking to yourself, then your conflict is internal. You are struggling to find some kind of solution or answer to a problem. You must search for and discover that answer or fail to do so during your monologue. That will provide you with your throughline. Your success or failure to do so by the end of your allotted time onstage will mark the ending of the story. You will need to make choices that clearly point out the important dramatic events during your journey. If you are talking to yourself, these dramatic events often consist of psychological obstacles that arise for your character. As they pop into your head, you must deal with them and overcome them. They are all dramatically important, so don't ice skate through them. You must engage in a struggle if your throughline is to be exciting.

If you are speaking to another character (and this is the case in most contemporary monologues), then the conflict is somehow between the two of you. Before you proceed any further in your work, you must identify the problem between the two of you and your purpose for speaking about it now. Only if you recognize what this conflict is, will you be able to make choices that help you overcome it. Only then will you be able to compellingly choose and play an objective. In a two-minute monologue, your need should be tremendous, and, in spite of the fact that you are alone onstage, your imaginary scene partner's resistance to your objective must be made apparent to the audience by the reactive choices you make. The more your imaginary partner resists, the greater the conflict, the better the story.

In other words, you must make choices for your imaginary scene partner as well as for yourself. You must decide who the character is and how he or she is reacting at every moment, and you must react to the other character. Then you must select and rehearse physical choices that let the audience know what you are seeing, hearing, and reacting to. You will be able to do that successfully only if you are absolutely specific. It might help you to rehearse your monologue with a real partner. You can then incorporate some of your partner's choices later when you are working alone. If you are able to turn your monologue into a dialogue, your work will be clear and alive moment to moment, specifically and believably.

A word of caution. It is sometimes necessary to cut a piece in order to make it fit specific time restrictions. Be very careful about cutting internally—that is cutting a line here and there. A well-written monologue by a skilled playwright has little fat. Most of it is essential. I have seen many student actors complain that they can't make a speech work, only to find out later that they have cut critical connective material. If shortening is necessary, it is often better to start the speech later, or end it sooner. A small acting **adjustment** can usually make a later start sound like the beginning, or an earlier end sound climactic. It is much more difficult to act a transition that no longer exists in the script.

Be sure to break your monologue into beats (the length of script during which you play a particular objective) and use each of your transitional moments. Every transition gives you the opportunity to demonstrate that you can act. This is so because every transition comes as the result of a situational change that you can react to—whether it is a victory or a defeat, an opportunity to react to new information, an in-the-moment discovery, or a mental short circuit. Two or three of these moments followed by a new objective clearly played in an already good story will work for you every time—guaranteed!

EXERCISE 18-8

Select a monologue to develop, and go through the following checklist step by step:

1. Define the conflict.

2. What does your character need from or want to do to the character being spoken to? Be specific.

3. Define the specific given circumstances surrounding the monologue. How can you use these specifics actively in the work?

4. Why are the stakes so high? If they are not, reconsider.

5. Locate the big events, dramatic moments, and so forth.

6. Divide and label the beats in terms of tactics and transitions.

7. Where and how does the listener react? How do you respond?

8. What physical choices will you make to tell the story effectively? These choices include gesture, movement, and business.

9. Where will your focus be? Why? At what points will you focus elsewhere? Why?

Performing the Audition

Once you have rehearsed your piece, it is your responsibility to remember and use the choices you have developed. Although your work will never be exactly the same twice, using the map you have developed in rehearsal will prevent you from generalizing, **indicating**, or simply playing emotional states. Be sure to go over your objectives, given circumstances, and important dramatic story moments before you go on. Always avoid thinking about the "e"-word (emotion). There will be plenty of that in you anyway. Your nervous energy almost guarantees it, but focusing on the things you need to do will keep your nerves from taking over.

What to Wear

At a general audition, it never hurts to look your best. If you are auditioning for a particular role, wearing something that suggests the part can be very helpful to your making the impression you want, particularly if, on first impression, that character seems a bit of a stretch for you physically. Never wear clothing that makes you feel uncomfortable. It will only affect your ability to relax into what you're doing—hard enough under the circumstances.

Focus

Where you should focus your eyes and energy in an audition has no absolutes. However, there are guidelines. It should always be in the direction of the auditors so that you can best be seen. Generally speaking, however, auditors do not like to be the focus of attention. It can distract them or make them uncomfortable. It can prevent them from watching critically or, should you have such luck or skill, as an audience. So, find a focus out front that is specific in location but not directly at an auditor. It is essential that you really see that spot selected as your actual scene partner. This will keep you focused and alive. It will help you remember to react and listen. It will help you avoid thinking about those judging you.

There are audition pieces that require actors to address the audience. In those cases, audience reaction is directly solicited and should be used. In other words, if you ask for a response from the audience, then you must react to the actual audience response. Otherwise the acting will seem false. Eye contact may be necessary in such cases, but you must be careful not to dwell on any one particular individual for too long. Again, the audience's comfort level can affect their perception of what they are viewing.

Presenting Yourself

Keep in mind that your introduction is an important part of your audition. The positive energy you can generate with your opening is essential. First impressions are real, and in a short audition they play a significant part of the whole picture created. A warm introduction, followed by a dramatic transition into the monologue, gives you an additional acting moment that can score points for you, especially if the contrast between you and your character is a big one. A strong, clear transition at the end of the piece to say "thank you" can again be an effective acting moment and should be there. Even if the entire monologue goes badly, you could still have scored two good acting moments. Money in the bank is not a bad thing. Finally, you must avoid helping the judges have a negative impression of you. Any anger, disappointment, or negative energy should be saved for a private time far away from the audition area. Your personal feelings don't belong on the stage, and that is where they are as long as you are still in the audition area.

Auditioning is a specialized skill that does not always reflect how good an actor really is. There are many mediocre actors who audition well consistently and manage to get part after part, only to later disappoint their directors, fellow actors, and eventually the audience. Obviously, there are also many fine actors who are simply unable to adequately demonstrate their talent in an audition situation, and, therefore, suffer as a result. But whether auditioning ultimately does you justice or not, it will remain a part of your life as long as you act. Therefore, it is up to you to master the learnable skills that are part of the auditioning process. It is up to you to learn to be smart about your work. That is what craft is all about.

EXERCISE 18-9

Present two contrasting pieces for your class as though it were an audition situation. Solicit feedback in the following areas:

- Appearance
- Personality
- Performance
    appropriateness of the piece
    effectiveness in selling you as an actor
    technical use of voice and movement

Summary

There are two basic kinds of auditions that actors must learn to handle—the reading, cold or prepared, and the monologue audition. Each of these auditions requires a specific set of skills that must be mastered—since for most actors, most of the time, it is through the audition process that they will get work. It is your responsibility at an audition to demonstrate that you are the best possible choice for a particular role. In some cases, that means you must figure out what roles you are best suited for. In others, it means that you must convince your auditors that you are the best for the role in which they see you. You have a chance of getting the role only if you convince your auditors that you can act believably, are exciting to watch, and are best suited for the role being cast. An audition requires the same level of preparation that preparing a role does. You must analyze, synthesize, and choose actions that demonstrate what you are thinking, feeling, as well as doing. You must create a story and tell it well in a brief amount of time. In short, you must be able to show them your best in an uncomfortable situation where your best will be difficult to conjure. In addition, you must also convince the auditors that they will want to work with you in a rehearsal situation. In other words, your audition begins at the moment you show up. Auditioning is a skill that must be mastered. Unless you do so, you will be far less likely to have the chance to demonstrate the other aspects of your acting skills that you have worked so hard to develop.

CHAPTER 19

Defining the Role

In the last chapter we covered the audition process and the ways an actor must approach that process. Let us assume now that you have gotten a role in a production that is about to start rehearsing. The fact that you have been selected indicates that the director and his or her production team not only saw the potential in your work, but also saw something in your audition that suggested that you could fulfill the demands of the character you have been cast as. In other words, your looks combined with the choices you made and your physical execution of those choices suggested the character the production team was searching for. You have already taken the first steps toward defining your character. Now it is time to make the rest of the journey.

Putting the Pieces Together

In the previous chapters of this book, we have explored the many individual pieces of the puzzle that actors must deal with when attempting to meet the definition of good acting. What remains now is to put all the pieces together to see how they fit. The best opportunity for doing so arrives when an actor is cast in a role in a play. Exercises, improvisations, monologues, script analysis, and scene work provide actors with a practice field to develop individual aspects of their game. But it is only during the rehearsal process for an actual production that actors have the chance to work all of their learned skills. They must be able to do so, however, in concert with the other actors sharing that stage, and in conjunction with everyone responsible for what happens on it. In other words, in the same way that you need to agree with your acting partner about the given circumstances of a scene, you must work on a production in total collaboration with the entire production team. Otherwise, the piece of the puzzle you represent will not fit into the overall picture.

Ultimately, it is the director's job to ensure that the collaborative effort necessary for a successful production happens. To be sure that it does, a director will take responsibility for the following:

- Interpreting the playwright's script

- Creating a unified vision of the script that can be turned into a production

- Communicating the story described in that script clearly and compellingly to an audience

- Ensuring that the play's meaning ultimately comes across to an audience

- Collaborating with designers to produce lights, costumes, a set, and sound effects that serve to enhance the play's concepts and meaning, and do so in a unified way

- Finding ways to get the cast of actors to translate the agreed-on interpretation of the script to an audience through their words and actions

In short, it is the director's job to create a unity of vision so that the fictional world of the play is a consistent and, therefore, believable one. This is no easy task since every individual brings his or her own ideas to a project. Consciously or not, every actor sees himself or herself as the most important element in the play, just as every designer sees his or her concepts as the ones that are the most beautiful or imaginative or useful. It is the director's job to cut through all that and mold a single whole that will be presented to an audience. But excellent directors are few and far between, so, ultimately, you must be ready and able to take responsibility for your part of the work because, in the end, it is you that will be standing in front of an audience. If you know how to do your job, you will usually be able to survive even the worst director and contribute effectively to the overall whole of the play. But whether your director is good or not, it will remain your primary responsibility to make sure that you accomplish the final point on the list—*to translate the agreed on interpretation of the script to an audience through your words and actions.*

Developing a role in a play can be a complicated endeavor even for the most skilled actors. Since so much of the acting process involves making the best possible choices at every given moment, working on a character who appears throughout the course of an entire play provides an actor with the opportunity to make and execute an almost infinite number of choices. Learning to do this efficiently and successfully will require a process that you will develop with time and experience. But in general most actors go through the following steps:

1. Research the play and its author.

2. Interpret and analyze the overall play and its constituent parts (scene, beats, moments) for meaning and story.

3. Find the **motivation** (the cause behind the need that cannot be played directly—see the glossary) and superobjective of your character.

4. Translate the story and superobjective of your character into a playable throughline of actions, physical and psychological, that tells your character's individual story while contributing at all times to the overall story and meaning of the play.

5. Convert all blocking—your own and that provided by the director—into useful playable actions that are interesting and clear, that help define your character, and, most importantly, that propel the story forward because they are consistent with your character's needs.

6. Develop your relationship with the actors/characters who share the stage with you so that the interaction is clear, compelling, and seemingly generated from each moment spontaneously—while, in reality, the result of your understanding of the story and the conflict of every scene.

7. Fine-tune the moments of the play so that the story is told with maximum effect.

8. Find the **externals** (the tangible aspects of any role including looks, movement, gesture, and voice) of the role you are playing, and combine them with the internals that you provide.

9. Adjust the pacing and tempo of your work according to the needs of the overall production as determined by the director.

10. Learn to play the play by being totally in the moment.

This chapter and the next concern themselves with characterization. Here, the focus will be on defining the role you will be playing through the actor's homework—the things an actor can do outside the rehearsal studio. In Chapter 20, the focus will shift from defining the role to developing the role before and during the rehearsal process.

Characters Serve the Play

I recently conducted a two-day seminar with a group of local professional film actors, most of whom had never had theatre training. The seminar was titled "Scene Study and Script Analysis," and most of these actors had no idea about the script analysis part of the class. As a credit to them, though, that is why most of them signed up. Early on in the first session, I asked the group how they approach a script in order to make the choices for their work. Several in the class looked back at me blankly, but those few who had an answer gave me variations on "I read the script to learn about how to do my character."

EXERCISE 19-1

Articulate in writing how you approach a script in preparation for doing a role in a play or a scene. Compare your approach with those of the members in your class. Draw conclusions.

After much discussion, it became clear to me that all of the members of my seminar shared the view that acting is about developing and playing a character. But none of them, even for a moment, ever stopped to entertain the idea that the characters they would be playing were part of a more important whole—the script and the story it contained. In their view of acting, they were not pieces of the puzzle, they were complete entities in and of themselves, and the script merely provided the landscape in which their characters could live and breathe. No wonder the scenes they put up later in the day made so little sense, and the characters they inhabited seldom seemed to have purpose, clarity, or direction.

It is essential for you to remember that the characters you play do not exist outside of the script in which they are found. If a character enters on page 3 and exits on page 37 of the script, that is the sum total of his or her existence. That character is there for those thirty-four or so pages because the playwright needed the character to be there—to serve the playwright's purposes, not your own. *A character interpretation that works only at the expense of the script is a badly flawed one.* You must begin your journey to find and play your character with that in mind.

Developing a character to play on the stage—or on screen for that matter—is a strange amalgam, combining the playwright's vision, suggested mostly through words, with the physical and emotional presence of the actor cast in the role and the choices that actor makes for that role. There is also a degree of identification that any actor shares with or brings to the character being played that adds dimension to the work as the role is developed. For these reasons, no two Macbeths or Hedda Gablers are ever quite the same. To some extent, however, actors play themselves in every role they take on since it is only through their individual intellect, emotional makeup, and experience that they can understand and communicate the characters they portray. But successful actors never forget that their first priority in the process of finding and developing a character is to understand the script, for by doing so, they have taken the first big step toward discovering who their characters are.

It will be necessary, then, in the early stages of preparation, to focus on the overall script, rather than on your character only. Your best chance of finding your way through the maze of possibilities is to step back and examine the whole map first, not just the area in which you and your character stand. Only when you can see the whole landscape can you begin to understand how your character individually must make his or her way through it. There are basically three viewpoints you need to consider when trying to analyze how a play script works—the author's, the audience's, and finally—when that other business has been taken care of—your character's.

Research and Analysis

Any smart actor will read the script of a play many times before beginning to work on his or her individual role. If you are not a "reader," the thought of doing that can be frightening. But if you are willing to read actively (thinking about everything that appears before your eyes and continuously asking the question "Why did the playwright put that here?"), you will avoid losing concentration and begin to develop your analytical abilities. Your task as an actor at this stage is really not unlike that of a detective or research scientist. Your job is to discover, take apart, and put together all the facts contained in the play script in such a way that you develop a clear sense of the material, the story of the play. Each time you reread your script, you can do so from a different angle in order to keep what you are reading fresh and alive.

EXERCISE 19-2

Read *Rules of Love,* the short play by Joe Pintauro found in the back of this text. Make a list of questions that reading the play actively brought to mind. Discuss the play and the items on your list with your class. Draw conclusions. Keep in mind that anything contained in a good play is there for a reason.

Reading for the Author's Viewpoint

Playwrights may write for several reasons. They may have a good story screaming to be told, or they may have been inspired by an interesting character. They might have something they need to say, either personally or as social or political commentary. Their source for ideas may be fact or fiction. But whatever the circumstances for the play's initial conception, the good playwright knows his or her work will be successful only if it is wrapped in a compelling story. But not all plays have the most obvious kind of cause-and-effect story propelling them. Some stories are character-generated; others focus on a particular idea or issue, and some on a more complex interweaving of many ingredients. Whatever the case, it is your job during the early stages of your investigation to figure out the play's meaning and its story, and, like a detective or scientific researcher, it sometimes pays to go to the source of the material—the author.

If you are working on a play by a well-known author, you have available to you an encyclopedia's worth of biographical and critical material about the playwright and his or her plays—material that can help you get started on the right road in your investigation. Today, libraries, bookstores, and the Internet all provide easy access into the minds and hearts of the playwrights you may be dealing with. From Chapters 15 and 16 you already know the importance of the time and place a playwright comes from or writes about, but making yourself familiar with the body of work of a particular playwright can be equally helpful in your investigation. Most playwrights have issues, themes, and stylistic characteristics that define them as unique artists and personalities. Knowing about these characteristics can keep you from misinterpreting a playwright's intention, voice, and style. Research can also help you understand the genre of play you are working on, and, by reading what others have successfully done with the material, you can gather clues that will later help you to make choices that will work for you as well.

Here is a list of questions related to playwrights and the times they live in or write about—questions that, when properly researched during your early stages of preparation, can help you get on the right track in developing your character's throughline of action.

- What themes or ideas is this playwright known for? Do any of those themes or ideas relate to the play you are working on? What is the central idea (or spine, or theme) of the play you are working on?

Many playwrights, intentionally or not, return to the same themes again and again throughout their body of work. This may be a case of writing about things they know, or it may be a result of personal, political, ethical, or social concerns. Sometimes a playwright will take a new twist on an old theme, and sometimes, as a result of personal growth or change, a playwright may take on a new viewpoint altogether. In either case, knowing this information through research can put you on the right track when trying to make sense of the play and your role in it.

- What do you know about the playwright's life, and how does that information color the play you are working on?

The ideas of playwrights, like those of most artists, are often strongly influenced by their life experiences. Learning about these experiences through research can clarify—or at least give clues to—the possible meaning of a play. For instance, knowing about Tennessee Williams's relationship with his own mother and sister might provide useful insight into interpreting and playing the roles of Amanda, Laura, and Tom when doing a production of *The Glass Menagerie*.

EXERCISE 19-3

1. Research the author of *Rules of Love*. Does any of the biographical information you discovered help you in your understanding of the play? Why or why not?

2. Select one of the following playwrights: Christopher Durang, Sam Shepard, Tennessee Williams, Eugene O'Neill, Harold Pinter, Eugène Ionesco, Bertolt Brecht, Henrik Ibsen, Anton Chekhov, August Wilson, Paula Vogel, Maria Irene Fornes, David Henry Hwang, Carol Churchill, or Jean Anouilh. Research the selected author. Then read one of the plays written by this author. How does the biographical information tie in with the play you have read?

- What do you know about the playwright's style? How does that connect with the play you are working on?

Many playwrights have distinct writing styles that can be confusing if the actor is not familiar with that playwright's work. Further, a misreading of that style can put an actor far off the track—a waste of time and energy, two commodities in limited supply during a rehearsal process. In simplest terms, it is useful to know that Christopher Durang writes scathing satirical comedies, or that strange things can happen when Sam Shepard is writing in the style of magical realism. By properly researching the work of a playwright and by doing some critical reading about that playwright's work, the smart actor can ensure he or she will be moving in the right direction.

EXERCISE 19-4

1. Research Joe Pintauro's style by focusing on critical reaction to his work. How does the critical research affect your analysis of the play? How does the research change your perception of the play, its characters, its meaning, and so forth?

2. Use your selected play and author from the previous exercise. Do some critical research into the author's style, and connect the critical research you have done to all aspects of your selected play. Describe the changes in your perception of the play that resulted from your investigation.

Reading for the Audience's Viewpoint

As you know by now, the ultimate test of the success of your work is through the audience. It is for the audience that theatre exists, that theatre is done. If your work as an actor is to be successful, you must make choices that serve the overall purpose of the play—which is always to entertain and enlighten the audience watching. That means that every one of your choices should serve to make the story clear and exciting, and to amplify, wherever possible, the ideas presented in the play, but never at the expense of the story itself. The safest way to ensure that all this happens is to interpret the script from the point of view of the audience. That is what a good director does, and it is what you must learn to do as well. Following is a series of questions that will help you investigate the story landscape of a play. These questions will work for most any play, but where examples are useful or necessary, I have chosen to use Shakespeare's *Macbeth*, a play probably familiar to most of you.

- What are the main conflicts in the play?

All plays have a story of some kind, and any story requires some element of conflict. It is the expectation of conflict, and later, its resolution that keeps an audience interested and attentive. Although in some types of plays, the conflict or conflicts immediately jump out at us, that is not true of all plays. But in either case it becomes your job to determine what the overall conflicts are in the play you are working on; only when you do so can the individual conflicts of your character and the acting objectives that spring from them be determined.

In the case of a play entitled *Macbeth,* for example, it is reasonable to conclude that the central conflict involves this eponymous Thane of Cawdor. (Though I'm being a bit tongue-in-cheek here, never underestimate the title of a play.) The character of Macbeth faces an enormous number of obstacles during the course of the play, but the central conflict centers on his obtaining and then holding onto the Scottish crown. The individual conflicts of the play—and there are many—all connect with this central one.

EXERCISE 19-5

1. List and describe the other conflicts found in *Macbeth.*
2. Describe the main conflict found in *Rules of Love.*
3. Describe the main conflict found in the work of your selected author.

- What is the relationship of the characters and their conflicts to the spine of the play?

Remember, in a well-crafted play all the dramatic elements are interrelated in order to produce an artistic whole. Good playwrights don't just throw obstacles in their characters' paths for the sake of entertainment value; rather, those conflicts arise directly from (or at least comment upon) the play's central idea. There are several thematic strains in *Macbeth* that work together through its story and characters, and vice versa. The ability of power to corrupt and the question of free will versus destiny, for instance, weave through the fabric of this play in the most beautifully intricate pattern. As actors, you must be able to find those connections and, ultimately, to communicate them to an audience.

EXERCISE 19-6

1. Describe how the character relationships in *Macbeth* are connected to the conflict and spine of the play.
2. Describe the connection between conflict, character, and spine in *Rules of Love.*

3. Describe the connection between conflict, character, and spine in the work of your selected author.

- What is the genre of the play, and how does that affect the storytelling?

Shakespeare calls *Macbeth* a tragedy, and the action of this play supports this assertion. The definition of tragedy tells us that a tragedy's central character should be of noble birth, and, as a result of some tragic flaw (or fate), should be brought down at the end of the play. According to the rules of tragedy, there should be **catharsis** when that point of the story is reached. In other words, the audience should have an intensely sympathetic response to what has happened to this central character. Knowing this about tragedy provides important clues for the actor playing Macbeth, particularly in terms of his dramatic throughline. The audience should sympathize with Macbeth's destruction—no easy task for the actor to accomplish considering all the horrible things Macbeth does over the course of the play. The actor portraying Macbeth must, even in the early stages of his preparation, begin to consider how he will be able to keep the audience caring about his character, so they will pity him when the cathartic moment arrives at the end of the play.

EXERCISE 19-7

1. List, describe, and justify several physical actions that Macbeth and Lady Macbeth could execute during the course of the play—actions that would, when combined, produce a cathartic reaction in the audience by the end of the play.

2. How would you describe the genre of *Rules of Love*? What does its genre suggest to you about character, plot, and so forth that will help make the play and your eventual choices work?

3. How would you describe the genre of your selected author's work? What does this genre suggest to you about character, plot, and so forth that will help make the play and your eventual choices work?

- What are the given circumstances of the play, and how do they affect the play's action and meaning?

An audience must be able to understand the world of the play. As I pointed out in Chapter 16, it is the actor's responsibility to make clear, as much as possible, the customs, beliefs, political systems, ethics, morals, and values of his or her character's world. Without that understanding, for example, there is no way that an audience could have a cathartic response to Macbeth's brutality, or even begin to understand why Macbeth felt the need to kill King Duncan in the first place.

EXERCISE 19-8

1. Describe the customs, beliefs, political system, ethics, morals, and values in the world of *Macbeth*. How do the answers you have come up with affect the play's action and meaning? Explain.

2. How do the given circumstances of *Rules of Love* affect its meaning, action, and characterization? Explain.

3. How do the given circumstances of your selected play affect its meaning, action, and characterization? Explain.

- What is the story of the play as witnessed by the audience? In other words, what happens?

The key words here are "as witnessed by the audience." Remember the danger of studying a play only from the perspective of the character you are playing. It is very important, particularly if you are not playing the character of Macbeth, to understand how the play works in totality, so that you will be able to better place the puzzle part that your character represents into the overall whole. The play, no doubt, looks very different from the vantage point of Macduff, Malcolm, Banquo, or even Lady Macbeth, but the actors playing those characters should be able to clearly articulate the story from the audience's perspective.

EXERCISE 19-9

1. Describe the dramatic action of *Macbeth* from the audience's point of view.

2. Describe the dramatic action of *Rules of Love* from the audience's point of view.

3. Describe the dramatic action of your selected play from the audience's point of view.

- What is the plot of the play—the sequence of events in detail?

Once you have tracked the overall story of the play, you are ready to examine the plot, event by event. You should be able to pinpoint the **inciting incident**, the one event that triggers everything else, and then follow the chain reaction of events until all the play's conflicts have been resolved. You should be very clear about the stages of the plot's development—the exposition, the rising action or complication, the climax, the falling action, and the resolution—and know exactly where they occur in the play. This information will contribute to your ability to make appropriate choices later, when developing the scenes you are in-volved in. Clearly, a conversation between Malcolm and Macduff coming at the climax of the play is more significant dramatically than one that occurs during the rising action.

EXERCISE 19-10

1. Make a chronological list of the action in *Macbeth,* event by event.

2. Make a chronological list of the action in *Rules of Love,* event by event.

3. Make a chronological list of the action in your selected play, event by event.

- What are the most dramatic moments of the play and why?

Young actors, and sometimes even more experienced ones, can make the mis-take of playing every moment as though it were the singular event of the play. Of course, by making everything equally important, you are actually diminish-ing the impact of any big moments when they come. It is essential that you be able to recognize the real turning points in the story of the play and be ready to play those for maximum effect. The thoughtful preparation you do during your analysis will carve the way for clearer, more exciting choices later, while mini-mizing the chances for overacting.

Once you have completed the preceding questions, you are ready to exam-ine the play from the point of view of your own character.

EXERCISE 19-11

1. What are the most dramatic events in *Macbeth*? Justify your answers.

2. What are the most dramatic events in *Rules of Love*? Justify your answers.

3. What are the most dramatic events in your selected play? Justify your answers.

Reading for the Character's Viewpoint

Once you know what the jigsaw puzzle looks like when completed, you are ready to examine your piece of the puzzle specifically. It is important to keep in mind that any particular character may not know the same things that other characters know, and certainly an individual character does not know all the things that the audience watching knows. On the other hand, a careful reading of the script might tell you that your character knows things that the audience, for plot purposes, might not yet know. All of this is important to your making the best possible onstage choices. Further, it is imperative that you keep in mind that you can only play the particular scene you are in. Knowing the ending of the play might be useful to you as an actor, but you must remember to play only what your character knows at any given moment of the story.

Following are some specific questions to help you in your character-centered analysis.

- What are both the story and the plot of the play from your character's point of view? How does this differ from the audience's point of view? What is the significance of these differences?

Before analyzing the story from a character's point of view, actors must remind themselves that characters don't usually see themselves as villains or heroes. Like most of us in real life, characters look at the world from their own viewpoints at the centers of their own stories. From this vantage point, they see their actions as both necessary and good. Even characters who are judged evil by their peers or by the audience seldom judge themselves as anything other than the protagonists of their own story.

From the point of view of Lady Macbeth, then, this play is a story about how a woman with a tremendous thirst for power loses that thirst as she begins to recognize the cost of quenching her desire. By going through the play event by event, the actor playing Lady Macbeth can discover her throughline of action—the things she specifically does scene by scene. For Macbeth the story is just the opposite. It is a story of how a man with a tremendous conscience and no thirst for power is transformed into an addict for the very thing that he at first had no interest in—ultimate power. Each is an intriguing story that intersects with the other, producing both terrific conflict and interesting throughlines. Malcolm's is a story of a prince with no political ambitions, converted into an excellent leader because of the actions of Macbeth. Banquo's is a story of a man uncorrupted by the temptations of power who, because of his conscience, is forced into sacrificing his life, but not his honor, to Macbeth. All the individual stories intersect and create conflict, like the weaving of a tapestry, while at the same time serving the overall story and the themes of this great play. This may all seem obvious now that the right questions have been asked and answered, but too often, without going through the work, the obvious remains undiscovered.

EXERCISE 19-12

1. Select a character from *Macbeth* other than the Macbeths themselves, and tell the story of the play from that character's point of view.

2. Tell the story of *Rules of Love* from the point of view of each of its characters. Compare the two stories. Connect the differences to the overall story. What have you learned?

3. Tell the story of your selected play from the point of view of one of its central characters. How is the story different from that individual's point of view? Connect the differences to the overall story. What have you learned?

- What is the superobjective of your character?

Though the characters themselves may be unaware of it, the actors playing those characters must discover or invent reasons for doing the things they do during the course of a play. Your throughline of action in a play dictates the overall actions you play out, but it is up to you to provide yourself and your character with both the motivation and the overall need that drives your character to do the things mandated in the script. You will not be able to play your motivation directly, but you can certainly go after the feeling of need it generates. I might never know that Lady Macbeth's mother made her feel helpless and insecure, but I will certainly recognize Lady Macbeth's need for power. Determining the single overwhelming need that drives your character to do the things he or she does (your superobjective) will help you to develop a strategy and make choices for every individual scene, beat, and moment in which you appear. This, in turn, will help you create both the clarity and seeming complexity you will want to bring to your performance and to your dramatic throughline.

EXERCISE 19-13

1. Select several characters from *Macbeth*. State the motivation and superobjective for each. Justify each of your choices. Discuss.

2. What are Jim's and Maisie's superobjectives in *Rules of Love*? Their motivations? Connect the two.

3. State the motivation and superobjective for the central character in the play you have selected. Justify your choices.

- What do you know about your character?

It's always fun to speculate about the hidden lives of the characters you play, but unless your speculations have direct usefulness in the work you will do onstage, they remain irrelevant to the work. The reasons that Duncan prefers Donalbain to Malcolm are only useful to the actors playing these roles if this background information can be converted into useful action onstage. The audience will not "see" such background information. So, although detailed character biographies can prove helpful to the actor when effectively constructed, when they are not so well constructed, they may be a distraction from the stories those characters are meant to tell. A good biography should lead to a more fully realized characterization in service of the script. Biographies that stand in the way of the story are better avoided or reconstructed in such a way that they serve the story.

Remember, however, that the script itself is chock full of character treasures that, after many careful readings, will surely be revealed to you. Much of what you need to know about the characters you will play can be mined through the following:

- What your character says

- What your character does

- What other characters say about your character

- What the playwright tells you directly or indirectly through stage directions and through the implied actions the dialogue suggests

EXERCISE 19-14

1. Select a character from *Macbeth*. Analyze that character using the approach suggested in the preceding list. Be sure to write down all references as you discover them. Discuss.

2. Select one of the characters from *Rules of Love*. Analyze that character using the approach suggested in the preceding list. Be sure to write down all references as you discover them. Discuss.

3. Choose one of the characters from your selected play. Analyze that character using the approach suggested in the preceding list. Be sure to write down all references as you discover them. Discuss.

- How does your character contribute to the play's overall spine or central idea?

This issue was addressed to some extent in the question about examining the story from an individual character's point of view, but there is another point to be made here. It is part of your obligation as an actor in service of the script to illuminate the author's themes as well as his or her story, wherever possible. By recognizing the places in the script where the author is making a thematic statement, it is possible to make choices that will help the audience recognize that idea. Once again, then, it becomes clear that as an actor playing a character, you must learn to operate on more than one level at all times. It is not enough to simply behave as a character, even if you are "completely inhabiting" that character. A part of you must always be available to serve both the story of the play and the ideas behind that story.

EXERCISE 19-15

1. Select several characters from *Macbeth*. Describe how each contributes to the central idea of the play. Be specific.

2. Describe how both Jim and Maisie contribute to the central idea of *Rules of Love.* Be specific.

3. Explain how several characters from the play you have selected contribute its central idea. Be specific.

Once you have completed your overall research and analysis of the play and how your character serves that play, you are ready to look more closely at the role you will be developing.

Summary

It is only during the rehearsal process, from pre-rehearsal preparation through the final dress rehearsal, that an actor has the opportunity to fully employ all the tools he or she has acquired through training. Developing and playing a role in a production provide the ultimate test of good acting—acting that is believable and that tells the best possible story while serving the script as well as the overall production goals of the director and the rest of the collaborative team. It is therefore the actor's responsibility to understand the overall story of the play, as well as the production concepts and goals established by the director, and to make choices during the rehearsal process that support the needs of the production.

Before any specific choices can be made or developed, the actor must understand the play from the viewpoint of the playwright, of the audience, and of the individual characters whose stories intersect to provide the conflict that powers the overall story of the play. The homework process that leads toward understanding may require a great deal of research. Ultimately, the actor must understand the playwright's purpose, the mechanics of the story being told, and how the characters interrelate to communicate the story and its meaning. He or she must understand the genre of the play being produced, as well as any stylistic characteristics of the play that might influence its ability to work effectively. Most importantly, the actor must be able to connect all the information gleaned from this research and make choices that will work within the collaborative framework of the individual production.

CHAPTER 20

Developing the Role: The Rehearsal Process

In Chapter 19 you learned some methods for analyzing the overall play and some tools for defining a particular role you might be playing. In this chapter you will learn more about the analysis process and the next steps necessary for developing a character. The focus here will be twofold: first, on a more specific scene-by-scene analysis of the play in order to determine a throughline of action for your character, and, second, on the continuing development of your character through the rehearsal process so that by the time you are ready to perform your work, you will have achieved the following goals:

- You will have created a performance that contributes directly to the success of the play because that performance is clear, compelling, and consistent with the needs of the production.

- You will have developed a character with physical, psychological, and emotional characteristics that are interesting, believable, and clear to the audience.

- You will have developed a character that well serves the overall story of the play and the playwright's meaning.

Before you are ready to sit down at the rehearsal table to begin the first reading of the play, however, there is one more step in the process of character analysis that the well-prepared actor must attend to.

The Throughline of Action

You will remember from Chapters 6, 7, and 8 that character is mostly communicated through the actions you choose to execute and the manner in which you execute them. Actions, which include all the things your character says as well as

232

acts out physically, are the tangible aspects of any performance. *Only through what is tangible will an audience ultimately come to know who your character is.* An audience cannot read a character's mind or look into a character's heart. An audience can only make assumptions and draw conclusions from what it sees and hears. Obviously, then, the actions you choose to present to an audience are extremely important. The actions that you select and perform are mostly generated as a result of the following:

- Determining the given circumstances at any particular moment of the play

- Determining the results of asking the "magic if"

- Determining what your character needs and what your character is willing to risk in order to achieve those needs

- Playing specific objectives

- Determining specific tactics to obtain those objectives

Discovering the Action

As an actor, you must take a fresh approach to each scene your character appears in. Finding and playing the actions dictated by your investigation of the elements listed earlier will help you create a throughline of action for your character. This throughline will not only define your character scene by scene, but will also suggest the changes that your character has undergone in the time that elapses between scenes. *By focusing on the particular tasks at hand in each scene and solving the particular problems in efficient ways, the actor as character creates a complex personality.* This process of creating complexity through simplicity might seem like cheating, but as I've said before, good acting is made up, at least in part, of illusion. Besides, working in this manner is far more reliable than trying to magically "become" the character as some of my film acting students have suggested.

EXERCISE 20-1

Reexamine *Macbeth* or another play you have recently worked on by focusing closely on the behavior of a particular character. Study the things the character actually does in each scene, and make a list of these specific actions. Then analyze the character in terms of these actions. How is the character's behavior different from scene to scene? Describe the differences. Does the changing behavior make sense in terms of the context of each scene? Explain. Describe and justify the throughline of action you observe. Draw conclusions.

Keep in mind that each scene in a play is a story unto itself, so you must analyze each scene in the same way that you analyze the overall play. It is a good idea to begin your scene-by-scene analysis of your character's throughline by selecting a scene that is immediately accessible to you—one that you feel you understand. The discoveries you make in this particular scene can help you more easily analyze other scenes that do not at first seem as accessible.

Following are some scene study questions that can guide you in selecting actions you can play in each scene—actions that will help you tell the story of the scene specifically and help you create and define your character while doing so.

- What are the given circumstances of the scene?
- What actually happens in the scene? Literally, what are the story events one by one?
- What is the conflict in the scene? Is there more than one?
- What are the most dramatic moments in the scene? What specifically leads up to these moments of drama?
- What is the climax of the scene? Why?
- What actions does your character actually perform in the scene?
- How does your character contribute to the conflict in the scene?
- What does your character need in this scene from the other character or characters?
- What stands in the way of getting what your character needs?
- What does your character do to get around these obstacles?
- How badly does your character need what is needed?
- What is your character willing to do to get what is needed?
- What discoveries does your character make during the scene?
- How does this new information affect your character? Does it change your character's behavior, way of thinking, needs?
- Can you identify places in the script where your character receives new information?
- Does this information somehow change what your character thinks or feels? Does this news signal a victory? A defeat? A reason for reevaluation? Something else?
- What internal changes does your character go through at these moments?
- Now that you have answered these questions, can you map a throughline of action for your character?

EXERCISE 20-2

1. Select an early scene from a play you have worked on recently or are currently working on. Analyze the scene using the preceding questions. Be specific.

2. Analyze the next scene in which your character appears. Compare your answers for the two scenes and draw conclusions.

3. Analyze *Rules of Love* (found in the back of this text) using the preceding questions. Answer the character-specific questions for both Jim and Maisie.

4. In a paragraph, tell the story of each character in *Rules of Love* based on the actions each executes and the manner in which each does so. Draw conclusions.

Scoring the Action

Once you have answered these questions, you can apply your answers directly to your script. Using a system of notation, or **scoring**, you can mark your script in such a way that, as in a musical score, the basic things you need to know for playing each scene will be included in your script, ready to be used—note by note, measure by measure.

Following is a sample system of notation for scoring a script. You can adapt or modify it for your own use. If the script you are working with does not belong to you, photocopy it so that you do not destroy the script for others who might use it later. Be sure to use pencil for all notations so that you can easily change them. As you continue to work on your script during the rehearsal process, you will learn more about the play, the scene, and your character. Your character will evolve as a result of collaborative input and your expanded understanding, and you will want to adjust your notations accordingly.

Notation System

1. **Write at the beginning of the scene your overall objective for the scene.** Make sure the objective contains a strong, specific verb, one that can be accomplished through the other actor in the scene—in other words, a goal or need that you can get from the other actor.

2. **Divide the scene into beats by drawing a line across the page after each beat ends.** At the beginning of each new beat on the left side of the page, clearly state the new objective being sought, and/or the new tactic being used.

3. **On the right side of your copy of the script, write an explanation for each transition.** It could be a discovery, a new idea, a defeat, a victory, and so forth.

4. **Also use the right side of the page to describe psychological and physical actions that you can use to make the story tangible to an audience.**

5. **Look at the other characters' lines, and circle any new information that your character did not previously know.** Remember, hearing this new information is actable.

6. **Note any stage directions hinted at through the dialogue.**

7. **Highlight or box the climax of the scene.** Remember, you must build dramatically toward this climax. The audience had better recognize the climax, or you are not doing your job of storytelling.

Here is a sample of what a scored page might look like for an actor playing Juliet.

Objective: To make Romeo feel loved so he will continue loving me.

Enter Romeo and Juliet aloft (at the window)

To convince Romeo that it is still night. Use nightingale to convince.

JULIET: Wilt thou be gone? It is not yet near day.

It was the nightingale, and not the lark,

That pierced the fearful hollow of thine ear.

Nightly she sings on yond pomegranate tree.

Believe me, love, it was the nightingale.

ROMEO: It was the lark the herald of the morn;

No nightingale Look, love, what envious streaks

Do lace the severing clouds in yonder East.

Night's candles are burnt out, and jocund day

Stands tiptoe on the misty mountain tops.

I must be gone and live, or stay and die.

Find ways to physically react to all evidence that day has arrived—play story of discoveries. Big react to "live or die."

JULIET: Yond light is not daylight: I know it, I.

It is some meteor that the sun exhales

To be to thee this night a torchbearer

And light thee on thy way to Mantua.

Therefore stay yet; thou need'st not to be gone.

Use meteor to convince.

ROMEO: Let me be ta'en, let me be put to death.

I am content, so thou wilt have it so.

I'll say yon grey is not the morning's eye,

'Tis but the pale reflex of Cynthia's brow;

Nor that is not the lark whose notes do beat

The vaulty heaven so high above our heads.

I have more care to stay than will go.

Come, death, and welcome! Juliet wills it so.

How is't, my soul? Let's talk; it is not day.

React to victory.

React: He loves me so much.

React: I could cause Romeo's death!

To make Romeo hurry to safety.	JULIET: It is, it is! Hie hence, be gone, away!	*Transition: I actually see outside light. It really is daytime. Oh God!! Help Romeo dress. Hurry!*
	It is the lark that sings so out of tune,	
	Straining harsh discords and unpleasing sharps.	
	Some say the lark makes sweet division;	
CLIMAX	This doth not so, for she divideth us.	
	Some say the lark and loathed toad change eyes;	
	O, now I would they had changed voices too.	
	Since arm from arm that voice doth us affray,	
	Hunting thee hence with hunt's-up to the day.	
	O, now be gone! More light and light it grows.	
	ROMEO: More light and light—more dark and dark our woes.	

	Enter Nurse (hastily).	*Transition: Nurse's arrival scares me. Listen. Discover how late it is. More need to hurry!*
To get information by listening completely.	NURSE: Madam!	
	JULIET: Nurse?	
	NURSE: Your lady mother is coming to your chamber.	
	The day is broke; be wary, look about.	
	(Exit.)	

To make Romeo know how much I love him.	JULIET: Then, window, let day in, and let life out.	*Transition: Go from listening to nurse to physically making Romeo move faster. Push him lovingly toward window.*
	ROMEO: Farewell, farewell! One kiss, and I'll descend.	
	(He goeth down.)	

To make Romeo agree to stay in touch; to delay him for a moment.	JULIET: Art thou gone so, love-lord, ay husband-friend?	*Discover what his leaving means, physically detain him because his leaving physically hurts so bad. React to victory.*
	I must hear from thee every day in the hour,	
	For in a minute there are many days.	
	O, by this count I shall be much in years	
	Ere I again behold my Romeo!	
	ROMEO: Farewell!	
	I will omit no opportunity	
	That may convey my greetings, love, to thee.	

	JULIET: O God, I have an ill-divining soul!	*Transition: Watch him leave; discover emptiness, get horrible thought.*
	Methinks I see thee, now thou art so low,	

To make Romeo understand my fear; make him comfort me.

As one dead in the bottom of a tomb.

Either my eyesight fails, or thou lookest pale.

ROMEO: And trust me, love, in my eye so do you.

Dry sorrow drinks our blood. Adieu, Adieu!

(Exit.)

Share fear; get comfort.

(*Romeo and Juliet,* Act III Scene 5)

EXERCISE 20-3

1. Score a section of *Rules of Love* for either Jim or Maisie. Trace the throughline of action in that section by reading the scene and using the notations you have written in. How does using the notations affect your reading? Be specific.

2. Apply the scene analysis questions listed earlier to the following scene. Be sure that you answer the questions specifically and thoroughly, as though you were playing Lady Macbeth.

3. Use your answers to the questions in Part 2 to score the scene.

Enter Macbeth.

LADY MACBETH: Great Glamis! Worthy Cawdor!

Greater than both, by the all-hail hereafter!

Thy letters have transported me beyond

This ignorant present, and I feel now

The future in the instant.

MACBETH: My dearest love,

Duncan comes here tonight.

LADY MACBETH: And when goes hence?

MACBETH: Tomorrow, as he proposes.

LADY MACBETH: O, never

Shall sun that morrow see!

Your face, my Thane, is as a book where men

May read strange matters. To beguile the time,

Look like the time; bear welcome in your eye,

Your hand, your tongue; look like the innocent flower,

But be the serpent under't. He that's coming

Must be provided for; and you shall put

This night's great business into my dispatch,

Which shall to all our nights and days to come

Give solely sovereign sway and masterdom.

MACBETH: We will speak further.

LADY MACBETH: Only look up clear.

To alter favour ever is to fear.

Leave all the rest to me.

Exeunt.

(*Macbeth,* Act I Scene 5)

Developing the Role through the Rehearsal Process

Once you have scored each scene in the manner suggested previously, your initial analysis of the play is essentially over. You are ready to begin your rehearsal process armed with enough information to prevent you from feeling lost, insecure, or stupid. Of course, all the work you have done is subject to change according to the concept of the director and the relationships that you develop with the actors playing the other roles.

The dynamics you and the other actors will bring to your individual roles cannot be predicted during your initial analysis, nor can the chemistry that will develop among you. The way you imagine a scene will be played out in your preliminary work cannot possibly anticipate the input that your fellow actors will provide. As when you do scene work for class, your own mental movie of the play and those individual movies that everyone else brings to the rehearsal process will be replaced by the new collaborative version. All concerned must be willing to adjust their individual work to this new reality. Your director will be there to help you all find this new collaborative vision. However, the preliminary work that you have completed will provide you with an excellent springboard for the next step in your creative process—the rehearsals themselves.

EXERCISE 20-4

As you have already learned, the casting of roles can strongly affect the choices that will work best to tell the story of a play.

1. Reimagine the scene from *Macbeth* with various physical types playing Macbeth and his wife. How would a very young couple in the roles of the Macbeths affect the story? An older couple?

An older Macbeth and a young Lady Macbeth? A physically un-
attractive Macbeth and a lovely Lady Macbeth? Other types?

2. Select another play and go through the same process as in Step 1.

The First Rehearsal

The rehearsal process usually begins with the director presenting his or her ideas
to the cast and to the rest of the production team. Included in these opening re-
marks will probably be the director's concept for the production, as well as his or
her ideas about the set, lighting, and costume design. If the designers themselves
are present, they will likely be given the opportunity to describe their work and
explain how their ideas fit into the overall project. If design models or diagrams
are available, they will be shared at this time to help make their plans clear. The
director may also share a preliminary vision of what the production might be
like by opening night and will certainly include an overview of how he or she
plans to work. At this time your director is also likely to summarize his or her expectations of you, your fellow cast members, and the design and production
team. If all this is laid out clearly in the beginning, there is less chance of misun-
derstanding and conflict later on. *It is your responsibility to make all your ideas and
suggestions fit into the director's overall vision.* You must be flexible and make adjustments to meet the expectations of the director. Any conflict during the rehearsal process should be reserved for the action of the play itself, where it will
help rather than hinder the eventual production.

Following the introductory notes, most first rehearsals begin with a reading
of the entire play. Since the cast members have not heard each other saying the
lines their characters speak, such a reading can be a nice icebreaker. You must remember that this reading is not intended to be a performance. You already have
the role, so don't feel you need to impress anyone. Use the reading for yourself—
to really listen to the words of the play and to your fellow actors. This will help
you begin tilling the soil that will lead to the growth of your performance. Feel
free to react to what you hear, but refrain from trying to "act." Remind yourself
not to make any value judgments at this point. This is just a reading. I have
acted in and directed productions where a standout reading by an actor turned
out to be the same performance the actor gave several weeks later. I have also
been involved in productions where an embarrassingly bad reader later turned in
a brilliant performance. So avoid making any judgments at the first read. Simply
listen, react, and learn.

Exploring the Script

Once the play has been read, some directors immediately start blocking the play.
As an actor I always hated that. For me, the reasons for moving onstage were al-

ways connected to what I was thinking, feeling, and doing from moment to moment. If I didn't yet know that, then blocking hindered rather than helped me when a director chose to jump right in. But time sometimes demands that a director work this way, and, if you have done your homework, you should not feel lost if your director plunges right into blocking.

Many directors, however, will choose to go through the script with their actors to help them develop the overall throughline of action. You may discover that you have to adjust your previously held ideas about your character, and even the play itself. You must be willing to do so. As part of your homework, you can reexamine your script, notating where necessary, to accommodate the vision of your director. But, by the time the director has worked through the script, you and your fellow actors should have a fairly unified idea of the conflicts in the play, your overall objectives, where beats begin and end, where the big dramatic moments potentially are, and what dialogue and action in the script specifically point up the play's central ideas. You may even acquire a sense of the music in the script itself. By music, I'm referring to the **pace** and **rhythm** of the play, which, as you develop your feel for the work as a whole, can help give you clues about your own **tempo** in a particular section of the play.

Keep in mind that the ideas developed during this part of the rehearsal process, even though they are now collaborative rather than just your own, are still subject to change later. Everyone, including your director, will continue to learn and make new discoveries as the work moves forward. This, in turn, will cause things to change again and again. Such changes are a necessary part of the process, and you must be willing to make the necessary adjustments. If the atmosphere that you help create is upbeat and supportive, you and your fellow actors will be receptive to each other. You will get ideas from them, and they from you, as well as from your director. This is an ideal arrangement.

Blocking the Play

During blocking rehearsals, your director will focus primarily on stage movement and the compositional aspects of the production. If the director is an actors' director, he or she will actively try to integrate the movement you are asked to make with your acting and storytelling needs. Such a director may also work with you to make organic choices, using your impulses as well as his or her own to help guide the creating of stage pictures and movement. If the director's background is less connected with the acting process, however, you may be left to figure out for yourself how your acting choices can fit in with the blocking you are given. Use your time during blocking rehearsals to try to do so.

Some actors waste valuable time during blocking rehearsals, mistakenly thinking that blocking is a task that must be patiently endured while waiting to get to the more valuable acting rehearsals that will follow. Remember, the arrangement of the visual elements in a production can make both aesthetic and storytelling statements. Try to see how the blocking is working in terms of the audience, but, more importantly, try to justify your movements and get those movements to help you tell the story you need to be telling.

In addition, always be sure to write down the blocking your director gives you. Note the when, the how, and the where specifically in your script—that is, mark exactly when in the script the movement takes place, how you are to execute the movement, and where you are onstage or where you move from and to. Never trust that you will remember a specific piece of blocking. By the time you rehearse for a few hours, the fog is likely to drift in. As part of your actor's homework, always go over the blocking you were given during rehearsals. This will not only help you to integrate it into your memory, it will also give you the opportunity to reexamine how you can use this blocking to help make your acting in this section of the script more clear and compelling onstage.

EXERCISE 20-5

1. Create blocking choices that will work for the *Macbeth* scene in Exercise 20-3. Make sure each action and movement contributes to the story of the scene for the character you have chosen. Mark your blocking into the script.

2. Select a section of *Rules of Love*. Follow the procedure described for Step 1.

3. Create blocking choices for the *Romeo and Juliet* scene reproduced earlier in this chapter. Follow the same procedure described for Step 1.

4. Select a scene of your own, and follow the procedure described for Step 1.

5. Create alternative blocking choices for one of these scenes. Compare and draw conclusions.

You will also need to consider some other aspects of blocking during this stage of rehearsals. For instance, you will not only need to consider how to justify the movements you are given in terms of playing your objectives, you will also need to consider the manner in which you execute those movements. The way you do what you do can be critically important in regard both to character and to storytelling. It is not, for example, enough to know that you cross from the sofa to the bar because you need to get away from your adversary. You must also know how you cross away. Do you go fast or slowly, upright or bent, with large steps or small? Where is your focus as you cross? On the floor, on the bar, or over your shoulder at your adversary? Any of these choices has the power to communicate information about what your character is thinking and feeling as well as who he or she is. You must use your rehearsal time to discover and make the choices that tell the audience what you need them to know.

EXERCISE 20-6

Reconsider the blocking choices you made in Exercise 20-5 by thinking about the manner in which you would execute them. Describe how this additional step enriches your ability to tell the story of the scene and of your character more effectively.

You must also begin to consider the gestures and business you can use to develop the externals for your character. Remember, these choices will help define who you are for your audience. As with movement, some of this may be provided by your director, but it is, to a large extent, your responsibility. No one knows your character better than you do, so be willing, even eager, to invent your character physically. Never be afraid to contribute your ideas, to try things out. Begin to explore your character's rhythms, defining gestures, and way of walking. Think about where your character's center of energy is. Is it in the abdomen, the head, the butt? How does your character listen, physically? Is the character a smiler or a frowner? Any of these questions could spark a defining choice in the creation of character. Always be on the lookout for physical clues.

Keep in mind that the movement, gestures, and business you and your fellow actors create are often as important to the storytelling as the words themselves. Audiences get the story as much with their eyes as with their ears, so don't minimize the importance of making and executing first-rate blocking choices.

EXERCISE 20-7

1. Explore and find a body of gestures for the character you have been working on in the previous exercises. Why would these gestures be appropriate and effective for that character?

2. People move at different rates of speed and have different rhythms for the things they do. Using the gestures you have already found, explore and find the appropriate tempo and rhythm for your character. Justify your choices.

3. Explore and find the walk and other physical characteristics that would be useful in telling the story of your character.

4. Consider the possibilities in your voice for telling the story of your character. Explore the use of pitch, tempo, and even tongue placement. What other elements in the voice might be useful?

5. Consider the character you are working on as he or she might be played by various famous actors—Dustin Hoffman, Daniel Day-Lewis, Anthony Hopkins, Glenn Close, Jennifer Jason Leigh, or Emma Thompson, for instance. What gestures, vocal work, and so forth might they employ? Explain your choices.

During your preparation work, you identified the big moments in the play and in each of its scenes. Those dramatic moments build logically out of the ongoing conflict that is being created. Transitional moments, however, may be more subtle. You must fully play these moments onstage as well as the bigger dramatic ones. Since there is no dialogue in a moment of transition, it is your responsibility to communicate the story of the transition through what you choose to do. Creating physical actions that communicate a specific thought or feeling can greatly enhance the effectiveness and clarity of the work. That, too, is something you must focus on during the blocking portion of rehearsal.

EXERCISE 20-8

Consider several transitional moments you have marked in the script you have been working on, and physicalize them. Make sure each transition you work on is clear and compelling. Does each have a beginning, a middle, and an end? Are your choices consistent with the physical character you have been developing?

Remember, rehearsing is not science. The bottom line is always "if it works, then it works." Rehearsing is a process that includes discovering, weighing, choosing, keeping, rejecting, and improving. Here is a list of items that first appeared in Chapter 14 for your consideration or reconsideration while blocking.

- *Work moment to moment.* Onstage as in life one thing leads to the next. You must not skip a step.

- *Every movement and gesture must be complete and full.* Blocking moments, like all acting moments, must have beginnings, middles, and ends. Be sure you act them.

- *Every journey onstage should have a purpose and a destination.* When actors cross away from something or someone onstage, they must remember that they are also moving toward something or someone else.

Workthroughs

Once blocking is completed, you will be working to develop the individual sections of the play. This is a stop-and-go process intended to fine-tune all the dramatic elements that combine to create compelling drama. It can be slow and painstaking, but the results are always worth it. During this part of the rehearsal process, you will continue to discover and develop the aspects of each scene that you considered in your individual preparatory work. You will also continue to learn things about your character that serve the overall story being told, and you will continue to find new ways of revealing to an audience the things you have learned about your character through what you say and do. You will also continue to make discoveries about the meaning of the play, which, in turn, may spark ideas about how to communicate those ideas through your character's actions.

In this stage of rehearsal, you will often work moment to moment, stopping whenever necessary to clarify and intensify what is happening between you and those you work with. You will have the opportunity to explore and to perfect the business that you have developed as part of the scene. When is the most effective moment to light the cigarette, reach for the drink, return to the newspaper, and so forth? How does your character inhale the cigarette, sip the tea, fold the newspaper? What does each piece of business and its execution contribute to the picture of the character you are painting?

EXERCISE 20-9

Return again to the scene you have been working on. Explore and find specific business that would be appropriate for that character to engage in. Find the appropriate manner for executing this business as the character.

Once the individual moments have been sharpened, you will be given a chance to work several moments together. Whenever there is new information, a discovery, a victory, a defeat, or an interruption in a scene, chances are there is also a good acting moment to be mined and polished. Eventually, you and your fellow actors will come to see your script, like a musical score, as a series of sections or beats, each with its own mini-story and characteristics. When you and your fellow actors reach this point, it is likely that strong, clear, and specific work will be taking place.

Memorization

By the time you have gotten through the entire script in this fashion, you will probably be surprised at how well you already know your lines. This phenomenon is both interesting and delightful. Rehearsing involves physical memory, emotional memory, and hearing memory, and this combination of memories greatly aids an actor's ability to learn the words. For this reason, it is likely you will be asked to be off book by the time you're ready for the second round of workthroughs. Whenever you are asked to be off book, though, be sure that you are ready. It is of no interest to those working with you that you are slow to memorize, or have difficulty with exact memorization. It is part of your job. What it takes to do your job is your business and your responsibility alone.

Keep in mind that you will lose some of your edge when first attempting to play off book, so work to know your lines so well that you could deliver them in an earthquake. Even if they seem fuzzy the first time through, they will get up to speed again surprisingly fast—because you know very well by now what is going on in each moment, beat, and scene.

EXERCISE 20-10

1. Memorize a passage from a play or poem.

2. Memorize another passage from that play or poem of equal length, this time using as many senses as possible to help you in the process. Discuss the differences. What have you learned?

Additional Workthroughs

Once you have worked through the play again, you will have become used to playing without your script. You will also have discovered new physical actions for your character based on suddenly working with two free hands—gesture and business choices that help you to define and develop your character.

You are probably now ready to run through sections of the script without interruption, and your director will want you to do so. This will allow you to better understand how things flow together. It will also help you start to feel the pace and rhythm of various sections of the play that, at this point, your director needs to focus on. During this time, you will have to adjust your individual work according to your director's need to establish the tempo of the play. It is the director's responsibility to orchestrate the pieces of the overall work into an effective whole, and the timing of the parts of the play as it moves toward its climax is an important element of effective storytelling.

Runthroughs

During the runthrough portion of the rehearsal process, you will have the chance to execute all you have learned without interruption. You will discover the kind of energy you will need to get through it all, and the kind of energy changes you will need to make as you go from one scene to another. You will also learn whether the biographical information you invented for your character takes you from one scene into the next effectively. You will find out if this information is specific enough to help you and the audience understand why your character behaves the way he or she does. If not, these runthroughs will tell you where you will have to make adjustments so that it will do so. Most importantly, the runthrough process will give you more and more opportunity to live as your character onstage from moment to moment. You will eventually be able to listen and react to your fellow actors without having to think about all the aspects of the performance that you worked so hard to create. As with the memorization of lines, you will eventually be able to carry out all of your actions without having to think about doing so. You will continue to make discoveries and choices for your character that come organically from each moment because at this point, to some degree, your physical, psychological, and emotional makeup is operating as your character. In short, you will be creating the illusion of living in the moment as your character because you have earned the ability to simply listen and react. At the same time you will learn to do so without compromising the pacing and tempo required of you by your director.

At the end of each runthrough, your director will give you notes and will expect you to absorb these notes and correct or adjust your work accordingly. If you do not understand a note, ask at the time it is given. Keep in mind that your director will have an enormous amount on his or her mind, and if you don't ask questions at the time the note is given, your director may forget what the note means later on. If your director gives you a note for correction or adjustment, do not spend rehearsal time explaining why you did what you did. It is irrelevant and a waste of time. If the note given seems to contradict an earlier note or agreed upon choice, know that rehearsing is a process—subject to change as new things develop. Just take in the note and make the adjustment. Know also that there is no correlation between the number of notes the director gives you and the quality of your work. A raft of notes can be inspired from a new good choice as well as from a failure to properly execute an old one. In addition, understand that your director is now primarily focused on making the overall play work, not on making sure you, as an individual, feel good; so do not expect your director to spend a lot of time at this point praising you. You must develop your ability to take notes in a non-critical way. You must always remember that you and your fellow actors are working together to achieve the best possible production. That means that you must never let your frustration, disappointment, or insecurity show. You must remain positive, attentive, and responsive.

Dry Tech and Technical Rehearsals

These rehearsals precede the final dress rehearsals. Dry tech is the rehearsal where all the technical elements of the production—particularly lighting and sound—are inserted where they will occur. Scene changes are also made at this time. This can be a difficult rehearsal, especially for actors, since there will be long stretches of time where you will be idle. If you're part of a large cast and/or a complex technical show, the difficulty is multiplied. It is important that you be psychologically prepared for such rehearsals. Use your time to adjust to the lights and sets whenever you can, but be focused and ready to do the work the director and production team need from you. This will help to minimize the outbursts of temper that sometimes accompany this stretch.

Most often the production team will work **cue-to-cue**—that is, you will only play the few lines leading up to a lighting change, sound cue, or set movement. These can be complicated or in need of fine-tuning, so you may have to repeat the cue several, if not many, times. In addition, the prop crew will be learning when and where to place and collect properties. By giving the crew the time they need to get it right during dry tech, the director can prevent the frustration of stopping for technical glitches later when you are running through the play. This time is particularly important for the stage manager who will be "calling" the show, or telling crewmembers when they must execute each individual cue.

The stage manager must practice calling these cues, and you must patiently allow for that time. Through all of this, you must be available to jump on and off the stage and in and out of your positions, while at the same time staying focused when you are not onstage. The process can be tedious, but avoid permitting any actor ego to infect your relationships with your collaborators.

The next step is running the play. This first run with the technical elements and, perhaps, the next couple of runs are also for the production team. You must understand this and do all you can to help. Mostly you need to be patient with their mistakes, maintain your concentration, and cooperate. If you do your part, the crew will quickly master the timing and flow of their responsibilities.

Dress Rehearsals

Even before dress rehearsal, you will have had several fittings for your costume or costumes. The designer will have conferred at great length with the director and, perhaps with you, about your character. Keep in mind that your costumes were designed to communicate your character to the audience, not necessarily to make you, the actor, look beautiful. Also remember that you will need time to adjust to the feel of your costumes and to discover how wearing each costume will physically help you reveal your character through action. Obviously, you will feel strange and perhaps even awkward at first, but give yourself time to explore and get used to this external part of your character. It is not unusual for a costume to provide just the catalyst you need to add the finishing touches to your characterization. If, however, you have a legitimate problem with your costume, share it with your director. He or she will want you to feel comfortable so that your work is the best it can be.

EXERCISE 20-11

1. Return to a monologue or scene you know well. Put together a costume appropriate for that character. Rehearse the work in costume, trying to find ways to physicalize the work in conjunction with what you are wearing. What new choices did you discover?

2. Repeat the procedure with another costume choice appropriate for the character. Compare. What have you learned?

At this point, there is nothing left for you to do but fine-tune your work. If you listen while onstage and continue to go back to your script to discover the little jewels that previous journeys there did not uncover, your work will continue to grow. In fact, it will never stop growing as long as you remain open and in the moment. During this last stage of rehearsals, your instincts will be more available to you than ever before, because you will be more relaxed and know your character better than ever before. Don't edit yourself, but realize that not everything you come up with will serve the play in the best possible way. It is your director's responsibility to continue to let you know what works and what doesn't. Allow the director to do his or her job by being receptive and cooperative. Understand that sometimes the addition of the technical elements alters what the director had previously thought, and you must be willing to make any necessary adjustments.

During the final dress rehearsals, your director will add in the curtain call. This may be an ensemble bow or one that recognizes individual performances, depending on the material as well as the production choices. In any case, remember that the curtain call is for the audience as much as it is for the actors. Even if you are not happy with the work you did on a particular evening, never let that show. You are being thanked and congratulated for the work you have done. Make sure the audience sees you graciously accept that thanks. If you're the kind of person who finds that difficult, then consider the curtain call part of your acting obligation, and act your way through it. It is your responsibility to give only the best of yourself at all times.

EXERCISE 20-12

Create a character based on a work of non-dramatic fiction or drawn from history. Use what you have learned about the creation of character from this chapter. Perform the work for your class.

Previews and Opening Night

If your rehearsal schedule includes one or more previews, you will have the opportunity to adjust your work in accordance with the way an audience responds to it. Since, ultimately, it is for the audience that you perform, you must acknowledge and learn from the way they react. This is particularly important in comedy and melodrama where an audience's reaction is not only palpable, but strongly contributes to the overall effect of the work. On the most basic level, learning where laughs are and where they surprisingly turn out not to be can be very helpful, as can perfecting that suspenseful moment. If there are several previews, you and the rest of the collaborative team will be able to draw some important conclusions about how an audience is likely to respond. As a result of these discoveries, your director may ask you to make some last minute adjustments in the work before you finally open.

By the time you reach opening night, you will probably be hearing far fewer notes than when you began rehearsals what seems so many centuries earlier. Know that you are now ready to perform your work for a paying audience and that it is the addition of this final, all-important element of theatre—through their energy as catalyst and theatrical partner—that will complete the work you have strived so hard to develop. It is they who will appreciate and respond to the magical, unique, and ephemeral fruit that your talent, craft, and dedication have built collaboratively during the rehearsal process. Take your bow, you deserve it.

Summary

In this chapter you have learned that the character you play must serve the overall script in which he or she appears. Character is created for the most part through the actions you execute and by the manner in which those actions are carried out. Every movement, gesture, and piece of business, and all other physical manifestations you create, should serve the telling of the overall story as well as the story of your character. A scene-by-scene approach to your work will lead you to a throughline of action that will be clear and exciting for the audience to watch. In addition, you have learned about the rehearsal process and about your responsibilities as that process unfolds. Further, you have learned about the ways you can develop your role efficiently and creatively while remaining fully collaborative during the weeks you work together to develop your performance.

CHAPTER 21

What You Need to Succeed

For over a decade now, I have been working in educational theatre. In my current position as director of acting programs at the University of Miami, I teach several levels of acting as well as script analysis. I also direct plays in addition to my administrative duties. I like my work very much. Most people who see my productions consider me a talented director. My students tell me what a fine acting teacher I am. I can't imagine myself doing anything else. Having a job in theatre where I get paid regularly to do things I love to do makes me feel fortunate.

I didn't always feel lucky, however. In fact it took me several years to come to feel the way I do now. For many years I wanted to make my living acting. I trained for it, I sacrificed security and family for it, I felt I had earned the right. But when I was thirty-six years old, I gave up acting professionally. After ten years at it, I quit. I couldn't make a decent living acting. I earned far more money with my "survival" jobs—as a houseboy, as a house painter, as a waiter, as a house cleaner, as a part-time professor of public speaking—than I earned as an actor. I never worked any of my survival jobs for free. But as a professional actor, in spite of the fact that I belonged to all the professional actors' unions, I often worked for little or no money just to get a chance to perform, just to be seen. But even the opportunity to work for free came too seldom to me, and I finally folded my hand.

Occasionally, I still do a commercial or film audition, and I have acted in a couple of productions since I've become a full-time teacher/director, working onstage with the students I teach or have taught. Once I appeared in a production of *Orphans* by Lyle Kessler, in which I played the adult lead. Two former students played the young men in the cast. Just after the production closed, I received a backhanded compliment from one of my acting students. "You were excellent," she told me. "In fact it was obvious that you were a professional actor and the other actors were not." In addition, she said that at intermission her father—who had met me—had asked her why I wasn't in the play after all. He apparently hadn't recognized me as my character onstage. But the comment I remember most was when she asked me why I still wasn't acting professionally since I was "too good to just be a teacher." To say her remark chilled me a bit would be an understatement.

The fact is that for years I asked myself the same question every day I was unemployed: "Why wasn't I acting professionally if I was so good? Why couldn't I get a job as an actor?" During those years, I never came up with an answer to the question. I simply repeated it like a mantra. But, maybe, I chose not to answer the question then because I was afraid of the answer. Today, because I am comfortable where I am, I can answer it, and I hope that what I say is helpful to every young actor who is reading this. If you are serious about a career in theatre, you must begin to think about some very important aspects of your possible life in the business—aspects as important as the question parents always ask me: "Does my kid have talent?"

Surprising though it may be, having talent and having what it takes to make it in the acting business are only distantly related. I remember reading about something Stella Adler, the legendary acting teacher, once said when asked who was the greatest talent of all her students. She might have said James Dean or Marlon Brando or Jack Nicholson since she had taught many of the greats of the postwar era. Instead, she declared that the finest actor she had ever taught was "Natso Lucky" (this was not the actual name she used but it was the name of an unknown). She, of course, was pointing out that talent is only one of a number of considerations that come into play when a young actor tries to "make it."

In one of the great all-purpose acting textbooks, *Acting Is Believing,* Charles McGaw refers to "the two t's"—talent and training. McGaw says that your talent is a given, what you have is what you have. Instead of worrying about one's talent, a young actor should focus on training to maximize the best possible use of that talent. This is excellent advice and will lead the actor to become the best possible actor he or she can be. Training is invaluable when an actor auditions or when he or she works on a role. But any actor who thinks that being a "good" actor is an automatic passport to success is very naive indeed. Had that been the case you would not be reading this chapter right now. I would have been too busy preparing some role or giving an interview to have written it.

So if it's not talent and training that make an actor successful, then what is it? I'll give you a hint. Be cynical. Brilliant reviews never put food on the table or paid the rent.

EXERCISE 21-1

Take a few moments to brainstorm. Compile a list of attributes that you think a successful actor must possess. Remember, "successful" here means "an actor who can make a living acting." (I should point out that there are many fine community playhouse and amateur or semi-professional actors who are "successful" in terms of their own definitions of the word.)

All right. Here is my top ten list in descending order of importance.

1. Luck

2. Knowing the right people

3. Having money or having someone to supply you with money between engagements

4. Looks

5. The willingness to see yourself objectively as a commodity

6. A healthy ego

7. Patience

8. A controlled aggressive streak with the ability to know when to pull back

9. The ability to avoid comparing yourself with other actors

10. Talent and training

I told you to be cynical. If you are to respect yourself as an artist, you must, of course, develop your talents through craft, but realize that much of your time in the profession will not be spent as an artist, but as a salesperson selling a single product—yourself.

EXERCISE 21-2

1. Make a list of the most successful actors you can think of. Examine your list. Are the actors on your list also the most talented actors you know? What do you think are the characteristics that have made them so successful?

2. Make a list of the most talented actors you can think of. Examine your list. What characteristics do you think keep them from being the most successful? In other words, why is Bruce Willis a bigger star than Robert Duvall or Gene Hackman? Why is Julia Roberts a bigger star than Meryl Streep or Glenn Close? Use the top ten list to help you. (Keep in mind, of course, that this is a relative question. The fact that the actors on your list have made your list at all means that they are already extremely successful in terms of the definition we are using.)

Let's examine my top ten list in a bit more detail.

Luck

Luck gets top ranking because, with it, your acting career can take off no matter how little talent you have and, without it, you'd just be another "Natso Lucky." You could also be born with any or all of the attributes for success on my top ten list. That, too, is a result of luck. Never underestimate the power of being six-foot-three with blue eyes and chiseled jaw, or growing up to look like Julia Roberts. There's luck again.

Being in the right place at the right time is a matter of luck. When I was in graduate school, the woman who always played the romantic female leads was beautiful. She was also over six feet tall. I was the obvious dashing male lead in my class—good-looking, athletic, and a pretty good actor. My only competition was another good-looking guy, far inferior to me in skills. He was much taller than I was, however, and he got the leads because he could reach that actress's lips without a stepstool. For three years I played character roles. Had another actress been in my class, had I gone to graduate school a year sooner or later, had my luck been better, I would have been Romeo instead of Father Lawrence, Dracula instead of Renfield, or Kilroy instead of A. Ratt.

I once heard a perhaps apocryphal story that Jack Nicholson discovered Mary Steenburgen one morning while ordering coffee in a Howard Johnson's. She was the waitress. A few weeks later she was playing opposite him in the western he directed, *Goin' South*. She is a fine actor, but no beauty; and, if the story is true, it was scrambled eggs and luck that jump-started her film career. Had she been working in the diner across the street, she'd be word processing the midnight-to-6-A.M. shift today.

EXERCISE 21-3

1. Are you lucky? Evaluate the part luck has played in your life.

2. Do you rely on luck to get you through your life? Explain.

3. Do you consider luck and fate obstacles that work against you? As forces that you must overcome? Do you ever find yourself railing against these forces? How do you handle these forces in your life as an ongoing issue?

Knowing the Right People

Jeff Bridges is a very fine and underrated actor. Michael Douglas—though less charismatic—may be a better actor than his father. Miguel Ferrer is not well known yet, but he works all the time in television and film. Natasha Richardson —as talented as she is beautiful. Bridget Fonda? Tori Spelling! Three guesses what all these actors have in common. (The answer, as Tori Spelling so clearly suggests, is not awesome talent and unrivaled beauty.)

In case you lead a very sheltered life, here is the answer: They all know someone in the business. This quality cannot be underrated in spite of what you hear on talk shows. Time and again actors declare in interviews that they made it on their own. In some cases, the talent inherited from their parents gives credence to this claim. But Jeff Bridges and Natasha Richardson were helped enormously by the fact that his father was Lloyd Bridges, and her parents are Vanessa Redgrave and the late director Tony Richardson. Michael Douglas did not suffer professionally from being the son of Kirk, and Bridget *is* a Fonda. Tori Spelling, I suspect, would not be on *90210* had her dad not owned the show.

Knowing someone in the business may not get you the role, but it gets you in the door. Even if you have talent and training, getting through the door—making contact with that agent—is one of the most difficult and trying aspects of being an actor. At this point you may want to stop reading and begin searching for show business parents. Or you might like to form some new acquaintances.

EXERCISE 21-4

1. Make a list of the people you know who could help you with your career. How can they help you? Be specific?

2. Do you know other people who have better connections in the business than you do? What are these connections? How does that make you feel?

3. Would you be willing to ask others you know to introduce you to someone they know in order to make a good connection? Why or why not?

Money to Sustain You

Most young actors who venture to New York or Los Angeles after graduating from some theatre school or university are no longer acting after five years or so. There are many reasons for this. Several are in my top ten list. But one of the things that wears actors out is finding rent money while unemployed as an actor. Since most actors must constantly give up their rent-paying jobs when cast in a play or film, the stress of constantly finding and losing jobs is incredibly draining. A rich parent or patron is very helpful in overcoming this obstacle. Since many of us are without that particular piece of luck, it is very important that—along with acting training—the young actor develop skills that will make him or her employable between acting jobs.

The most common job-between-jobs for an actor is probably waiting tables. If you are good at it, you can make a lot of money and maintain flexible hours. However, the work is not for everyone. If you know that this occupation is not for you, think about alternatives before you make the move to one of the coastal meccas. During my acting career, I did several things for money that I could never have dreamed of doing. In addition to those I mentioned earlier, I was a building superintendent, a skyscraper window washer, a flower delivery boy, a catering waiter, a wheelchair pusher, a library alphabetizer, a proofreader, a freshman English teacher, and a judge for oral interpretation contests. I never did word processing, but, like waiting tables, it offers a good deal of flexibility at a very decent hourly wage. You must, however, have solid skills, so learn them before applying.

Looks and the Willingness to Recognize Yourself as a Commodity

I'm combining numbers 4 and 5 on my list because they're so closely related. By looks, I don't necessarily mean physical beauty, although I couldn't argue with beauty's power in the marketplace anymore than I'd argue against being six-foot-three and built like an Adonis. What I do mean is having a look that is marketable. Do you look like a gangster, a jolly fat guy, a young mother, a prostitute, an egghead? Agents can sell you if they can pigeonhole or type you in a particular way. Most actors bridle at this idea, but, nevertheless, it is a reality of the acting business. It is important for you to know how you'd be perceived by those selling and buying you. Once you understand this, you are more likely to get in the door and sell yourself. Then, when you make some money for agents, they'll try to sell you some more. That's good business—theirs and yours.

EXERCISE 21-5

1. List the actors that you are most like and explain why. Don't be modest; don't lie to yourself. Evaluate yourself as honestly as possible.

2. Type yourself, and write a brief description of how you look and how you would come off to others in an interview.

3. List the kinds of roles you could be cast in. Think in terms of movies, television, commercials, and theatre. Justify your opinions.

4. What are the great roles that you are right for, or will someday be right for? Justify your answers.

5. Ask someone you trust to answer the previous questions with regard to you. Compare their answers to your own. Draw conclusions.

I'm about five-foot-nine, fairly good looking as I mentioned, but I have a thick lower lip. I used to get sent out for commercials very regularly for a while. But I did not have tremendous success as a commercial actor in spite of the fact that I often read very well (according to the casting directors). Once, while I was auditioning as a young father in a Pampers commercial, I was told that my lips were too sensual for me to play a young father. (Now I'm an older father and my lips seldom affect my performance.) Another time, while auditioning for the role of a young, sexy guy in a Miller Beer commercial, I was told that my lips were distracting. I offered to cut them off, but the casting director said it would be easier to cast someone else.

In my first few years as a professional actor I got a lot of work as young executives and lawyers on soap operas and in industrial films, often playing much younger than I was. A few years later, I looked too old to get that kind of work, but agents told me that I looked too young to be believed as an established lawyer or executive. To conclude, I didn't seem to fit well into any of several molds in my thirties, and therefore—in spite of my talent, training, and good looks—acting work was difficult to find. My balding roommate with a developing beer belly (who will come up again later) was becoming more employable as a type with each pint of Cherry Garcia he swallowed and each hair that took a powder.

Some of you are no doubt thinking, "I'm gonna be an actor. I'll be able to play all kinds of roles. That's my job." That is positive actor thinking, and it suggests that you have a healthy attitude about your abilities. That is another important quality we'll be discussing later. But the fact is, as so many fine unemployed character actors will tell you, today there are actors available, perfect for any kind of role. If a role calls for an ugly, middle-aged Irish guy with a limp and lisp, there's an ugly, middle-aged Irish actor with a limp who can play him. If the role calls for an underweight, albino African American who can wrestle in Greco-Roman style, there's a fine underweight, albino African American actor who can wrestle in Greco-Roman style to play him. In fact, not long ago, I heard character actor Ned Beatty tell an interviewer that he knew he had arrived when he read a character description for a movie that called simply for a "Ned Beatty" type. So work on your craft. Develop your skills and broaden your range. But know how you will most often be seen. Don't fight it, because it could be your meal ticket.

For years my roommate fought his image. "I'm no fat guy!" he would often exclaim. "I'm James Dean!" On the inside, my roommate was James Dean, and for years he had a flair for self-destruction. He refused to do commercials because whenever his agent sent him up for them, he found himself surrounded by middle-aged men or fat men or ugly men. "That's not me!" he chanted. "I'm James Dean!" And so for years James Dean moved furniture instead of acting. Lived like a pauper instead of acting. Got angry instead of acting. Once he even turned down an interview with Oliver Stone, who was casting *Wall Street* at the time, because he heard that Josh Mostel, a decidedly overweight actor, was up for the same role. When my roommate saw the film, he could have kicked himself because the role was not for a fat actor; it was for a good actor, and the good actor who got the role happened to be fat. Don't fight how you are seen. You won't win, but it could defeat you if you try. Actors need to work. Accept the facts of the business.

A Healthy Ego

The most brutal aspect of being an actor has to be the fact that in order to do your art, someone must give you a job. The composer composes, the writer writes, the painter paints. The creative process can be fully engaged in spite of what others think, in spite of whether someone else hires you. It is true that all artists have an equal chance of starving, but actors are in the unenviable position of starving without having had the opportunity to create. Of course, they can work on monologues or take acting classes, but that is not the same thing as working on a role and doing it in full context or in front of an audience.

It is also true that, for the actor, rejection can be far more damaging emotionally than for other artists. When you reject the work of a painter or composer, it is clearly the work that is the issue. The painting or composition is a tangible commodity separate from the creator. The actor and his or her work, however, are one and the same. When you don't like my work as an actor it is me that you have rejected. Bruce Miller was wrong for the role. Bruce Miller was unconvincing. Bruce Miller obviously does not have the looks or skills to adequately fulfill the demands of Hamlet.

Not only can the criticism of an actor be brutally ugly, it is also ironic. Those nasty blurbs about the actor Bruce Miller came, let's remember, after six weeks of hard work. And that came after a giant victory—I auditioned for the part and got it because some director or casting agent thought that I, above literally hundreds of other fine actors, could do the role better. If I was really wrong for the role, is it my fault some jerk cast me in it? If I was unconvincing after the director and casting agent thought I was very convincing at the audition, is that my fault or the fault of the director who directed me badly? If my looks and skills are wrong, can I be held responsible for knowing that? Should I have turned down the job if I did?

It doesn't really matter, because you *will* be blamed. You may also be blamed if a play is poorly written or underrehearsed or badly cast or badly directed. That is the nature of the beast. The bottom line is that this will happen to you. Every actor has gotten bad notices at one time or another. Many actors always get bad notices, yet continue to find work. Some actors get fine notices and seldom work. There are no rules. There is no real fairness.

So you must be strong. You must believe in yourself. That may mean believing in your talent, your training, your connections, your looks, or any combination of the above. If you spend time, energy, and emotion downing yourself, all that you are doing is shortening your life expectancy in the business. Your getting or not getting any particular role may or may not have anything to do with you. A role might already have been cast; the director may just be looking for new ideas, not actors; you might not be right physically for the role. Or any of a thousand other things. The point is that you have no control over any of these reasons. You can't afford to waste energy over it. Getting down only weakens you for the next time and shortens your life expectancy in theatre.

Of course, there is the possibility that not getting the role was your fault. Perhaps you *were* terrible. Even if that was the case, though, what good does it do to suffer over it? Anyone can have a bad audition. If it was not your day, then bury it—now it's past. But if you always think you're terrible, then you have a problem much bigger than lack of talent. If you are so bad that you can't believe in yourself, then get out of the business because there is only hardship and pain in front of you. However, if you do believe in yourself and your talent, but you have this bad emotional circuitry that causes you to punish yourself any time you come up short, change it! Now! Mastering your self-abuse is far more important than talent, looks, voice production, technique, who you know, and so on. You *must* believe in yourself. You must be your own best friend and nurturer. The world of theatre is too damn hard to survive it any other way.

Statistically, survival in the world of theatre and film is a very bad bet anyway. Ninety percent of those who go to New York at twenty-one to be actors are out of the business by the age of twenty-six, mostly because of broken hearts and broken spirits. When getting a job means paying the rent, and failing to get it means the wolf's at the door, fun is minimal. It's tough to keep an upbeat attitude.

Most of you reading this chapter are young actors just beginning a life in the theatre. Here's some useful advice: Keep it fun while you can, while there are no bills to pay, while life pressures are still in the background. Subdue that ego, and train yourself to find the joy in the work you do in theatre. If you learn to do so, you will possess a skill as valuable as any you'll learn in acting class. Make sure when you get the role, you're happy about it even if it's not the role you wanted. Remember you're working. Make sure that opportunities to rehearse and the time spent in the studio are joyous even when it's not going right. This is what you love to do, so love it even when you're not perfect. Finally, if when you're working on a scene or rehearsing, you find yourself resenting it, think about doing something else in life, because you're supposed to be happy at this moment.

EXERCISE 21-6

1. Evaluate your ability to take criticism. Do you see criticism as a positive force? Can you accept it without emotion? Can you convert criticism into positive action?

2. Evaluate your ability to take rejection. Does it make you withdraw, or make you more determined? Find examples from your life. If it makes you withdraw, what are you planning to do about it? How?

3. Do you avoid things you are not good at? Or do you work even harder to master them? How does it make you feel when everyone around you is better at something than you are? How does it make you react? Find examples from your life.

4. Ask yourself the following question: Is acting really fun for you? I mean really fun? Fun enough to sustain you through all the potential pain and disappointment that exists out there as a genuine possibility?

Patience

Remember that roommate of mine who kept doing everything possible to keep himself from succeeding? Well, he's beginning to succeed. In his mid- to late-forties, after over twenty years in the business, I see him everywhere. On a

Rolaids commercial, as a cop in a John Sayles movie, working in a film with Al Pacino, Jack Lemmon, and Ed Harris. I even saw his snarling face and balding head staring at me from the Sunday *New York Times*. His picture was part of a giant ad for a David Rabe play.

There are two reasons that it's happening for him after all these years. In the first place, he's now willing to play the game. He's discovered that doing a commercial, even if it means auditioning with fat guys, can be more rewarding than moving furniture for a buck. He is now willing to talk to Oliver Stone. He's probably even polite to strangers. But the second reason he's working now is patience. My roommate has stuck with it. There are a lot fewer actors in their late forties than in their twenties. The competition has thinned out, like my roommate's hair. Actors have given up. Some have moved on to live normal lives—lives with steady paychecks and families where goals *can* be reached through hard work and persistence.

But twenty years' worth of contacts give an actor a better chance of knowing influential people in the business—people who know who you are, people who see you as a type or as a product (even if you don't), people who could help you, people who might even have learned to recognize your talent and training. For some this never happens, but patience in the business substantially increases your chances. My own acting mentor began seriously pursuing his professional acting career in his late sixties. He's doing very well, working steadily. He's happy because he recognizes that he's too old to play Hamlet and he's okay with that fact. It may not happen for you quickly. Accept that truth, but only stay with it if there's absolutely nothing else for you. Otherwise it can be poison.

EXERCISE 21-7

1. Evaluate your patience level. Do you want it all now, or are you willing to work for things that are not handed to you? Give examples to prove your position. Ask a friend to evaluate your patience level. Compare the evaluations. What does this all mean?

2. Do you audition for the work or for the part? What does this mean about you? When you fantasize about your future, do you think of yourself as a star or as an actor? What does this all mean?

Aggressiveness

Aggressive patience is the oxymoron of the acting business. In order for people in the business to notice you, they have to see you in something and be impressed. If agents think you have something they can sell, they will help you. Waiting for your chance requires tremendous patience, but the aggressive actor will try to impress an agent or director with persistence and determination while patiently waiting for the big break. This requires guts and ego. How many times are you willing to have an agent refuse to see you? How many postcards are you willing to send? How willing are you to schmooze and fawn at interviews? Can you make an impression in two or three minutes, convincing someone who has seen a hundred people before you that you are special? How good are you at pushing people into helping you? How good is your ability to recognize when you've pushed someone far enough? How long can you continue to do these things? You may have to continue doing them for a very long time—while sustaining your energy and optimism. That's what it may take to succeed.

In my own graduate school class, there were two people more aggressive than the rest of us. Though they both possessed a charming side and could be great fun, the rest of us grew to hate them. They were out for themselves bigtime. There was nothing, even in graduate school, that they wouldn't do to get a role or to make themselves look better than anyone else when onstage. They were willing to kiss up to anyone at any time if they thought it would profit them somehow. Truly, they were the living embodiments of the Ann Baxter character in *All About Eve.*

Of the twelve in my class, these two actors have had the most successful professional careers. Obviously, many successful actors have great integrity and are wonderful people, but there are many like the ones I have described. Play the game, but keep your integrity.

EXERCISE 21-8

1. Evaluate your own aggressiveness. Give examples.

2. Ask someone else to evaluate your aggressiveness. Does this quality remain an asset, in that person's opinion, when dealing with others? When do you start to rub people the wrong way?

3. Compare yourself to the examples given earlier. Where do you fit in? Realistically, evaluate your ability to do what is necessary to get work. What do you need to do to improve with regard to your ability to take charge of yourself and your career?

Avoiding Comparisons

The other day, after a cold reading exercise, a student who works as hard as any I have ever worked with came up to me at the end of class. He had read during the exercise and had not done particularly well, a result more of his lack of reading skills than any shortcoming specific to the acting department. He was very upset and wanted to ask me something. Finally he got it out.

"How am I doing?" he asked. "I mean in class. I mean, you know, acting is everything to me and I know my reading sucked, and, like, I'm worried about if . . . you know, am I gonna make it or not . . . cause, like, other guys in the class . . . you know . . . did a lot better than I did in the reading."

This is what I told him: "Look at your acting now, and then think about your acting when you came here in September. Think about where you will be as an actor in June. Forget everything else. It doesn't matter if others read better, it doesn't matter if someone else gets a role you want this year or next year. Right now you should be thinking about becoming the best actor you can be. You'll never be anyone but yourself; you're stuck with you. If you can't cold read too well, work on it. It's important to be able to read if you're an actor. It'll help you get work. So work on it. But no matter how well you read, no matter how well you act, if you're wrong for something, you won't get it. If you're right, and if you're lucky, you will get it. But being the best or worst in your high school or college class is meaningless. It won't get you work. Agents and casting directors don't care if you played Macbeth in high school. What matters is paying the rent when you're a working actor. Spend your time preparing for that!"

That's what I told that student.

EXERCISE 21-9

1. How much time do you spend comparing yourself to others—in your work, in other aspects of your life? How much time do you spend saying "if only" or wishing you could change something about yourself?

2. Make a list of the things you'd like to change about yourself. Examine the list.

3. What things are changeable? Are you willing to do what is necessary to change the things you can change? How will you do it? When will you begin? What keeps you from starting now?

4. What things are not changeable? Why? How will you deal with this? When will you begin to deal with this? Why didn't you say "right now"?

5. Do you see the importance of asking yourself these questions? Explain the importance—to yourself and to someone else.

And that brings me to the last item on my list.

Talent and Training

You can't learn luck or buy it. Some people won't play with their looks, although in some cases modifications can help a career. Whether you know people who can help you at the start or meet them as you go, you'll still have to show something when you get through that agent's door. That may happen sooner or later depending on how you've mastered the sales aspect of your career and on how aggressively you handle your professional connections. If your spirit, ego, and sense of humor are all intact when the moment finally happens for you, what you do for the agent boils down to two things—whether you look right and whether you act right. That means talent and training.

An agent may not know good acting from bad. For a particular role, how you look may be more important than what you can do. But you have no control over these things. So in the end, it all boils down to what you can show when you're asked to show it. In the end, for most of us, it all boils down to those "two t's."

If you possess a prodigious talent, you may intuitively be able to make exciting and believable acting choices when you walk through the casting agent's door. You may be able to create moments that are clear, specific, bold, and logical. Your voice and body may naturally transform into the personification of the character you are reading for. No matter what the rigors of the role, your body may be naturally prepared to take them on. Your emotional range may permit you to be totally available for any situation. Instinctively, you may perceive the differences between a character living now, or a century ago, or in the Middle Ages. Your sensitivity to poetic language may be so strong that it falls from your lips with beauty and clarity. You may automatically intuit a playwright's purpose and how your character serves it. In every acting situation your mind, body, and spirit may be ready to work—automatically.

If this is not the case, however—and the chances that you fall into this second category of actor are strong—then it's time to recommit yourself to that second "t." Training—rigorous, dedicated, and disciplined—will go a long way toward getting you ready for the moment when your big opportunity arrives. Keep in mind, of course, that you never stop learning. Acting, like all other art forms, is an ongoing process of development. The more you learn, the more you need to learn. For instance, each time I pick up a favorite book on acting, it says something new to me. What I have learned since the last time I read it both changes and deepens what the book is saying to me and what I can do with what it says. As a developing artist, you too, hopefully, will have the same experience.

So—better get back to work. Keep reading. Keep working hard on your craft. It may take a while before the other nine items on my list start to kick in!

Summary

It will take more than talent and training if you are to have a successful career. You will need to decide for yourself the definition of "success," of course, but for many people in the business, a successful career is one where you regularly have the opportunity to do the work and be paid for it. The opportunity to work at what you love is *almost* pay enough. But the reality is that bills must be paid, and when an actor can work and be paid for that work, many would consider themselves lucky. Indeed, luck is a quality that most successful actors possess at least to some degree. If you are to succeed, you will also need patience, a healthy ego, and an ability to pursue your goal doggedly and without letup. It will also help if you know someone who can help you along the way, either with connections or with money to sustain you through the tough times. A marketable skill to provide money for yourself is also an asset. You also need to be realistic about who you are and how the world perceives you. In short, you will need to do three things. First, you must learn to be absolutely honest about the art, the craft, and the business you might either already be in, or may someday enter. Second, you must, wherever possible, be willing to change the things about you that will keep you from succeeding. Finally, you must continue to develop your craft, both because it is part of your artistic makeup to want to do so and because it is a necessary part of your growth as an artist.

Rules of Love

Joe Pintauro

Setting: *A confessional booth*

(Father Jim McGrath, a Roman Catholic priest, walks to midstage, turns his back to the audience, genuflects, then walks to a chair. He sits, partially facing the audience, in what would be a confessional booth in a church. He's wearing a cassock, the long black gown that a priest often wears. Underneath, he wears trousers, socks, and shoes, all black, and a white tee shirt. He places a lavender or purple stole to hang from his neck like an open necktie—it's just a purple satin ribbon about two inches wide and a yard or so long. The priest and penitent are separated by a wall with a sliding door which he opens to talk to the confessing person. Even with this sliding door open, there is a metal screen between the two, and over the screen a black piece of silk to insure anonymity. So, the priest would face forward, at most just cocking his ear toward the voice of the penitent. On stage the whole setup may be represented simply by a chair with a back, in which the priest sits sideways, so that the penitent may use the back of his chair as a priedieu. Maisie kneels on a red velvet pad. The actors' behavior will indicate that they are enclosed and cannot see one another. She may talk to his face now and then, figuring out its whereabouts in the dark, but the priest keeps his profile to her, never risking to identify her, or any penitent, for this would violate the penitent's rights.)

(Maisie walks on, her footsteps echoing toward the would-be booth. She carries a suitcase which she leaves outside the area of confession. Cautiously, she steps inside and kneels. We see the priest's profile and Maisie almost faces the audience as she is about to speak through the silk-shrouded screen into his ear. He blesses her with his right hand, making a cross in the air. He does this blindly, then urges her to pronounce the opening words.)

PRIEST: Bless me Father . . .

WOMAN: Bless me Father for I have sinned. My last confession was two years ago.

PRIEST: Speak louder please?

WOMAN: My last confession was two years ago.

PRIEST: Okay. Two years ago. (*Silence*) Are you there?

WOMAN: I'm here. I was . . . afraid at first . . .

PRIEST: Did you say afraid? I'm sorry, once again I can't . . .

WOMAN: I said I was afraid, but . . .

PRIEST: What are you afraid of?

WOMAN: I have committed a very grave sin, Father.

PRIEST: Alright.

WOMAN: And by afraid, I meant simply that I was nervous about coming here.

PRIEST: I'm not going to hurt you.

WOMAN: I know.

PRIEST: So take your time. (*Silence*) Uh . . . now, your sins?

WOMAN: I . . . I've fallen in love.

PRIEST: That's no sin.

WOMAN: With a priest.

PRIEST: Uh . . . Even so, that's no sin per se.

WOMAN: We've had sex fifteen, maybe twenty times.

PRIEST: Oh . . . (*Now he recognizes the voice.*) Let me explain something: after a person confesses a sexual sin to a priest, if that priest follows up with an intimate act with that person, the priest cannot be forgiven except by the Pope. It's called solicitation.

WOMAN: I know about that.

PRIEST: But . . . it ends the relationship. Don't you understand? And it ties his hands because he can't . . . stop you from doing something foolish. *For God's sake! Find another priest to confess to!*

WOMAN: There are no other priests hearing confessions tonight.

PRIEST: Well, come back tomorrow.

WOMAN: I want to confess to you, Father. I know what I'm doing.

PRIEST: Alright. Say what you want to say.

WOMAN: At times I feel absolutely no guilt whatever for this relationship. I have the purest memories. Other times, the whole thing's a bummer. Every morning I wake up hating myself. I feel dirty.

PRIEST: You shouldn't.

WOMAN: Convince me.

PRIEST: (*Shifts uncomfortably*) Do you have any other sins to confess?

WOMAN: Yes, sins against myself. Selling myself cheap. I don't mean literally, although sometimes I did feel like a piece of meat.

PRIEST: Don't say that.

WOMAN: Why else would I come here if I didn't feel that way? God, if there's one true sin that I should confess, it's the fact that I tried with all my power to get him to leave the priesthood.

PRIEST: Easy . . .

WOMAN: If God hates me for that he has a perfect right to.

PRIEST: There's no hate in God.

WOMAN: Promise me that?

PRIEST: Yes. I promise.

WOMAN: I was alone for too long Father . . .

PRIEST: You don't have to . . .

WOMAN: . . . and here was such a beautiful man worth caring for, and he wanted me. I did *not* go after *him*. I just couldn't resist his attention to me.

PRIEST: Isn't that what most people yearn for?

WOMAN: It was so damn egotistical.

PRIEST: No it wasn't.

WOMAN: I thought I could accomplish what God had failed to.

PRIEST: And what was that?

WOMAN: To get the guy off that ice-cold mountain he was sitting on all alone, like a lost little boy, afraid to love, afraid to touch.

PRIEST: Maybe you succeeded.

WOMAN: I don't think so.

PRIEST: A person's changed for the rest of his life by such a thing.

WOMAN: What such a thing?

PRIEST: Love.

WOMAN: Well that's nice to hear.

PRIEST: Don't hurt this man. Maisie?

WOMAN: Don't use my name.

PRIEST: Don't punish him for his predicament. He suffers a lot because of his love for you. He needs your help.

WOMAN: That's why I came here.

PRIEST: How old are you?

WOMAN: Oh stop.

PRIEST: How old?

WOMAN: Thirty.

PRIEST: What took the woman so long to fall in love? Okay? What the hell was she doing before this? Eh? An attractive woman like you? Afraid of men, right? So you go after the least available guy, the least experienced? Hmmmn? Someone unmarried, but someone promised to God for the rest of his life?

WOMAN: I . . . did not . . . pursue you.

PRIEST: Bullshit. And one sexual conquest over this priest wasn't enough. You had to have twenty-seven.

WOMAN: Was it twenty-seven? I wasn't counting.

PRIEST: I was. And on top of that you wanted him for *life*. He's God's property.

WOMAN: I'm sure you'll never miss such a woman.

PRIEST: How dare you address me directly.

WOMAN: I don't have a church to hide behind.

PRIEST: Do you realize that I cannot give you absolution unless you're prepared to avoid the occasion in the future?

WOMAN: You mean avoid him?

PRIEST: Precisely.

WOMAN: I know the rules.

PRIEST: Well, shouldn't you *think* about this?

WOMAN: I . . . got a job in another city. My plane leaves in a couple of hours.

PRIEST: (*Shocked*) I see. Alright then. Do you have any other sins you wish to place before God?

WOMAN: You're really not going to stand up and fight for me?

PRIEST: What the hell do you mean?

WOMAN: You're not going to throw over all these cockamamie regulations and grab me and take the both of us out of here?

PRIEST: Shut up. You can't do this.

WOMAN: We can do whatever we want! What do *you* want to do?

PRIEST: (*Formal*) Do you have any other sins you wish to place before God?

WOMAN: Shit. I've told you all my sins.

PRIEST. Then, for your penance, please attend Mass and offer it up for the spiritual welfare of this priest, and of yourself.

WOMAN: He needs it more than I.

PRIEST: Think of the years I worked to be what I am and you expect me to flush this down the drain in a minute? For what? And don't say love. I became a priest for love.

WOMAN: Bullcrap.

PRIEST: Every day's an act of love for me. Many others depend on me.

WOMAN: I was one of many?

PRIEST: Yes. In a manner of speaking. In another sense . . . You meant more to me than the whole . . .

WOMAN: The whole what? Jim?

PRIEST: The whole . . . lot of them.

WOMAN: Oh Jim . . .

PRIEST: Don't *call* me that in here.

WOMAN: Do you want me to move away?

PRIEST: I can't answer that in here. The minute you stepped in here everything changed for us. I don't know what I think. Please . . .

WOMAN: Do you love me?

PRIEST: God, yes I do. Of course, but I can't help us now. You've destroyed everything beyond your realization. You *ended* it. It's terrible what you did, Maisie. (*Pause*)

WOMAN: It's terrible what you did.

PRIEST: For your penance go to Mass and offer it up for the welfare of this priest. . . . You might remember him often that way.

WOMAN: I will remember him often. I promise you that.

PRIEST: Thank you . . .

WOMAN: Thank you, Father . . .

PRIEST: You're welcome.

WOMAN: Goodbye, Father.

PRIEST: Now recite your Act of Contrition. (*He raises his hand, whispering the words of absolution in the old Latin form, overlapping her Act of Contrition.*) Ego te absolvo ab omnibus censuris et peccatis, in nomine patis et filio et spiritus Sancti. . . . Amen.

Woman: Oh my God I am heartily sorry for having offended Thee, and I confess all my sins because I dread the loss of heaven and the pains of hell. But most of all, because they offend Thee, my God, who art all good and deserving of all my love . . . I firmly resolve, with the help of Thy grace, to confess my sins, do penance, and to amend my life. Amen. (*She stands up and leaves the confessional booth. She lifts her suitcase as if to exit church. Jim steps out of the booth, calling out in a loud voice.*)

PRIEST: Which city?

(*The Woman says nothing, but turns to continue on her way.*)

PRIEST: (*Angrily, loudly*) Which . . . city?

WOMAN: (*Smiling*) Chicago. (*Exit. Lights fade on Jim.*) END

GLOSSARY

absurdism A style of dramatic writing in which human existence is portrayed as absurd, meaningless, and without logic.

action The physical or psychological activity an actor actually engages in; the through-line of dramatic action in a play.

adjustment When an actor responds to a new or spontaneous way that his or her fellow actor plays a particular moment; when an actor adjusts his or her physical position to accommodate a new position by a fellow actor in order to be in a physical position conducive for the audience's viewing.

Adler, Stella One of the great American acting teachers of the twentieth century. Founding member of the Group Theatre along with Lee Strasberg, Robert Lewis, Sanford Meisner, Harold Clurman, and Elia Kazan.

aesthetic distance A term referring to the audience's ideal position for taking in a play—somewhat empathetic but also able to judge the work intellectually.

analysis and synthesis The intellectual tools necessary for taking a script apart and putting it together in such a way that the play will work effectively for an audience.

audience A group of people joined as one to witness a singular event.

audition An acting situation in which you try out for a role in a play. You must not only prove that you can act, but you must also convince your auditors that you are right for the role and the production and that you are desirable to work with.

beat The section of script during which a single objective is played.

beginnings, middles, ends The necessary ingredients for all storytelling—actions, moments, beats, scenes, and plots all have them.

blocking The physical ingredients of storytelling onstage—movement, gestures, and business.

business, stage Any ongoing activity actors engage in while fulfilling their acting tasks onstage.

catharsis The release of emotion by an audience resulting from a sympathetic response to a tragic character's downfall.

classical A term originally referring to the plays of ancient Greece and Rome, but now referring to all plays from other periods.

cold reading An audition in which you are asked to read from a scene without having the opportunity to fully prepare.

collaboration A term referring to the fact that theatre cannot be done alone. It requires a group of artists, onstage and off, who must work together to produce a consistent and shared vision of a play.

comedy A genre of play with a humorous content that usually centers on and makes comments about the shortcomings in our human natures. Classical comedy usually focuses on mistaken identity and the need to find a way to bring its young lovers together in marriage by the end of the play.

composition The picture created when the set, props, and actors are all present in the scene.

conflict When two opposing forces collide; the engine of all drama; the first element actors must discover about the story they are telling.

contemporary A play set in or near to the time in which we currently live.

contextual meaning The circumstances within which a particular line is delivered.

controllable One of the qualities of a theatrical performance referring to the fact that the performer must each time be able to perform his or her work in the same manner as it was rehearsed so that there is consistency and reliability in the performance.

conventions, theatrical An accepted set of rules that are applied consistently to theatre in general, or to a particular play or production.

craft The elements or tools of acting that can be learned and mastered—as opposed to talent, which cannot.

criticism Objective feedback based on what worked and what did not.

cue-to-cue A rehearsal where actors are asked to play only the moment leading up to and during a section of the play where lighting, sound, or set elements are added or taken away.

defeats The moments onstage when an actor as character realizes his or her objective cannot be achieved. This moment will be followed by a transition to a new beat or objective.

discoveries Any new information an actor as character learns—information that he or she can and should react to.

drama From the Greek word, *dran,* which means action. Drama also refers to a genre of play that is serious and seemingly real.

elements of drama As defined in Aristotle's *Poetics,* action, dialogue, character, idea, music, and spectacle.

elevated language Dialogue that is more poetic than the language of ordinary life.

emotional memory The use of personal memory to create an emotion that can be applied to an acting situation.

emotional truth The product of an actor who can find and produce honest emotions within himself or herself that serve the acting moment the actor is creating.

endowment Giving an object specific emotional meaning that can be tapped into for acting purposes.

ephemerality The characteristic of theatre that refers to the fact that once a theatre performance is over, unlike other art forms, it is gone forever.

expressionism A style of writing in which the playwright portrays a reality as seen through a particular character's eyes.

external technique The outside-in approach to acting in which an actor focuses first on what his or her character needs to be doing rather than what the character is thinking or feeling.

externals The tangible aspects of any role including looks, movement, gesture, and voice.

farce A comic genre of play in which the laughs are produced through the broad, ridiculous, life-and-death choices of its characters. The comedy is often physical and desperate, the laughs coming more from the characters' actions than from the witty dialogue.

figurative language Language poetic in nature that expresses a thought or feeling in a non-literal way.

first read A fully prepared reading, one that has been carefully rehearsed, but has not yet been put on its feet.

fourth wall The imaginary separation between the actors onstage and the audience watching a production. The actors do not acknowledge the presence of the audience.

genre A particular type or category of play—such as tragedy, comedy, farce, melodrama— or of film—such as the action picture, historical epic, teenage comedy.

gesture A specific physical action that communicates emotion, information, or attitude.

given circumstances The who, what, when, and where of a play or scene.

head-first acting A term coined for this book suggesting that good acting requires analysis and synthesis, and that often the best choices that serve the story must be thought out rather than simply inspired.

idea One of Aristotle's six elements of drama referring to the thematic elements that make up a play.

immediacy The characteristic of theatre that refers to the fact that an audience is right there viewing the event and, through its interaction with the performers, is affecting the performance itself.

implied action Any playable action that is suggested through dialogue but not stated as a stage direction specifically.

inciting incident An event that is the catalyst for the action of a play.

indicating When a performer physically demonstrates what he or she is thinking or feeling rather than committing to it and doing it in a believable manner.

inner monologue The subtext that an actor goes through while acting a role; the thoughts and feelings that may be as important to the role as the dialogue itself.

intention Another word for acting objective, or action, that an actor pursues while onstage.

internal technique The inner part of acting referring to drawing from the actor's real feelings to portray a character.

journey The combined series of changes an actor undergoes as a character while pursuing his or her overall objectives through tactics that will lead to fulfilling those needs. Also the throughline.

justification Acting a line or moment in such a way that it is not only believable and clear, but that makes sense in terms of its literal, contextual, and subtextual meaning as well.

listening A basic requirement for an actor if he or she is to be believed; refers to the need to be connected at every moment with the other actors sharing the stage.

literal meaning The meaning of a line of dialogue without considering its contextual and subtextual meaning.

"magic if" Acting tool invented by Stanislavski in which the actor asks, "What would I do if I were the character in this situation?"

magical realism A style of playwriting in which the action seems realistic; yet strange, often unexplained and symbolic events keep occurring. In *Buried Child* by Sam Shepard, for instance, Tilden brings onstage a crop of corn from the visible field behind the house that has been fallow for years. This is both impossible and real in the context of the play.

Meisner, Sanford One of America's great acting teachers who sprang from the Group Theatre of the 1930s. His focus on the subject of listening and being in the moment provided many great acting exercises widely used in current teaching.

melodrama A genre of play characterized by a plot-driven story in which the characters are often two dimensional, but the conflict between the forces of good and evil create compelling suspense.

Method, the Internal approach to acting based on emotional truth and sense memory; developed by Lee Strasberg based on early writings of Stanislavski.

modern A term referring to plays written in a style meant to reflect the reality in which we live. Today the term generally refers to the plays of the early modern European writers of the latter part of the nineteenth century such as Ibsen, Strindberg, and Chekhov.

moment The smallest unit of dramatic action that can be acted.

moment to moment Refers to the ability of the good actor to adjust his or her work in accordance with the way his or her acting partner is behaving at a particular moment.

monologue A sustained speech delivered by an actor without interruption, or a sustained speech delivered by an actor spoken without the physical presence of another actor.

motivation The reason a character pursues a particular superobjective. The motivation cannot be played directly; rather, it can be used as a detective device to find the need. My motivation for wanting to be a star, for example, is that I was ignored as a child. I cannot play my past onstage. However, this motivation translates into the superobjective—to make the world pay attention to me.

movement When actors move from one place to another onstage.

naturalism A style of writing and theatre sometimes known as "heightened realism," where everything could be mistaken for reality itself, even without suspension of disbelief.

negative choices Tactics used by an actor that do not help get what he or she needs.

new information Anything a character finds out onstage that can change what he or she thinks, feels or does; information that an actor should respond to onstage.

objectives The needs an actor playing a character pursues at all times while onstage.

obstacles The things in a scene or play that keep a character from fulfilling his or her objectives. They provide conflict and heighten the stakes of a situation by creating conflict and upping the risk factor.

operative words Words in dialogue that are intentionally stressed to make a line's context or subtext clear.

organic Acting choices that spring spontaneously from doing the work itself, rather than being imposed from the outside.

pace The speed at which you pick up your cue and deliver your next line of dialogue.

personal space Any acting setting where a character controls the privacy. No one is permitted there without the owner's approval. A bedroom or private office would be examples.

physical action The actual things a character does onstage. They demonstrate what a character is thinking and feeling as well as make the story clear to an audience.

positive choices The choices an actor makes in pursuit of his or her objective that actually work to get the character closer to fulfilling that need.

presentational Refers to a style of acting or theatre in which the performers onstage acknowledge that the audience is present.

private space Any acting setting to which access is restricted. Not everyone is permitted to go or be there, but it is space that may be expected to be shared—a work office, a living room, or a kitchen.

psychological action Refers to the thought process of a character, sometimes expressed through what that character says, that must be somehow translated into tangible action so that the audience watching will understand what those thoughts are.

public space Any acting setting where people are free to come and go and to observe each other—a public library, a bus terminal, and a school yard, for instance.

realism A style of playwriting or theatre that attempts to make the audience believe that what they are seeing is real with a minimum of suspension of disbelief.

relationship An acting tool to help define the connection between characters onstage, to get insight into the dynamics that affect the way a scene might work.

repeatable One of the desired qualities in an acting choice. Actions should be repeatable so that there is consistency and reliability in any performance.

repetition games Acting exercises invented and developed by Sanford Meisner in which dialogue is repeated with the purpose of developing an actor's ability to listen onstage.

representational Refers to a style of acting or theatre that does not acknowledge the presence of an audience and that tries to create the illusion of reality onstage.

rhythm The pattern of changes in tempo that, when combined, serve to keep an audience's attention (for instance, a slow intimate scene followed by a fast scene of major conflict).

risk A basic acting tool for producing compelling acting; making choices for a character that are dangerous for him or her and therefore interesting.

score and scoring A map of an actor's role in a play, or the process of developing such a map, composed of the sequential listing of actions and objectives to be played, along with all other pertinent information.

selectivity and control The characteristics necessary to the production of all good art. In terms of acting process, to some degree all acting choices must be thought out and contribute to the story being told. Random or spontaneous choices do not necessarily do so.

sense memory The use of our strong powers of recall relating to smell, sound, taste, touch as well as sight to enhance the emotional power of an acting moment or situation.

sides Small sections of a script usually distributed to actors to read in an audition situation.

spectacle One of the six elements of theatre as defined by Aristotle, referring to all the visual ingredients of a performance. These include set, lights, and costume.

spine A term coined by Harold Clurman referring to the central idea of a play that, like a spine, serves to hold the play together while all other parts are connected to it.

stakes What is at risk for the actor as character at any given moment or overall in a play. They make the acting situation more interesting.

Stanislavski, Constantin The Russian theatre director, actor, and teacher most responsible for the manner and technique in which acting craft is taught.

Strasberg, Lee The legendary American acting teacher who developed the "Method."

style The result of recognizing, defining, and using a set of characteristics and conventions shared by a set of characters in a play; the created world of the play.

substitution A technique by which an actor replaces or enhances the acting situation he or she is in emotionally by replacing it with a parallel one from his or her own life to increase the intensity and truth of the acted moment.

subtext The meaning of a line of dialogue in terms of the acting objective being pursued.

superobjective The overall need that an actor as character pursues during the course of a play.

suspension of disbelief The term referring to the fact that an audience never completely forgets that what they are watching is fictional. Yet, when the performance is working, the audience will pretend that it is real, at least while in the act of watching.

tactics The specific things an actor as character does to get what he or she needs from another character. These tactics can be quickly replaced by the actor if they prove ineffective.

tangible Referring to things that can actually be seen by the audience.

tempo The overall rate of speed at which a play or section of a play is played. (Note that this definition is different from Stanislavski's use of the term, but this meaning reflects the term's most common use in theatre today.)

theatre The unique art form where human beings perform as human beings and set out to imitate or represent our humanness by using our bodies, voices, intelligence, and spirit to another group of human beings who witness the event.

theatrical event A live performance that happens in continuous action in front of audience members who share the experience together. Once the shared experience is over, it will never be repeated, or even if it is, it will never be exactly as it occurred at that time.

theatricalism A style of playwriting or theatrical production that acknowledges the presence of the audience watching and makes that audience a direct part of the action onstage.

throughline The combined series of actions that are mapped out in a script by an actor in working out his or her character's story moment by moment, scene by scene.

tragedy A genre of play in which the central character or protagonist is destroyed irrevocably through fate or because of some inherent quality that causes his or her downfall. Tragedy is intended to produce in an audience an empathy or understanding resulting from the moral dilemma of the central character that is shared or understood by the audience.

transitions The actable moments when one objective is given up and replaced with a new one. This transition occurs when an objective is won, lost, or abandoned because of a discovery, an interruption, or the arrival of new information.

victories The actable moments when objectives are obtained.

SUGGESTED READINGS

Books on Acting

Acting Is Believing, Charles McGaw
Acting One, Robert Cohen
Acting: Onstage and Off, Robert Barton
Acting Power, Robert Cohen
Acting: The First Six Lessons, Richard Boleslavski
Advice to the Players, Robert Lewis
An Actor Prepares, Constantin Stanislavski
Building a Character, Constantin Stanislavski
Creating a Role, Constantin Stanislavski
High Concept, Lo Tech, Barbara Carlisle and Don Drapeau
Let the Part Play You, Anita Jesse
The Monologue Workshop, Jack Poggi
A Practical Handbook for the Actor, Melissa Bruder et al.
Respect for Acting, Uta Hagen
The Sanford Meisner Approach, Larry Silverberg
Sanford Meisner on Acting, Sanford Meisner and Dennis Longwell
Stanislavski in Rehearsal, Vasily Osipovich Toporkov
To the Actor, Michael Chekhov
Training an Actor, Sonia Moore

Books on Acting Style

Acting Shakespeare, Robert Cohen
Acting with Style, John Harrop and Sabin R. Epstein
Classical Acting, Malcolm Morrison
The Rediscovery of Style, Michel Saint-Denis
Style: Acting in High Comedy, Maria Aitken
Style for Actors, Robert Barton

Books on Training the Voice and Body

Acting through Exercises, John L. Gronbeck-Tedesco
The Actor and His Text, Cecily Berry
Body Wisdom: The Use and Training of the Human Body, Arthur Lessac
Creating a Character: A Physical Approach, Moni Yakim
The Expressive Body, David Alberts
Freeing Shakespeare's Voice, Kristin Linklater
Freeing the Natural Voice, Kristin Linklater
Movement Training for the Stage and Screen, Jean Sabatine
The Use and Training of the Human Voice, Arthur Lessac
Voice and the Actor, Cecily Berry

Books on Script Analysis

The Actor's Script, Charles Waxberg
Backwards and Forwards, David Ball
Script Analysis, David Grote
Script Analysis for Actors, Directors, and Designers, James Thomas

Books on Directing

The Art of Directing, John W. Kirk and Ralph A. Bellas
Creative Play Direction, Robert Cohen
Directing Plays, Stuart Vaughan
The Director's Voice, Arthur Bartow
On Directing, Harold Clurman
Play Directing, Francis Hodge
A Sense of Direction, William Ball

Books on Understanding Theatre

The Creative Spirit, Stephanie Arnold
The Essential Theatre, Oscar Brockett
Life of the Drama, Eric Bentley
Theatre, Robert Cohen
Theatre: A Way of Seeing, Millie Barranger
Theatre: Choice in Action, Arden Fingerhut
The Theatre Experience, Edwin Wilson
The Theatrical Imagination, Jeffrey H. Huberman, James Ludwig, and Brant L. Pope

Books on Interviews with Actors

The Actor Speaks, Janet Sonnenberg
Actors: A Celebration, Rita Gam
Actors on Acting, Toby Cole and Helen Chinoy
Conversations in the Wings, Roy Harris
The Player, Lillian Ross and Helen Ross

Books on the Meaning and Philosophy of Theatre

The Empty Space, Peter Brook
Lies Like Truth, Harold Clurman
The Theatre and Its Double, Antonin Artaud

Books about the Profession of Theatre

Acting Professionally, Robert Cohen
Being an Actor, Simon Callow
Letters from an Actor, William Redfield
Next Season, Michael Blakemore (a novel)
Setting Free the Actor, Ann Brebner
The Working Actor, Katinka Matson

Books on Theatre Criticism

The Collected Works of Harold Clurman, Harold Clurman
Curtains, Kenneth Tynan
The Dramatic Event, Eric Bentley

Books on the History of Twentieth Century American Theatre

The Fervent Years, Harold Clurman
A Life, Elia Kazan
Method Actors, Steven Vineberg
Mind Bends, Arthur Miller

Books on Auditioning

Audition: Everything an Actor Needs to Know to Get the Part, Michael Shurtleff
Auditioning for the Musical Theatre, Fred Silver
How to Audition, Gordon Hunt

Books on the Method

All About Method Acting, Ned Manderino
A Dream of Passion, Lee Strasberg
Method—or Madness?, Robert Lewis
On Method Acting, Edward D. Easty

Books on Film Acting

Acting in Film, Michael Caine
Secrets of Screen Acting, Patrick Tucker

Books on Acting Theory and Training

The End of Acting, Richard Hornby
True and False, David Mamet

Books about Acting Shakespeare

Acting in Shakespeare, Robert Cohen
Acting Shakespeare, Bertram Joseph
Playing Shakespeare, John Barton

Books on Acting for Musical Theatre

The Complete Singer-Actor, H. Wesley Balk
On Singing Onstage, David Craig

BIBLIOGRAPHY

Aristotle. *Poetics*. Trans. Kenneth A. Telford. Chicago: Gateway, 1968.

Barranger, Millie. *Theatre: A Way of Seeing*. Belmont, CA: Wadsworth Publishing Company, 1995.

Barton, Robert. *Acting: Onstage and Off*. Fort Worth: Harcourt Brace and Company, 1993.

Barton, Robert. *Style for Actors*. Mountain View, CA: Mayfield Publishing Company, 1993.

Bentley, Eric. *The Dramatic Event*. Boston: Beacon Press, 1954.

Bentley, Eric. *The Life of Drama*. New York: Atheneum Publishers, 1964.

Brockett, Oscar G. *The Essential Theatre*. New York: Holt, Rinehart and Winston, Inc., 1988.

Brook, Peter. *The Empty Space*. New York: Atheneum Publishers, 1968.

Bruder, Melissa, et al. *A Practical Handbook for the Actor*. New York: Vintage Press, 1986.

Clurman, Harold. *The Fervent Years*. New York: Harcourt Brace Jovanovich, Inc., 1975.

Clurman, Harold. *On Directing*. New York: Macmillan Publishing Company, 1972.

Cohen, Robert. *Acting One*. Palo Alto, CA: Mayfield Publishing Company, 1984.

Cohen, Robert. *Acting Power*. Palo Alto, CA: Mayfield Publishing Company, 1978.

Cohen, Robert. *Theatre*. Mountain View, CA: Mayfield Publishing Company, 1988.

Cohen, Robert, and Harrop, John. *Creative Play Direction*. Englewood Cliffs, NJ: Prentice-Hall, Inc., 1974.

Felnagle, Richard H. *Beginning Acting*. Englewood Cliffs, NJ: Prentice-Hall, Inc., 1987.

Fingerhut, Arden. *Theatre: Choice in Action*. New York: Harper Collins College Publishers, 1995.

Grote, David. *Script Analysis*. Belmont, CA: Wadsworth Publishing Company, 1985.

Hagen, Uta. *Respect for Acting*. New York: Macmillan Publishing Company, 1973.

Harrop, John, and Epstein, Sabin R. *Acting with Style*. Second Edition. Englewood Cliffs, NJ: Prentice-Hall, Inc., 1990.

Kazan, Elia. *A Life*. New York: Alfred A. Knopf, Inc., 1988.

Kirk, John W., and Bellas, Ralph A. *The Art of Direction*. Hudson, IL: Ad Hoc Productions, 1989.

McGaw, Charles, and Clark, Larry D. *Acting Is Believing*. Fort Worth, TX: Harcourt Brace and Company, 1996.

Meisner, Sanford, and Longwell, Dennis. *Sanford Meisner on Acting*. New York: Vintage Press, 1987.

Moore, Sonia. *Training an Actor*. New York: Penguin, 1979.

Shurtleff, Michael. *Audition: Everything an Actor Needs to Know to Get the Part*. New York: Walker and Company, 1978.

Silverberg, Larry. *The Sanford Meisner Approach*. Lyme, NH: Smith and Kraus, Inc., 1994.

Stanislavski, Constantin. *An Actor Prepares*. Trans. Elizabeth Reynolds Hapgood. New York: Theatre Arts Books, 1936.

Stanislavski, Constantin. *Building a Character*. Trans. Elizabeth Reynolds Hapgood. New York: Theatre Arts Books, 1949.

Stanislavski, Constantin. *Creating a Role.* Trans. Elizabeth Reynolds Hapgood. New York: Theatre Arts Books, 1961.

Thomas, James. *Script Analysis for Actors, Directors, and Designers.* Woburn, MA: Butterworth-Heinemann, 1999.

Tucker, Patrick. *Secrets of Screen Acting.* New York: Routledge Publishing, 1994.

Waxberg, Charles. *The Actor's Script.* Portsmouth, NH: Heinemann Educational Books, Inc., 1998.

Whelan, Jeremy. *Instant Acting.* Cincinnati, OH: Betterway Books, 1994.

CREDITS

Chapter 15   p. 154 From *Speed the Plow* by David Mamet. Copyright © 1985, 1986, 1987 by David Mamet. Used by permission of Grove/Atlantic, Inc. p. 155 From *The Dumb Waiter* by Harold Pinter. Copyright © 1960, 1988 by Harold Pinter. Used by permission of Grove/Atlantic, Inc. p. 156 From *Sarita* by Maria Irene Fornes. Copyright © 1986 Maria Irene Fornes. Reprinted with permission from The Johns Hopkins University Press. p. 158 From *Curse of the Starving Class* by Sam Shepard. Reprinted with permission from Bantam Books. p. 158 From *The Glass Menagerie* by Tennessee Williams. Copyright © 1945 by Tennessee Williams and Edwina D. Williams. Copyright renewed 1973 by Tennessee Williams. Reprinted by permission of Random House, Inc. p. 159 From *Long Day's Journey into Night* by Eugene O'Neill. Copyright © 1955 by Carlotta Monterey O'Neill. Reprinted with permission from Yale University Press.

Chapter 21   p. 265 From *Rules of Love* by Joe Pintauro. Copyright © 1989 by Joe Pintauro. Reprinted by permission of William Morris Agency, Inc., on behalf of the author. All rights reserved. Caution: Professionals and amateurs are hereby warned that *Rules of Love* is subject to a royalty. It is fully protected under the copyright laws of the United States of America and of all countries covered by the International Copyright Union (including the Dominion of Canada and the rest of the British Commonwealth), the Berne Convention, the Pan-American Copyright Convention, and the Universal Copyright Convention, as well as all countries with which the United States has reciprocal copyright relations. All rights, including professional/amateur stage rights, motion picture, recitation, lecturing, public reading, radio broadcasting, television, video or sound recording, all other forms of mechanical or electronic reproduction, such as CD-ROM, CD-I, information storage and retrieval systems, and photocopying, and the rights of translation into foreign languages are strictly reserved. Particular emphasis is laid upon the matter of readings, permission for which must be secured from the author's agent in writing. Inquiries concerning rights should be addressed to: William Morris Agency, Inc., 1325 Avenue of the Americas, New York, NY 10019, Attn: Gilbert Parker.

INDEX